WINE FOLLY

LIFE IS TOO SHORT TO DRINK BAD WINE.

–Anonymous

WINE FOLLY
The Essential Guide to Wine

MADELINE PUCKETTE AND JUSTIN HAMMACK

AVERY

an imprint of Penguin Random House

New York

AVERY

An imprint of Penguin Random House LLC
375 Hudson Street
New York, New York 10014

Most Avery books are available at special quantity discounts for bulk purchase
for sales promotions, premiums, fund-raising, and educational needs.
Special books or book excerpts also can be created to fit specific needs.
For details, write SpecialMarkets@penguinrandomhouse.com.

Library of Congress Cataloging-in-Publication Data

Puckette, Madeline, author.
  Wine folly : the essential guide to wine / Madeline Puckette and Justin Hammack.
    p.   cm
  ISBN 9781592408993 (paperback)
  1. Wine and wine making.   I. Hammack, Justin, author.   II. Title.
  TP548.P793   2015   2015025749
  641.2'2—dc23

Printed in the United States of America
7 9 10 8
Book design by Madeline Puckette

Contents

INTRODUCTION

Like wine? Want to know more about it? This book is for those of us who need simple guidance to get over the challenges of getting into wine. It contains practical knowledge that is immediately useful to help you find and enjoy great wine.

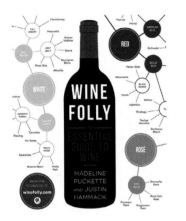

This guide is small on purpose. It's a visual reference guide designed specifically for everyday wine drinkers. Within these pages you'll find:

› Wine fundamentals
› How to taste, handle, and store wine
› A compendium of 55 different types of wine
› 20 detailed wine maps

Want more? Go online.

http://winefolly.com/book

› Hundreds of articles
› How-to videos
› In-depth resources
› Poster guides and maps

Access Wine Folly's extensive resources free online. The site is supported by hundreds of thousands of subscribers and is used by consumers and professionals alike.

WHY LEARN ABOUT WINE

Perhaps you want to stock up on delicious value wines. Or maybe you want to navigate a restaurant wine list with confidence. Learning about wine starts with the realization that the wine world is a lot bigger than we think:

There are over a thousand wine varieties to choose from . . .

There are thousands of wine regions with unique wines . . .

Every day, an average of 600 new wines are released . . .

Fortunately, wine isn't overwhelming when you have a solid foundation. A good foundation leads to informed purchases and better-tasting wine.

THE CHALLENGE

Complete the following challenges and you will gain confidence both in choosing and tasting wine.

Taste at least 34 of the 55 wines included in this book (just not all at once!). Take great **tasting notes** (pg. 21).

Try at least 1 wine from each of the **12 countries** (pgs. 176–217).

Learn how to **blind taste** (pgs. 12–21) your favorite single-varietal wine.

Fundamentals

Wine Basics

WHAT IS WINE

Definition of wine, grape varieties, regions, and what's inside a single bottle of wine.

WINE BOTTLE FACTS

On drinking, sulfites, bottle sizes, and ways that bottles are labeled.

BASIC WINE CHARACTERISTICS

Definitions of the 5 basic traits of wine: alcohol, acidity, tannin, sweetness and body.

INSIDE A BOTTLE
OF WINE

5 GLASSES
5 OZ / 150 ML

WATER

ALCOHOL

ACIDS, MINERALS
GLYCEROL, SUGAR

1 GLASS
DRY WINE

10%	11%	12%	13%	14%	15%	16%	ABV
105	120	135	150	165	180	195	CALORIES

WHAT IS WINE?

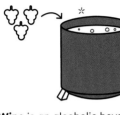

Wine is an alcoholic beverage made with fermented grapes. Technically, wine can be made with any fruit, but most wines are made with wine grapes.

VITIS LABRUSCA

VITIS VINIFERA

Wine grapes are different than table grapes. They are much smaller, they have seeds, and they are also sweeter than table grapes.

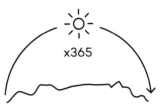

x365

Grapevines take a year to grow grapes. The harvest in the northern hemisphere is Aug.–Oct., and the harvest in the southern hemisphere is Feb.–Apr.

Vintage refers to the year when the grapes were harvested. Non-vintage (NV) wines are a blend of several harvests.

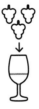

A **single-varietal wine** is made with one grape variety (e.g., Pinot Noir, pg. 100).

A **wine blend** is made by mixing several wines together (e.g., Bordeaux blend, pg. 134).

A temperate climate is where grapes grow best. In North America, grapes grow from northern Mexico to southern Canada.

Regions with **cooler climates** make wines that taste more tart.

Regions with **warmer climates** make wines that taste more ripe.

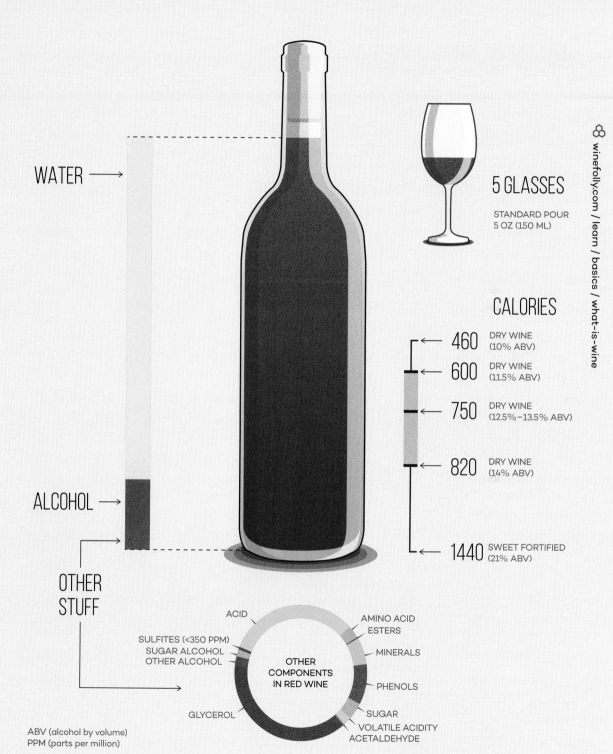

WATER →

ALCOHOL →

OTHER STUFF →

5 GLASSES

STANDARD POUR
5 OZ (150 ML)

CALORIES

460 DRY WINE
(10% ABV)

600 DRY WINE
(11.5% ABV)

750 DRY WINE
(12.5%–13.5% ABV)

820 DRY WINE
(14% ABV)

1440 SWEET FORTIFIED
(21% ABV)

winefolly.com / learn / basics / what-is-wine

OTHER
COMPONENTS
IN RED WINE

ACID

AMINO ACID

ESTERS

MINERALS

PHENOLS

SUGAR

VOLATILE ACIDITY

ACETALDEHYDE

GLYCEROL

SULFITES (<350 PPM)
SUGAR ALCOHOL
OTHER ALCOHOL

ABV (alcohol by volume)
PPM (parts per million)

5

WINE BOTTLE FACTS

DRINKING FACTS

STANDARD BOTTLE SIZE
A standard 750 ml bottle contains 5 servings of wine.

STANDARD WINE POUR
A standard pour is 5 oz (150 ml) and contains an average of 150 calories and 0–2 grams of carbs.

HEALTHY DRINKING
The National Cancer Institute recommends that women have no more than 1 drink per day and men have no more than 2.

A GLASS A DAY
If you drink a glass of wine every night of your adult life, you will drink over 4,000 bottles of wine.

A bottle of wine contains the fermented juice of *Vitis vinifera* grapes. Besides fermented grape juice, there is also a small portion of sulfur dioxide (aka "sulfites") added as a preservative.

SULFITE FACTS

Sulfites affect about 1% of the general population, and wineries are required to label their wines if they contain more than 10 ppm (parts per million). In the US, wine has no more than 350 ppm sulfites and organic wine has no more than 100 ppm. In comparison, a can of Coke contains 350 ppm of sulfites, french fries contain 1,900 ppm, and dried fruit contain about 3,500 ppm.

WINE BOTTLE SIZES

| 187.5 ml | 375 ml | 500 ml | 750 ml | 1.5 L (2) | 3 L (4) | 4.5 L 6 STANDARD BOTTLES | 6 L 8 STANDARD BOTTLES | 9 L 12 STANDARD BOTTLES | 12 L 16 STANDARD BOTTLES | 15 L 20 STANDARD BOTTLES |
| SPLIT | DEMI/HALF | JENNIE | STANDARD | MAGNUM | DOUBLE MAGNUM | JEROBOAM | IMPERIAL | SALMANAZAR | BALTHAZAR | NEBUCHADNEZZAR |

3 EXAMPLES OF HOW WINE IS LABELED

winefolly.com / learn / basics / wine-label-101

BY VARIETY

Wines can be labeled by grape variety. This German wine has the name of the grape variety—Riesling—listed on the label. Each country requires a minimum percentage of the variety in the wine in order for it to be listed on the label:

75% USA, CHILE

80% ARGENTINA

85% ITALY, FRANCE, GERMANY, AUSTRIA, PORTUGAL, NEW ZEALAND, SOUTH AFRICA, AUSTRALIA

BY REGION

Wines can be labeled by region. This French wine is labeled as a Bordeaux Supérieur. If you learn about Bordeaux, you will learn that this region grows primarily Merlot and Cabernet Sauvignon and blends them together. Wines labeled by region are common in:

FRANCE

ITALY

SPAIN

PORTUGAL

BY NAME

Wines can be labeled with a made-up name. More often than not, a named wine is a blend of grape varieties that is unique to the producer. Named wines are occasionally found on single-varietal wines in order to differentiate between the wines that the producers make.

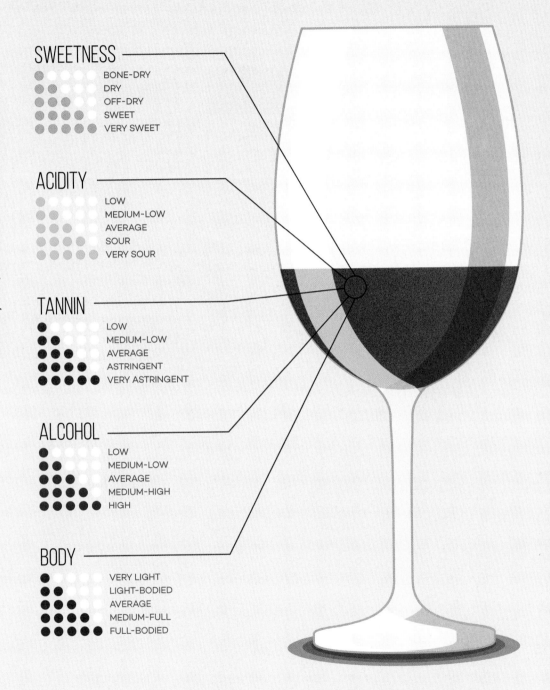

SWEETNESS
- BONE-DRY
- DRY
- OFF-DRY
- SWEET
- VERY SWEET

ACIDITY
- LOW
- MEDIUM-LOW
- AVERAGE
- SOUR
- VERY SOUR

TANNIN
- LOW
- MEDIUM-LOW
- AVERAGE
- ASTRINGENT
- VERY ASTRINGENT

ALCOHOL
- LOW
- MEDIUM-LOW
- AVERAGE
- MEDIUM-HIGH
- HIGH

BODY
- VERY LIGHT
- LIGHT-BODIED
- AVERAGE
- MEDIUM-FULL
- FULL-BODIED

BASIC WINE CHARACTERISTICS

There are 5 characteristics that help define the profile of a wine: sweetness, acidity, tannin, alcohol, and body.

SWEETNESS

Sweetness in wine is derived from residual sugar (RS). Residual sugar is the leftover sweetness when not all the grape must is fermented into alcohol.

We describe sweetness as a taste that ranges from bone-dry to very sweet. It's good to know that a technically dry wine can contain up to a half tea-spoon of sugar per glass. See the chart below for standardized vocabulary to describe sweetness.

LOWER ACIDITY   HIGHER ACIDITY

PERCEIVED SWEETNESS: At the same sweetness level, wines with lower acidity taste sweeter than wines with higher acidity.

SWEETNESS LEVELS

Sweetness levels in still wines can result in additional calories per 5 oz glass:

BONE DRY	DRY	OFF-DRY	SWEET	VERY SWEET
0 cal.	0–6 cal.	10–21 cal.	21–72 cal.	72–130 cal.
less than 1 g/L RS	*1–10 g/L RS*	*17–35 g/L RS*	*35–120 g/L RS*	*120–220 g/L RS*

Sparkling wine sweetness levels shown in teaspoons of sugar and calorie levels per 5 oz glass:

BRUT NATURE	EXTRA BRUT	BRUT	EXTRA DRY	DRY	DEMI-SEC	DOUX
0–2 cal.	0–5 cal.	0–7 cal.	7–10 cal.	10–20 cal.	20–30 cal.	30+ cal.
0–3 g/L RS	*0–6 g/L RS*	*0–12 g/L RS*	*12–17 g/L RS*	*17–32 g/L RS*	*32–50 g/L RS*	*50+ g/L RS*

LEMON
2 pH

YOGURT
4.5 pH

ACIDITY RANGE OF WINE:
Wine ranges in acidity from
2.5 pH to 4.5 pH. A wine with
a pH level of 3 has ten times
more acidity than a wine with
a pH level of 4.

STEMS
SKINS
SEEDS

GRAPE TANNIN: Tannin comes
from skins, seeds, and stems.
Grape tannin is bitter and
astringent but contains high
levels of antioxidants.

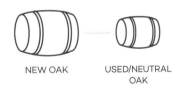

NEW OAK

USED/NEUTRAL
OAK

OAK TANNIN: New oak barrels
impart more tannin into wine than
used oak barrels.

ACIDITY

Acids are the primary attribute that contribute to
wine's tart and sour flavor. Most acids in wine come
from grapes including tartaric, malic, and citric acid.
Like many fruits, wine lies on the acid side of the pH
scale, ranging from about 2.5–4.5 pH (7 is neutral).

One useful thing to know about acidity in wine is
that, as grapes ripen, they become less acidic. Thus,
a wine from a cooler climate where it's hard to ripen
grapes will produce wines with higher acidity.

TANNIN

Tannin is a naturally occurring polyphenol found in
plants. Tannin is unique to red wine, since white
wines ferment without skins. In wine, tannin is not
necessarily a flavor but a textural astringent taste.

Tannin comes from two sources: grape skins and
seeds, and from new wood barrels.

To taste tannin in wine, focus on the texture on your
tongue. A high tannin wine will remove proteins
from your tongue, causing a drying and puckering
sensation. This sensation is often described as
"grippy." High tannin wines act as palate cleansers
to rich, fatty meats; cheeses; and pasta dishes. This
is why they are often served with food.

ALCOHOL

The alcohol in wine comes from yeast converting grape must (sugar) into ethanol. Alcohol may also be added to a wine, which is called fortifying.

Alcohol plays an important role in wine aromas. It's the vehicle by which aromas travel from the surface of the wine to your nose. Alcohol also adds viscosity and body to wine. You can sense alcohol in the back of your throat as a burning sensation.

A "HOT" WINE: Alcohol level is often described as a temperature because of how it feels in your throat. A "hot" wine has higher alcohol.

LOW	MEDIUM-LOW	MEDIUM	MEDIUM-HIGH	HIGH
●	● ●	● ● ●	● ● ● ●	● ● ● ● ●
Below 10% ABV	10–11.5% ABV	11.5–13.5% ABV	13.5–15% ABV	Over 15% ABV

BODY

Body is not a scientific term, but a categorization of style from lightest to boldest. The four characteristics of sweetness, acidity, tannin, and alcohol each affect how light or bold a wine will taste.

TIP: Imagine the difference between light- and full-bodied wines like the difference between skim and full milk.

 LIGHTER WINES
MORE ACIDITY
LOWER ALCOHOL
LESS TANNIN
LESS SWEET

 BOLDER WINES
LESS ACIDITY
HIGHER ALCOHOL
MORE TANNIN
MORE SWEET

You can use terms like "light-bodied" or "full-bodied" to describe the style of wine you want to drink.

Tasting Wine

The 4-step wine tasting method is a professional tasting technique that focuses a taster's ability to separate and identify key characteristics in a wine and improve flavor and taste memory.

HOW TO TASTE
WINE

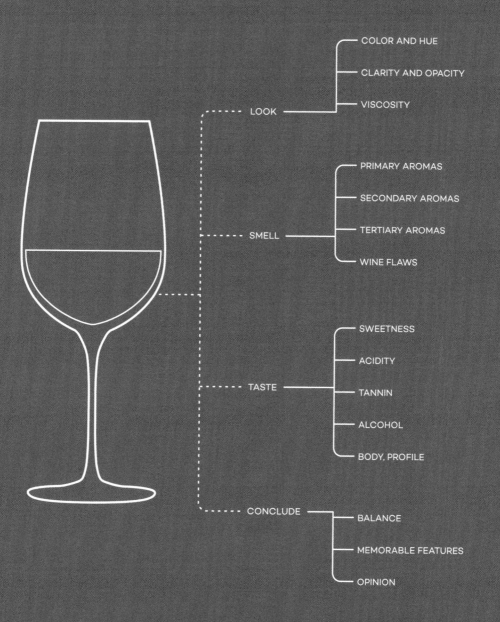

LOOK
- COLOR AND HUE
- CLARITY AND OPACITY
- VISCOSITY

SMELL
- PRIMARY AROMAS
- SECONDARY AROMAS
- TERTIARY AROMAS
- WINE FLAWS

TASTE
- SWEETNESS
- ACIDITY
- TANNIN
- ALCOHOL
- BODY, PROFILE

CONCLUDE
- BALANCE
- MEMORABLE FEATURES
- OPINION

HOW TO TASTE: LOOK

The 4 steps of wine tasting are: **look**, **smell**, **taste**, and **conclude**.

HOW TO TASTE WINE: LOOK

The color in wine is a scientifically complex topic. Fortunately, a seasoned taster can learn to identify clues about a wine just from inspecting the **color**, **intensity**, **opacity**, and **viscosity.**

For a tasting size, pour a 3 oz (75 ml) serving. Attempt to view the wine with natural light over a white surface, such as a napkin or a piece of paper.

INSPECT: Angle the glass over a white backdrop and inspect the color, intensity, and hue at the rim of the glass.

SWIRL: Swirl the wine to see the viscosity. Viscous wines have higher alcohol and/or residual sugar.

COLOR: We look at the hue and compare it not necessarily to all wines but to other examples of the same wine—in that way we can see how it differs in terms of both variety and production.

INTENSITY: Observe the wine from the rim to the middle. You will see small differences in color and clarity of a wine based on several factors, including variety, production, and age.

WINE TEARS: Wine "legs" or "tears" is a phenomenon called the Marangoni effect caused by fluid surface tension. Slow-moving "tears" indicate higher alcohol levels but do not signify quality.

THE COLOR OF WINE

winefolly.com / learn / basics / tasting-wine / wine-color

CLEAR: UN-OAKED AND
COOL CLIMATE WINES

HUE: GREEN TO COPPER

DEEP GOLD: OAK-AGED
AND LATE HARVEST WINES

PALE PLATINUM: A nearly clear white wine that refracts in the light will likely be young and not aged in oak.

MEDIUM LEMON: Several white wines have green hints in their color, including Grüner Veltliner and Sauvignon Blanc.

DEEP GOLD: Oak aging will often give a white wine a deeper golden hue due to the natural oxidation that happens while it ages in barrels.

PALE COLOR:
LESS PIGMENT

A RED TINT:
HIGHER ACIDITY

A BLUE-VIOLET TINT:
LOWER ACIDITY

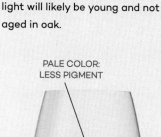

PALE GARNET: Pale red wines contain less of the red pigment anthocyanin. Pinot Noir, Gamay, Grenache, and Zinfandel are naturally more pale in color.

MEDIUM RED: Wines that tint red typically have higher acidity than wines that tint blue-violet. Merlot, Sangiovese, Tempranillo, and Nebbiolo tend to tint red.

DEEP PURPLE: Opaque red wines contain more pigment. Aglianico, Malbec, Mourvèdre, Petite Sirah, Syrah, and Touriga Nacional contain more anthocyanin.

15

HOW TO TASTE: SMELL

SMELL: Hold your glass just under your nose and sniff once to "prime" your nose. Then swirl your wine once and smell again. This time, smell the wine longer and slower but just as delicately. Switch between sniffing and thinking.

AROMAS: Move your nose to different positions around the glass. Rich fruit aromas are generally found on the lower lip, and floral aromas and volatile esters can be smelled on the upper lip of the glass.

LEARN TO SWIRL: Swirling wine releases aroma compounds into the air.

OVERLOADED?: Neutralize your nose by sniffing your forearm.

PERFUME: Avoid wearing strong scents when actively tasting wine.

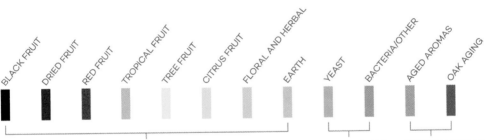

BLACK FRUIT · DRIED FRUIT · RED FRUIT · TROPICAL FRUIT · TREE FRUIT · CITRUS FRUIT · FLORAL AND HERBAL · EARTH · YEAST · BACTERIA/OTHER · AGED AROMAS · OAK AGING

PRIMARY AROMAS · SECONDARY AROMAS · TERTIARY AROMAS

PRIMARY AROMAS: Primary aromas come from grapes. Each variety has a range of possible aromas. For example, the white wine variety Sauvignon Blanc often smells like gooseberry or fresh-cut grass. Primary aromas range depending on the climate where the wine was made and how long the wine has aged.

SECONDARY AROMAS: Secondary aromas come from winemaking, specifically, from reactions caused by wine yeast and bacteria.

For example, the aroma of butter found in Chardonnay is from a special bacteria.

TERTIARY AROMAS: Tertiary aromas come from aging and controlled interaction with oxygen. For example, the nutty flavors in vintage Champagne and Sherry are from years of aging.

WINE FAULTS: Some aromas you will encounter are faults. It's useful to learn them in order to know a good wine from a bad one.

HOW TO IDENTIFY WINE FAULTS

winefolly.com / learn / basics / tasting-wine / wine-faults

"Corked"

aka TCA Taint, 2,4,6-Trichloroanisole

Most corked wines smell strongly of wet cardboard, wet dog, or a musty cellar. Sometimes, however, a corked wine will just lack aromas and have very subtle musty aromas. Don't worry, you can return a faulty wine.

Reduction

aka Mercaptans, Sulfur Compounds

Reduction in wines smells like boiled garlic and cabbage. It happens when a wine doesn't receive enough oxygen in bottle. Decanting should improve the smell, or you can stir your wine with a pure silver spoon.

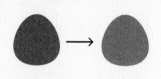

Oxidized

aka "Maderized"

Oxidized wines smell flat and are brown in color, much like an apple. Red wines will taste dry and bitter due to phenols (e.g., tannin) interacting with oxygen. Oxidized white wines typically have an apple cider–like odor.

UV Damage

aka "Light Strike"

Light strike happens when wines sit under supermarket lighting for too long or are exposed to sun. Light strike causes reduction. Avoid light damage by storing your wines in the dark, and avoid "shelf-aged" bottles.

Heat Damage

aka "Cooked," "Maderized"

Wine starts to deteriorate quickly at 82°F and cooks at around 90°F (32°C). Cooked wines can smell pleasant, like caramel and cooked fruits, but they will taste flat with no beginning, middle, or end. Heat damage also causes browning.

Spritz and Bubbles

(in a non-sparkling wine)

Occasionally, wines will ferment again in the bottle. This is easy to identify by the presence of spritz in a wine that's supposed to be still. These wines will also typically be a little hazy, due to yeast and protein particles.

HOW TO TASTE: TASTE

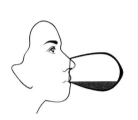

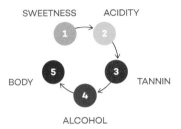

SWEETNESS   ACIDITY

1   2

5   3

BODY   4   TANNIN

ALCOHOL

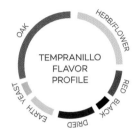

TEMPRANILLO FLAVOR PROFILE

OAK · HERB/FLOWER · RED · BLACK · DRIED · EARTH · YEAST

TASTE: Try coating your mouth with a larger sip of wine followed by several smaller sips so that you can isolate and pick out flavors.

Try to pick out at least 3 fruit flavors and 3 other flavors—one at a time.

TIP: Spitting is more common at professional tastings.

IDENTIFY: Identify where the basic wine traits hit your palate:

Sweetness is toward the front.

Acidity makes your mouth water.

Tannin is textural and dries your mouth out like wet tea bag.

Alcohol feels like heat in the back of your throat.

PROFILE: Now that you've tasted the wine, create a mental profile (or write one down) of the wine. Try to organize the flavors and aromas by their category. For example, if you taste vanilla, it might be due to oak.

TIP: You can cross-reference the variety section of this book for hints on how to categorize flavors.

WINE EVOLVES ON YOUR PALATE

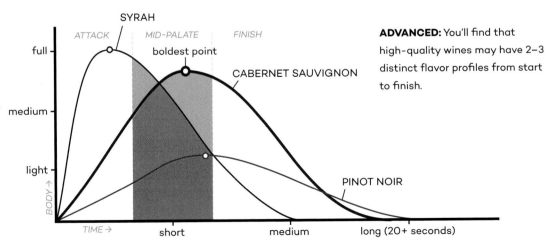

SYRAH

ATTACK   MID-PALATE   FINISH

full —

boldest point

CABERNET SAUVIGNON

medium —

light —

BODY →

PINOT NOIR

TIME →   short   medium   long (20+ seconds)

ADVANCED: You'll find that high-quality wines may have 2–3 distinct flavor profiles from start to finish.

TASTE PREFERENCES ARE GENETIC

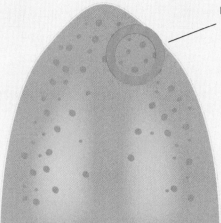

How many taste buds
are within the area
of one hole punch
on your tongue?

winefolly.com / learn / basics / tasting-wine / palate-test

NONSENSITIVE

HYPERSENSITIVE

Nonsensitive

10–25% of people

Less than 15 taste buds. You can handle spicy food and love the richest, boldest flavors. Bitterness doesn't bother you because you can't taste it at all. You're primed for drinking the most intense wines in the world.

FACT: Asians, Africans, and South Americans have a higher proportion of supertasting genetics than Caucasians.

Average Taster

50–75% of people

15–30 taste buds. You can taste bitterness like tannin just fine, but it doesn't make you wince in pain. You're capable of loving most wines. Improve your palate simply by slowing down and paying attention to nuances.

FACT: Women are over two times more likely to be supertasters than men.

Hypersensitive

"Supertaster": 10–25% of people

30+ taste buds. Everything tastes intense: salty, sweet, sour, oily, and bitter. You are not a fan of bitterness. The good thing is, sensitivity makes you a more conscientious eater. You'll lean toward delicate, smooth wines.

IDEA: The #1 way to improve your sense of taste is to spend more time smelling and identifying aromas.

HOW TO TASTE: CONCLUDE

bleh   meh   yeah   last meal

BALANCE: Now that you've tasted the wine, you can evaluate it. Do all the traits in the wine balance one another?

TIP: A wine that's out of balance will have characteristics that overpower other flavors in the wine, for example, a jarring acidic flavor that dominates the taste.

IMPROVE YOUR MEMORY: Note a few key traits of the wine and commit them to memory:

Traits or flavors specific to the grape variety.

Flavors or traits unique to the region, vintage, or producer.

YOUR OPINION: Take your time with wines that you enjoy. Identify what you prefer about them over other wines. You'll find yourself to be more articulate when seeking new wines.

At Wine Folly, we use a simple 4-point rating system with a focus on drinkability. A "last meal" is so good you can die happy.

BLIND TASTING

Practice blind tasting with your friends. Have your friends each bring a bottle of wine in a bag or wrapped in aluminum foil. Then pour tastes of each wine and go around the table discussing characteristics to identify each wine.

TIP: It's easiest to start blind tasting with single-varietal wines. Then work up to blends.

TIP: Set up your tasting in a well-lit room to improve your visual assessment.

TASTING IDEAS

REGIONAL COMPARISON: Try the same variety over several regions to see how geography influences flavor.

VINTAGE COMPARISON: Find a series of vintages by a producer for a specific wine to learn how wine changes year to year.

QUALITY COMPARISON: Put together a lineup of similar wines that vary in price to see how quality varies.

HOW TO WRITE USEFUL TASTING NOTES

DUNN VINEYARDS CAB. HOWELL MTN.
2002, TASTED 2009 W/ J. & D.

HAZY RUBY TO GARNET RIM.
VERY BRIGHT. MED. VISCOSITY WITH
STAINED TEARS.

BOLD AROMAS. DRIED BLACK CURRANT,
RED PLUM, TRICOLOR PEPPER, SAGE,
CRUSHED GRAVEL, CEDAR PLANK &
LICORICE. ALL WRAPPED UP IN
WINTERGREEN.

TASTED LIGHTER THAN EXPECTED
MODERATE ACIDITY, MODERATE FINE
TANNIN. TASTED OF BLACK CHERRY,
WINTERGREEN & RARE STEAK.
SMOKY SWEET FINISH.

DRANK ON EQUINOX. WONDER IF THAT
HAS ANYTHING TO DO WITH IT. SERVER
BUTCHERED THE CAPSULE. IT WAS
CUTE.

WILL TRY TO SAVE NEXT BOTTLE FOR 2015!

WHAT YOU TASTED/DRANK
Producer, region, variety, vintage,
and any special designation.

WHEN YOU TASTED IT
Wine changes as it ages.

YOUR OPINION
This is what really matters.

WHAT YOU SAW
Will help identify winning themes.

WHAT YOU SMELLED
Be specific.

TIP: Try listing the most obvious
flavors first. This helps create a
hierarchy of importance.

WHAT YOU TASTED
Since we "taste" so much with our
nose, add structural notes here, as
well as anything unique that you
didn't get in the smell.

WHAT YOU DID
Because wine is an experience.

TASTING PLACE MATS: Available
in our resources section online:

http://winefolly.com/resources/tasting-mats

Handling Wine

WINE GLASSES	Different types of wine glasses and tips on picking glassware.
SERVING WINE	How to open and decant still and sparkling wines.
WINE TEMPERATURE	Wine temperature best practices.
WINE STORAGE	Tips on storing wine short and long term.

SPICY RED
(SYRAH)

LIGHT WHITE
(SAUVIGNON BLANC)

TULIP
(SPARKLING)

SWEET FORTIFIED
(PORT)

BOLD RED
(BORDEAUX)

BOLD WHITE
(MONTRACHET)

FLUTE
(SPARKLING)

SWEET WHITE
(SAUTERNES)

AROMATIC RED
(BURGUNDY)

ROSÉ & AROMATIC WHITE

COUPE
(SPARKLING)

DRY FORTIFIED
(SHERRY)

STEMLESS RED

STEMLESS WHITE

STEMLESS SPARKLING

WINE GLASSES

There are many different wine glasses to choose from. Here are a few facts about wine glasses to help you decide what glassware is best for you.

Hold stemmed glasses by the stem and close to the foot.

Lead-free crystal glassware is dishwasher-safe.

Leaded crystal contains anywhere from 1% to 30% lead oxide. Fine crystal is 24% or more. Leaded crystal is not hazardous unless wine is stored in it for many days.

Buying wine glasses? Stick to 2 glass styles most suited to your drinking habits.

Stemmed vs. stemless? Stems do not affect aroma or taste.

CRYSTAL VS. GLASS

Crystal stemware refracts light due to its mineral content. Minerals also strengthen crystal, allowing it to be spun very thin. Traditionally, crystal glassware is leaded, but today there are several lead-free options made with magnesium and zinc. Most lead-free crystal is dishwasher safe. However, leaded crystal glasses are porous and should be hand washed with fragrance-free soap.

Standard glass is technically more fragile than crystal but it's spun thicker to make it more durable. Regular glass is dishwasher-safe.

HOW THE SHAPE AFFECTS TASTE

The bowl of a glass affects aroma intensity while the rim affects how much wine hits your palate.

IDEAL FOR DELICATE, AROMATIC WINES

IDEAL FOR SPICY, BOLD WINES

A LARGE ROUND BOWL collects more aromas from the larger exposed wine surface.

A NARROW BOWL collects less aromas and has less wine surface exposed to air.

CHOOSING GLASSWARE

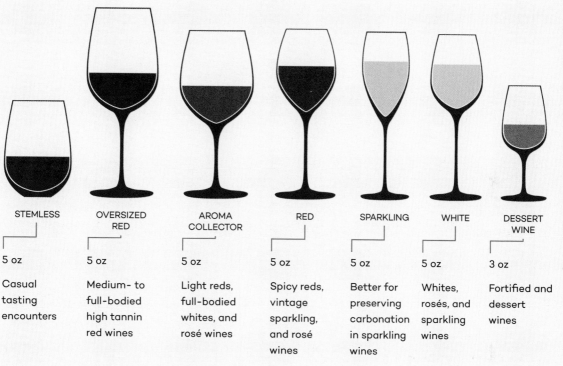

STEMLESS	OVERSIZED RED	AROMA COLLECTOR	RED	SPARKLING	WHITE	DESSERT WINE
5 oz	5 oz	5 oz	5 oz	5 oz	5 oz	3 oz
Casual tasting encounters	Medium- to full-bodied high tannin red wines	Light reds, full-bodied whites, and rosé wines	Spicy reds, vintage sparkling, and rosé wines	Better for preserving carbonation in sparkling wines	Whites, rosés, and sparkling wines	Fortified and dessert wines

winefolly.com / learn / basics / handling / wine glasses

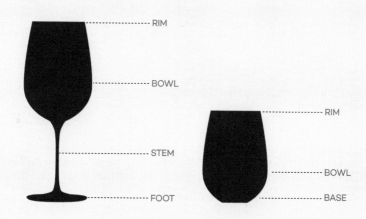

RIM

BOWL

STEM

FOOT

RIM

BOWL

BASE

SERVING WINE

The fundamentals of opening, pouring, serving, and decanting wine:

OPENING STILL WINE

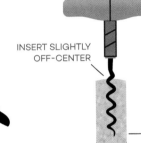

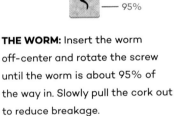

INSERT SLIGHTLY
OFF-CENTER

95%

5 OZ
150 ML

REMOVE THE FOIL: It doesn't matter if you cut the foil above or below the lip, although tradition is to cut below.

THE WORM: Insert the worm off-center and rotate the screw until the worm is about 95% of the way in. Slowly pull the cork out to reduce breakage.

STANDARD POUR: The standard serving size for wine is about 5–6 oz or 150–180 ml. Dry wines average 130–175 calories per glass depending on alcohol level.

OPENING SPARKLING WINE

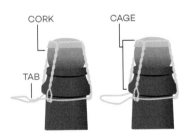

CORK

CAGE

TAB

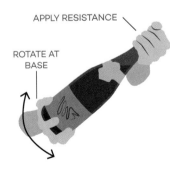

APPLY RESISTANCE

ROTATE AT
BASE

HOLD BOTTLE
AT AN ANGLE &
IT WON'T
BUBBLE OVER

45°

THE CAGE: Remove the foil and untwist tab 6 times. Keep your thumb on cage and cork—they will come off together.

TWIST: With 1 hand firmly holding the cork and cage, use your other hand to rotate the bottom of the bottle.

RELEASE: When the cork pushes, resist it and slowly release it. Keep bottle at an angle for a second or two after you remove the cork.

AERATING WINE TO IMPROVE FLAVOR

Decanting introduces oxygen to wine. This simple step oxidizes stinky aroma compounds into less detectable smells. It also reduces the concentration of certain acids and tannins, making wine taste smoother. In short, it's magic.

WHICH DECANTER?: Get one you love. It's wise to get one that's easy to fill, pour, and rinse. A wine aerator is technically more efficient although not as stately.

"CORNETT"   "SWAN"   "DUCK"   AERATOR   STANDARD

WHAT TO DECANT: All red wines can be aerated. An aerated wine won't store open for long, so be sure to decant only what you plan to drink.

POUR: For increased air-to-wine contact, pour wine so it distributes on the sides of the glass as it fills.

WAIT: The bolder and more concentrated the wine, the longer you should wait. 15–30 minutes is a good starting point.

TIP: Smell sulfur? Don't worry, it's not sulfites. It just means your wine is "reductive" (see Wine Faults, pg. 17). Decanting will improve the smell and so will stirring the wine with a silver spoon.

WINE TEMPERATURE

SERVING TEMPERATURE

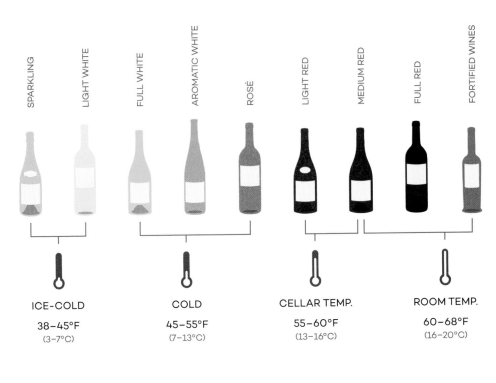

| SPARKLING | LIGHT WHITE | FULL WHITE | AROMATIC WHITE | ROSÉ | LIGHT RED | MEDIUM RED | FULL RED | FORTIFIED WINES |

ICE-COLD
38–45°F
(3–7°C)

COLD
45–55°F
(7–13°C)

CELLAR TEMP.
55–60°F
(13–16°C)

ROOM TEMP.
60–68°F
(16–20°C)

It's useful to note that wines served at room temperature are served at 60–68°F, which is cooler than most homes.

TOO COLD: Your wine might be served too cold if it's lacking aroma and tastes sour. This is a common problem for white wines stored in the refrigerator. Cup the bowl with your hands to warm your glass.

TOO HOT: Your wine might be too hot if the aroma burns your nose and smells medicinal. This is common with higher alcohol red wines that are stored in ambient home temperatures. Cool the bottle for 15 minutes.

STORING OPEN WINE

Wines quickly deteriorate when exposed to oxygen or ambient home temperatures. So store open wines in a chiller at 50–55°F (10–13°C). If you don't have a wine chiller, store open wines in your fridge and let them warm up for about an hour before serving.

VACUUM CAP

Recorking a wine stops outside oxygen from getting in, but it won't remove the oxygen inside. A wine preserver such as a vacuum pump or argon gas preserver will keep your wine fresh longer.

	1–3 DAYS
	1 WEEK
	3–5 DAYS
	1 WEEK
	1 WEEK
	3–5 DAYS
	3–5 DAYS
	3–5 DAYS
	1 MONTH

AGING WINE

The ideal storage temperature is 50–55°F and 75% humidity.

Wine ages four times faster stored in a pantry or closet. Bottles stored in variable temperature environments are also more likely to develop wine faults. So if you plan to age wine for longer than a year, look into purchasing a wine fridge or related cellaring solution.

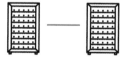

THERMOELECTRIC (SHORT TERM)   CONDENSER (LONG TERM)

There are 2 types of wine fridges: thermoelectric and condenser. Thermoelectric chillers fluctuate with temperature but are more quiet. Condenser-type chillers are louder and require maintenance intervals but are more temperature accurate.

✗	**82°F** 28°C	Wine cooks
⚠	**70°F** 21°C	Entering danger zone
✓	**50–55°F** 10–13°C	Ideal temp. range
⚠	**46°F** 8°C	Entering danger zone
✗	**32°F** 0°C	Wine freezes

29

Food and Wine Pairing

FLAVOR PAIRING THEORY

CHEESE PAIRING

MEAT PAIRING

VEGETABLE PAIRING

HERB/SPICE PAIRING

Food pairing is the practice of creating harmonious pairings by considering flavor, texture, aroma, and intensity. Learning to pair wine with food opens up a new range of wines to enjoy and explore.

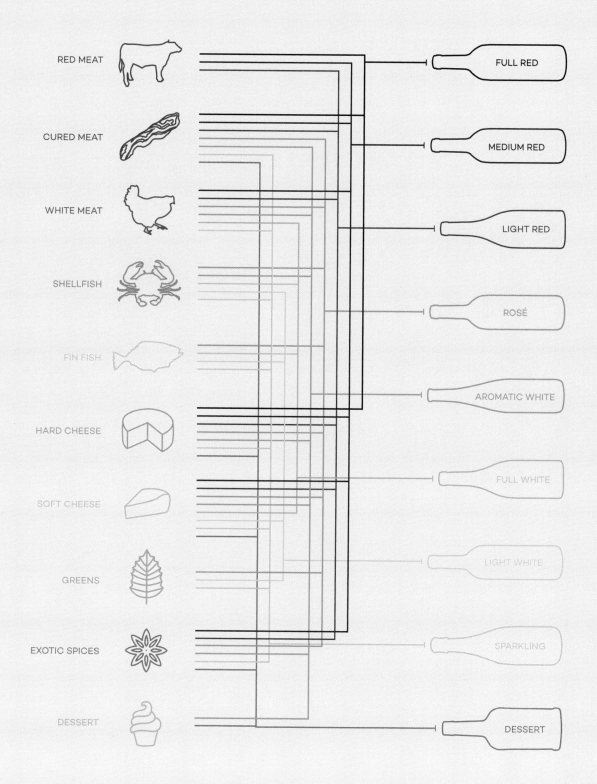

RED MEAT

CURED MEAT

WHITE MEAT

SHELLFISH

FIN FISH

HARD CHEESE

SOFT CHEESE

GREENS

EXOTIC SPICES

DESSERT

FULL RED

MEDIUM RED

LIGHT RED

ROSÉ

AROMATIC WHITE

FULL WHITE

LIGHT WHITE

SPARKLING

DESSERT

FLAVOR PAIRING THEORY

Flavor pairing is the practice of finding what foods go well together by paying attention to taste, aroma, texture, color, temperature, and intensity.

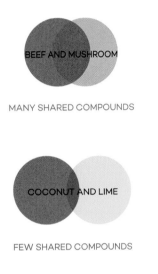

MANY SHARED COMPOUNDS

FEW SHARED COMPOUNDS

CONGRUENT VS. COMPLEMENTARY

Flavors match together in a congruent or complementary manner. Congruent pairings have many shared compounds that combine together and intensify. Complementary pairings oppose and counteract each other to create balance.

You can create amazing pairings by employing congruent pairings to amplify harmonious flavors and complementary pairings to counteract discordant flavors.

FOOD AND WINE PAIRING TIPS

ACIDIC FOOD: High acidity foods make lower acidity wines taste flat. Match high acidity foods with high acidity wines.

RICH FOOD: A high tannin red wine acts as a palate cleanser to rich, fatty proteins.

SPICY FOOD: A cold sweet wine with low alcohol will counteract the burn of spiciness.

PUNGENT FOOD: Pungent flavors like Gorgonzola match with wines that have higher acidity and sweetness.

BITTER FOOD: Bitter foods magnify the bitterness of tannin. Try pairing bitter foods with low or no tannin wines with salinity and sweetness.

SWEET FOOD: Sweet foods often make dry wines taste bitter. Try matching sweet foods with a sweet wine.

WINE PAIRING CONSIDERATIONS

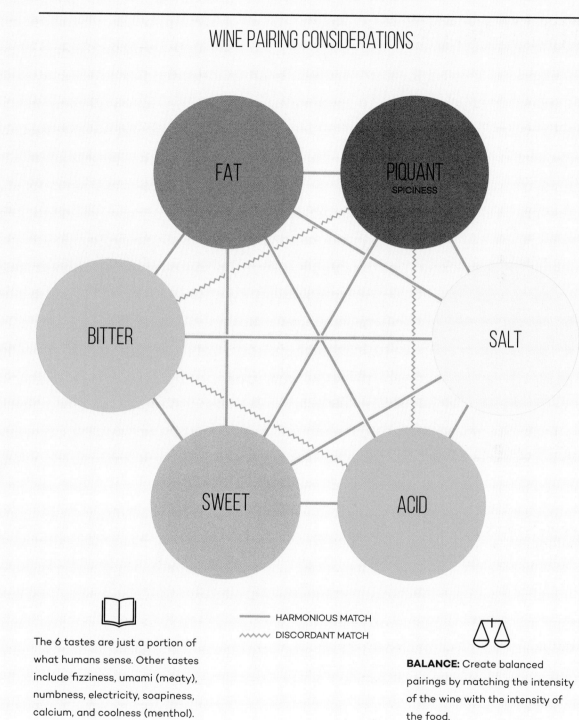

FAT

PIQUANT
SPICINESS

BITTER

SALT

SWEET

ACID

—— HARMONIOUS MATCH

∿∿∿ DISCORDANT MATCH

The 6 tastes are just a portion of what humans sense. Other tastes include fizziness, umami (meaty), numbness, electricity, soapiness, calcium, and coolness (menthol).

BALANCE: Create balanced pairings by matching the intensity of the wine with the intensity of the food.

CHEESE PAIRING

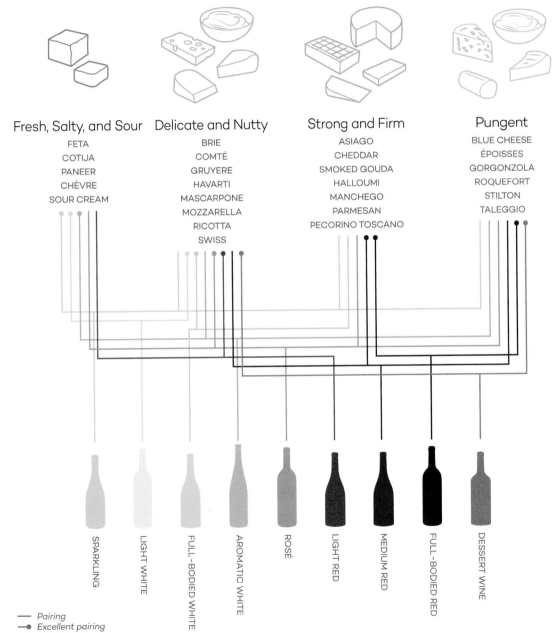

Fresh, Salty, and Sour
FETA
COTIJA
PANEER
CHÈVRE
SOUR CREAM

Delicate and Nutty
BRIE
COMTÉ
GRUYERE
HAVARTI
MASCARPONE
MOZZARELLA
RICOTTA
SWISS

Strong and Firm
ASIAGO
CHEDDAR
SMOKED GOUDA
HALLOUMI
MANCHEGO
PARMESAN
PECORINO TOSCANO

Pungent
BLUE CHEESE
ÉPOISSES
GORGONZOLA
ROQUEFORT
STILTON
TALEGGIO

SPARKLING
LIGHT WHITE
FULL-BODIED WHITE
AROMATIC WHITE
ROSÉ
LIGHT RED
MEDIUM RED
FULL-BODIED RED
DESSERT WINE

— Pairing
—● Excellent pairing

MEAT PAIRING

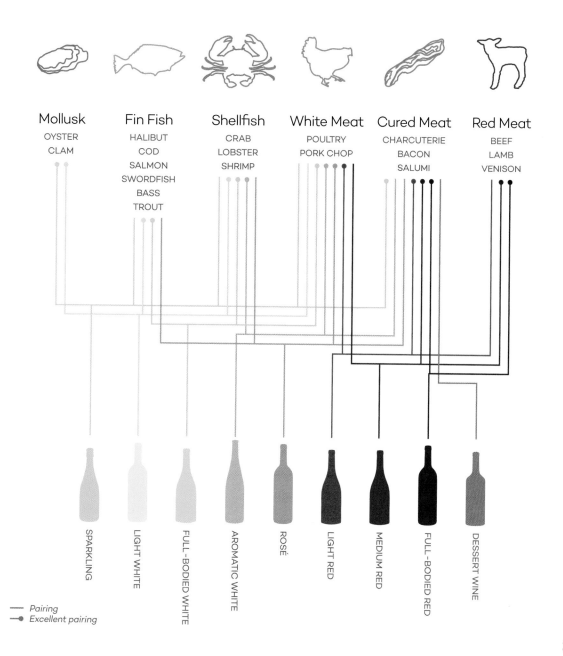

winefolly.com / learn / basics / food-and-wine / meat

Mollusk
OYSTER
CLAM

Fin Fish
HALIBUT
COD
SALMON
SWORDFISH
BASS
TROUT

Shellfish
CRAB
LOBSTER
SHRIMP

White Meat
POULTRY
PORK CHOP

Cured Meat
CHARCUTERIE
BACON
SALUMI

Red Meat
BEEF
LAMB
VENISON

SPARKLING
LIGHT WHITE
FULL-BODIED WHITE
AROMATIC WHITE
ROSÉ
LIGHT RED
MEDIUM RED
FULL-BODIED RED
DESSERT WINE

— Pairing
•— Excellent pairing

VEGETABLE PAIRING

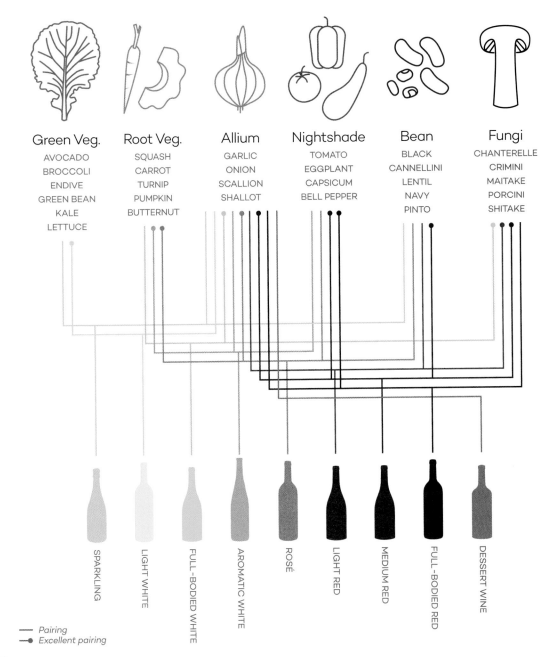

Green Veg.
AVOCADO
BROCCOLI
ENDIVE
GREEN BEAN
KALE
LETTUCE

Root Veg.
SQUASH
CARROT
TURNIP
PUMPKIN
BUTTERNUT

Allium
GARLIC
ONION
SCALLION
SHALLOT

Nightshade
TOMATO
EGGPLANT
CAPSICUM
BELL PEPPER

Bean
BLACK
CANNELLINI
LENTIL
NAVY
PINTO

Fungi
CHANTERELLE
CRIMINI
MAITAKE
PORCINI
SHITAKE

SPARKLING

LIGHT WHITE

FULL-BODIED WHITE

AROMATIC WHITE

ROSÉ

LIGHT RED

MEDIUM RED

FULL-BODIED RED

DESSERT WINE

— Pairing
—● Excellent pairing

HERB/SPICE PAIRING

winefolly.com / learn / basics / food-and-wine / herb-spice

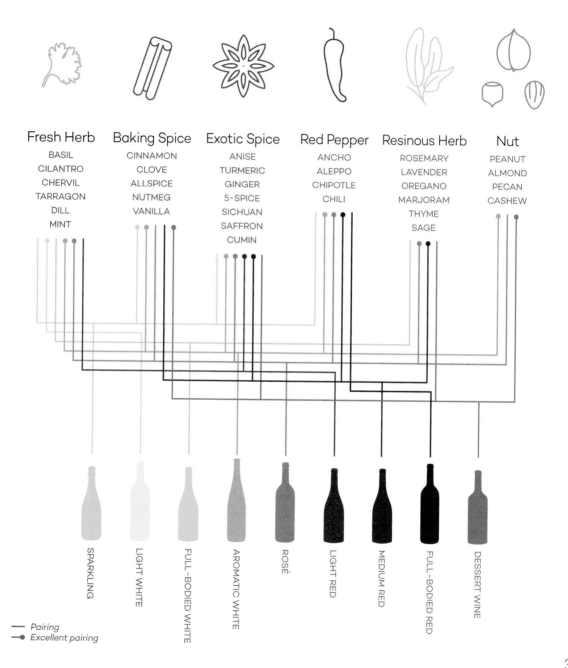

Fresh Herb
BASIL
CILANTRO
CHERVIL
TARRAGON
DILL
MINT

Baking Spice
CINNAMON
CLOVE
ALLSPICE
NUTMEG
VANILLA

Exotic Spice
ANISE
TURMERIC
GINGER
5-SPICE
SICHUAN
SAFFRON
CUMIN

Red Pepper
ANCHO
ALEPPO
CHIPOTLE
CHILI

Resinous Herb
ROSEMARY
LAVENDER
OREGANO
MARJORAM
THYME
SAGE

Nut
PEANUT
ALMOND
PECAN
CASHEW

SPARKLING
LIGHT WHITE
FULL-BODIED WHITE
AROMATIC WHITE
ROSÉ
LIGHT RED
MEDIUM RED
FULL-BODIED RED
DESSERT WINE

— Pairing
—• Excellent pairing

37

Styles of Wine

Styles of Wine

SPARKLING WINE

LIGHT-BODIED WHITE WINE

FULL-BODIED WHITE WINE

AROMATIC WHITE WINE

ROSÉ WINE

LIGHT-BODIED RED WINE

MEDIUM-BODIED RED WINE

FULL-BODIED RED WINE

DESSERT WINE

Wines in this book are organized from lightest to boldest within nine different styles. This categorization method is designed to help you quickly identify what a wine tastes like without having to try it. Occasionally, you may come across a wine that doesn't fit neatly into this categorization method. It is an exception to the rule.

SECTION DETAILS

CHARACTERISTICS
See pgs. 8–11 for details.

NAME

PRIMARY FLAVORS

aka (ALSO KNOWN AS)
Other varietal names or regional names that are synonymous with wine.

PRONUNCIATION

SANGIOVESE

🔊 "San-jo Vay-zay"
aka: Chianti, Brunello, Nielluccio, Morellino

🍃 VARIETY

🍷 WINE/BLEND

WINE FOLLY LINK
Where to go online for more information.

wfolly.com / variety / sangiovese

PROFILE

FRUIT	●●● ●●
BODY	●●● ●●●
TANNIN	●●● ●●
ACIDITY	●●● ●●●
ALCOHOL	●● ●

DOMINANT FLAVORS

RED CURRANT · ROASTED TOMATO · RASPBERRY · POTPOURRI · CLAY POT

ADDITIONAL FLAVORS
See pg. 16 for details.

POSSIBLE FLAVORS

POSSIBLE FLAVORS
Find out more about flavors and aromas on pg 16.

PRIMARY
- ■ BLACK FRUIT
- ■ DRIED FRUIT
- ■ RED FRUIT
- TROPICAL FRUIT
- TREE FRUIT
- CITRUS FRUIT
- FLORAL / HERBAL
- EARTH / OTHER

SECONDARY
- YEAST
- BACTERIA / OTHER

TERTIARY
- ■ OAK
- OTHER TERTIARY

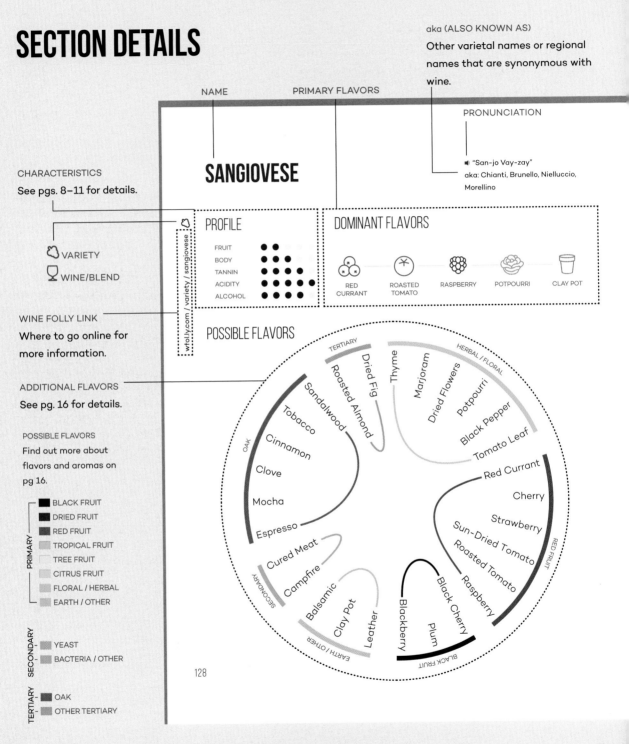

128

42

WINE STATISTICS

Distribution and total world acres/ha (hectares) based on statistics from 2010–2014.

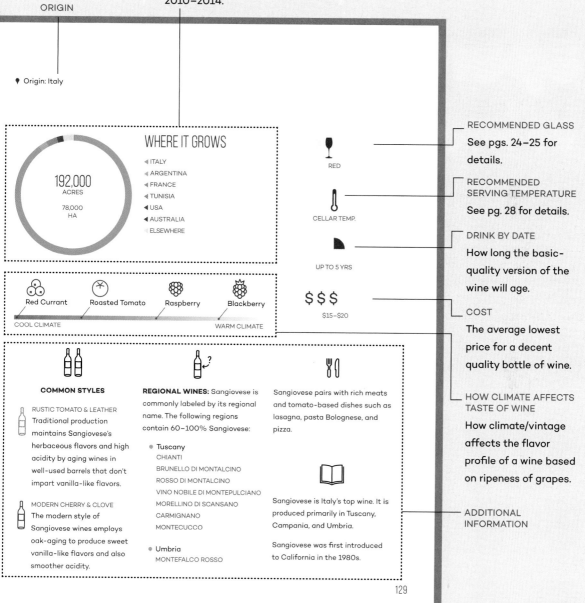

Origin: Italy

WHERE IT GROWS

192,000
ACRES

78,000
HA

◄ ITALY
◄ ARGENTINA
◄ FRANCE
◄ TUNISIA
◄ USA
◄ AUSTRALIA
◄ ELSEWHERE

Red Currant   Roasted Tomato   Raspberry   Blackberry

COOL CLIMATE   WARM CLIMATE

RED

CELLAR TEMP.

UP TO 5 YRS

$ $ $
$15–$20

RECOMMENDED GLASS

See pgs. 24–25 for details.

RECOMMENDED SERVING TEMPERATURE

See pg. 28 for details.

DRINK BY DATE

How long the basic-quality version of the wine will age.

COST

The average lowest price for a decent quality bottle of wine.

HOW CLIMATE AFFECTS TASTE OF WINE

How climate/vintage affects the flavor profile of a wine based on ripeness of grapes.

ADDITIONAL INFORMATION

COMMON STYLES

RUSTIC TOMATO & LEATHER Traditional production maintains Sangiovese's herbaceous flavors and high acidity by aging wines in well-used barrels that don't impart vanilla-like flavors.

MODERN CHERRY & CLOVE The modern style of Sangiovese wines employs oak-aging to produce sweet vanilla-like flavors and also smoother acidity.

REGIONAL WINES: Sangiovese is commonly labeled by its regional name. The following regions contain 60–100% Sangiovese:

● Tuscany
CHIANTI
BRUNELLO DI MONTALCINO
ROSSO DI MONTALCINO
VINO NOBILE DI MONTEPULCIANO
MORELLINO DI SCANSANO
CARMIGNANO
MONTECUCCO

● Umbria
MONTEFALCO ROSSO

Sangiovese pairs with rich meats and tomato-based dishes such as lasagna, pasta Bolognese, and pizza.

Sangiovese is Italy's top wine. It is produced primarily in Tuscany, Campania, and Umbria.

Sangiovese was first introduced to California in the 1980s.

129

Sparkling Wine

CAVA

CHAMPAGNE

LAMBRUSCO

PROSECCO

Sparkling wine is carbonated by yeast fermenting in an airtight container. The 2 most common sparkling winemaking methods are called "traditional method" and "tank method." Sparkling wine is produced throughout the world and often follows the same winemaking methods and grape varieties found in Champagne.

DIFFERENT SPARKLING WINEMAKING METHODS

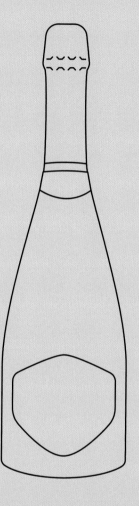

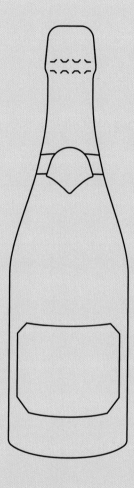

TANK "CHARMAT" METHOD

EXAMPLE: Prosecco, Lambrusco

BUBBLES: Medium-size, spritzy bubbles and 2–4 atmospheres of pressure

TRADITIONAL METHOD

EXAMPLE: Champagne, Cava, Crémant, US sparkling wine, Metodo Classico (Italy), Cap Classique (South Africa)

BUBBLES: Small, persistent bubbles and 6–7 atmospheres of pressure

CAVA

🔊 "kah-vah"

🛢 Traditional Method

winefolly.com / learn / wine / cava

PROFILE

FRUIT

BODY

DRY

ACIDITY

ALCOHOL

DOMINANT FLAVORS

QUINCE — LIME — YELLOW APPLE — PEAR — ALMOND

POSSIBLE FLAVORS

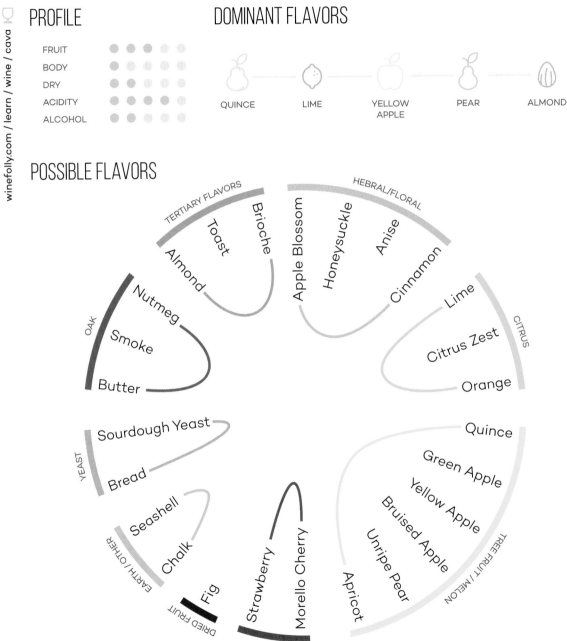

TERTIARY FLAVORS
- Almond
- Toast
- Brioche

HEBRAL/FLORAL
- Apple Blossom
- Honeysuckle
- Anise
- Cinnamon

CITRUS
- Lime
- Citrus Zest
- Orange

OAK
- Nutmeg
- Smoke
- Butter

TREE FRUIT / MELON
- Quince
- Green Apple
- Yellow Apple
- Bruised Apple
- Unripe Pear
- Apricot

YEAST
- Sourdough Yeast
- Bread

EARTH / OTHER
- Seashell
- Chalk

DRIED FRUIT
- Fig

RED FRUIT
- Strawberry
- Morello Cherry

📍 Origin: Spain

~79,000
ACRES

32,000
HA

WHERE IT'S MADE

◀ PENEDÈS, SPAIN
◀ [ELSEWHERE IN SPAIN]

SPARKLING

ICE-COLD

UP TO 2 YRS

$ $ $ $ $
$5–$10

Quince   Lemon   Orange   Apricot

COOL VINTAGE   WARM VINTAGE

winefolly.com / learn / wine / cava

CAVA GRAPES: There are 3 primary grapes of Cava:

MACABEO
(aka Viura, Macabeu)
adds floral, apricot, and berry flavors.

XARELLO
adds acidity.

PARELLADA
adds quince, apple, and citrus flavors.

QUALITY LEVELS: There are 3 quality levels, indicated by a sticker or band on the bottle:

CAVA (STANDARD)
9 months min. aging

RESERVA
15 months min. aging

GRAN RESERVA
30 months min. aging and vintage dated

Cava is versatile with food because of its palate-cleansing effect. Try it with chili, huevos rancheros, nachos, tacos, and hush puppies.

Cava DO (Denominación de Origen) is the only Spanish wine classification for a style of wine rather than a region. Still, around 95% of the production is in the Penedès region of Spain.

CHANPAGNE

◀) "sham-pain"

🛢 Traditional Method

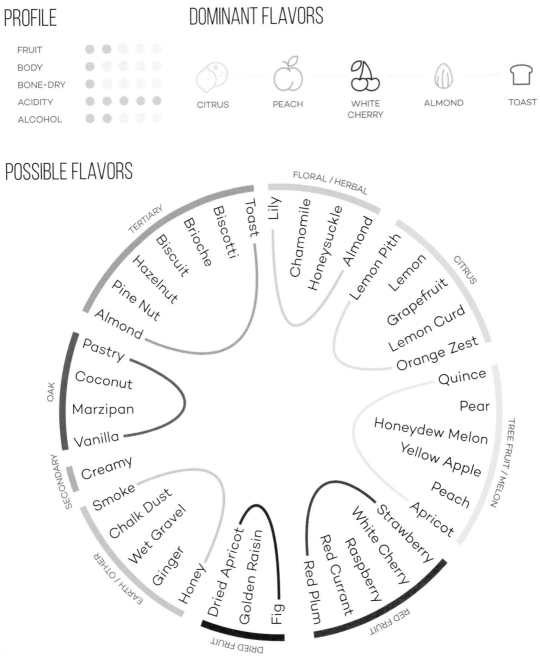

PROFILE

FRUIT	●	●	●	○	○
BODY	●	●	○	○	○
BONE-DRY	●	●	○	○	○
ACIDITY	●	●	●	●	●
ALCOHOL	●	●	○	○	○

DOMINANT FLAVORS

CITRUS · PEACH · WHITE CHERRY · ALMOND · TOAST

POSSIBLE FLAVORS

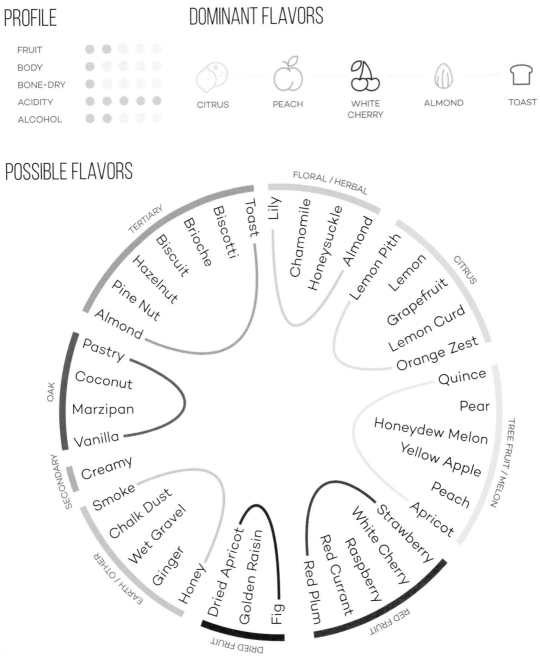

FLORAL / HERBAL: Lily, Chamomile, Honeysuckle, Almond

CITRUS: Lemon Pith, Lemon, Grapefruit, Lemon Curd, Orange Zest

TREE FRUIT / MELON: Quince, Pear, Honeydew Melon, Yellow Apple, Peach, Apricot

RED FRUIT: Strawberry, White Cherry, Raspberry, Red Currant, Red Plum

DRIED FRUIT: Dried Apricot, Golden Raisin, Fig

EARTH / OTHER: Honey, Ginger, Wet Gravel, Chalk Dust, Smoke

SECONDARY: Creamy

OAK: Pastry, Coconut, Marzipan, Vanilla

TERTIARY: Toast, Biscotti, Brioche, Biscuit, Hazelnut, Pine Nut, Almond

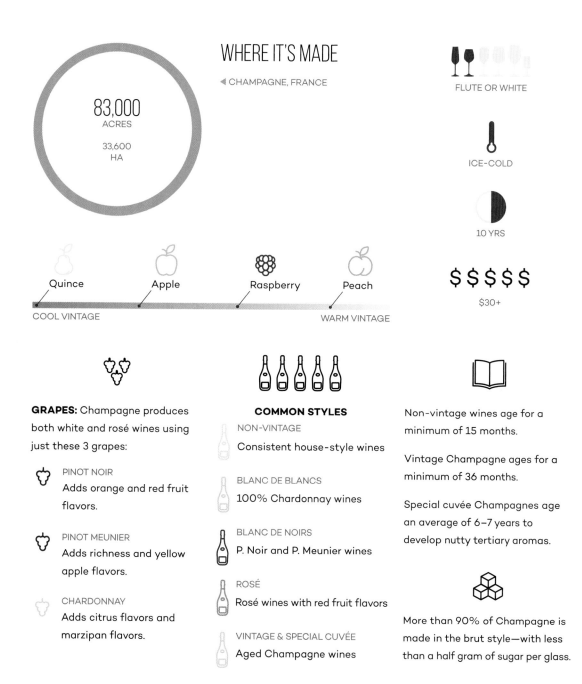

Origin: Champagne, France

WHERE IT'S MADE

◄ CHAMPAGNE, FRANCE

83,000
ACRES

33,600
HA

FLUTE OR WHITE

ICE-COLD

10 YRS

$ $ $ $ $
$30+

Quince   Apple   Raspberry   Peach

COOL VINTAGE   WARM VINTAGE

GRAPES: Champagne produces both white and rosé wines using just these 3 grapes:

PINOT NOIR
Adds orange and red fruit flavors.

PINOT MEUNIER
Adds richness and yellow apple flavors.

CHARDONNAY
Adds citrus flavors and marzipan flavors.

COMMON STYLES

NON-VINTAGE
Consistent house-style wines

BLANC DE BLANCS
100% Chardonnay wines

BLANC DE NOIRS
P. Noir and P. Meunier wines

ROSÉ
Rosé wines with red fruit flavors

VINTAGE & SPECIAL CUVÉE
Aged Champagne wines

Non-vintage wines age for a minimum of 15 months.

Vintage Champagne ages for a minimum of 36 months.

Special cuvée Champagnes age an average of 6–7 years to develop nutty tertiary aromas.

More than 90% of Champagne is made in the brut style—with less than a half gram of sugar per glass.

winefolly.com / learn / wine / champagne

LAMBRUSCO

🔊 "lam-broos-co"
🛢 Tank "Charmat" Method

PROFILE

FRUIT
BODY
OFF-DRY
ACIDITY
ALCOHOL

DOMINANT FLAVORS

STRAWBERRY   CHERRY   BOYSENBERRY   RHUBARB   HIBISCUS

POSSIBLE FLAVORS

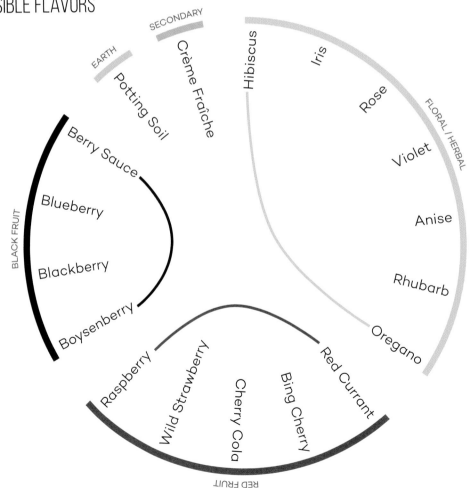

SECONDARY

EARTH

Crème Fraîche

Potting Soil

Berry Sauce

Hibiscus

Iris

Rose

FLORAL / HERBAL

Violet

Anise

Rhubarb

Oregano

BLACK FRUIT

Blueberry

Blackberry

Boysenberry

Raspberry

Wild Strawberry

Cherry Cola

Bing Cherry

Red Currant

RED FRUIT

📍 Origin: northern Italy

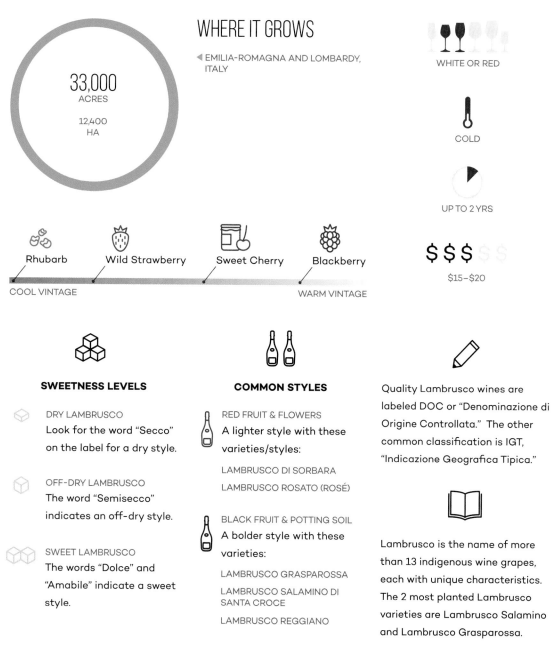

33,000
ACRES

12,400
HA

WHERE IT GROWS

◀ EMILIA-ROMAGNA AND LOMBARDY, ITALY

WHITE OR RED

COLD

UP TO 2 YRS

$ $ $ $ $
$15–$20

Rhubarb   Wild Strawberry   Sweet Cherry   Blackberry

COOL VINTAGE   WARM VINTAGE

SWEETNESS LEVELS

DRY LAMBRUSCO
Look for the word "Secco" on the label for a dry style.

OFF-DRY LAMBRUSCO
The word "Semisecco" indicates an off-dry style.

SWEET LAMBRUSCO
The words "Dolce" and "Amabile" indicate a sweet style.

COMMON STYLES

RED FRUIT & FLOWERS
A lighter style with these varieties/styles:
LAMBRUSCO DI SORBARA
LAMBRUSCO ROSATO (ROSÉ)

BLACK FRUIT & POTTING SOIL
A bolder style with these varieties:
LAMBRUSCO GRASPAROSSA
LAMBRUSCO SALAMINO DI SANTA CROCE
LAMBRUSCO REGGIANO

Quality Lambrusco wines are labeled DOC or "Denominazione di Origine Controllata." The other common classification is IGT, "Indicazione Geografica Tipica."

Lambrusco is the name of more than 13 indigenous wine grapes, each with unique characteristics. The 2 most planted Lambrusco varieties are Lambrusco Salamino and Lambrusco Grasparossa.

PROSECCO

🔊 "pro-seh-co"
🛢 Tank "Charmat" Method

PROFILE

FRUIT
BODY
DRY
ACIDITY
ALCOHOL

DOMINANT FLAVORS

GREEN APPLE — HONEYDEW MELON — PEAR — HONEYSUCKLE — CREAM

POSSIBLE FLAVORS

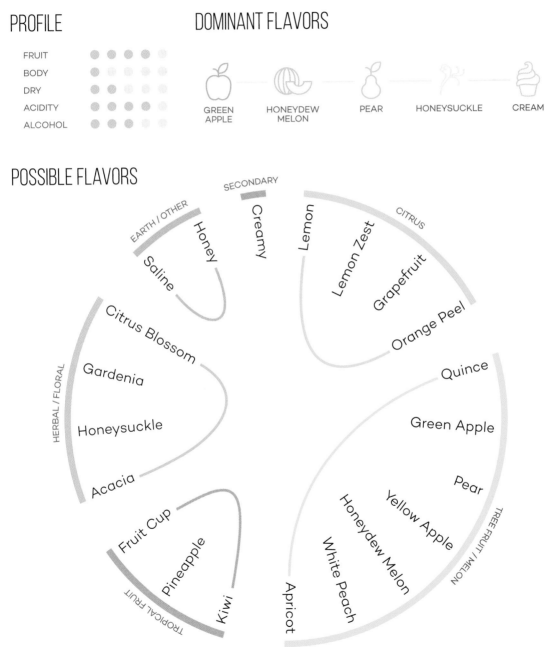

SECONDARY
Creamy

EARTH / OTHER
Honey
Saline

CITRUS
Lemon
Lemon Zest
Grapefruit
Orange Peel

HERBAL / FLORAL
Citrus Blossom
Gardenia
Honeysuckle
Acacia

TREE FRUIT / MELON
Quince
Green Apple
Pear
Yellow Apple
Honeydew Melon
White Peach
Apricot

TROPICAL FRUIT
Fruit Cup
Pineapple
Kiwi

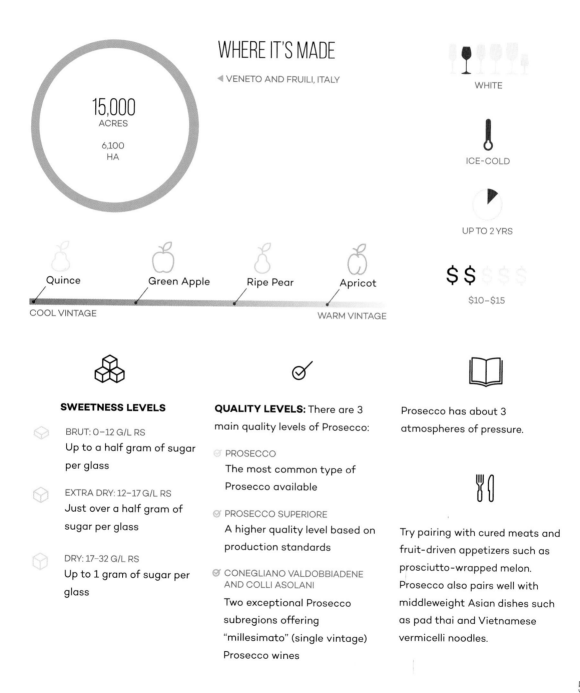

♥ Origin: northern Italy

WHERE IT'S MADE

◄ VENETO AND FRUILI, ITALY

15,000
ACRES

6,100
HA

WHITE

ICE-COLD

UP TO 2 YRS

$ $ $ $ $
$10–$15

Quince — COOL VINTAGE

Green Apple

Ripe Pear

Apricot — WARM VINTAGE

SWEETNESS LEVELS

BRUT: 0–12 G/L RS
Up to a half gram of sugar per glass

EXTRA DRY: 12–17 G/L RS
Just over a half gram of sugar per glass

DRY: 17–32 G/L RS
Up to 1 gram of sugar per glass

QUALITY LEVELS: There are 3 main quality levels of Prosecco:

⊘ PROSECCO
The most common type of Prosecco available

⊘ PROSECCO SUPERIORE
A higher quality level based on production standards

⊘ CONEGLIANO VALDOBBIADENE AND COLLI ASOLANI
Two exceptional Prosecco subregions offering "millesimato" (single vintage) Prosecco wines

Prosecco has about 3 atmospheres of pressure.

Try pairing with cured meats and fruit-driven appetizers such as prosciutto-wrapped melon. Prosecco also pairs well with middleweight Asian dishes such as pad thai and Vietnamese vermicelli noodles.

53

Light-Bodied White Wine

ALBARIÑO

GRÜNER VELTLINER

MUSCADET

PINOT GRIS

SAUVIGNON BLANC

SOAVE

VERMENTINO

Light bodied white wines are known for their dry and refreshingly tart flavor. Most light-bodied white wines are meant to be enjoyed young when they have maximum acidity and bold fruit.

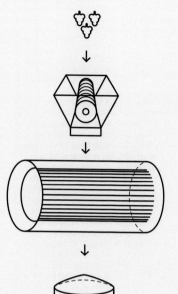

White or red wine grapes are collected and sorted.

Grape bunches are destemmed.

Grapes are pressed and separated from skins and seeds.

Juice ferments into wine without skins.

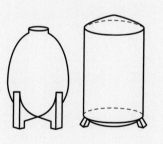

Wine is kept cool in storage tanks to settle and stabilize for a short period of time.

Wines are clarified, bottled, and released shortly thereafter.

ALBARIÑO

🔊 "alba-reen-yo"
aka: Alvarinho

PROFILE

FRUIT
BODY
DRY
ACIDITY
ALCOHOL

DOMINANT FLAVORS

LEMON — GRAPEFRUIT — NECTARINE — MELON — WET GRAVEL

POSSIBLE FLAVORS

HERBAL / FLORAL
Lily
Citrus Blossom

EARTH / OTHER
Saline
Quinine
Crushed Gravel
Minerals
Beeswax

Lime Zest
Lemon
Lemon Peel
Grapefruit Pith
Grapefruit
Orange Peel
Tangerine
CITRUS

TROPICAL FRUIT
Papaya
Peach
Nectarine
Apple
Honeydew Melon
TREE FRUIT / MELON

📍 Origin: Northern Portugal

19,000
ACRES

~7,700
HA

WHERE IT GROWS

◀ SPAIN
◀ PORTUGAL
◀ USA
◀ ELSEWHERE

WHITE

ICE-COLD

UP TO 2 YRS

$ $ $ $ $
$15–$20

Lemon   Grapefruit   Melon   Peach

COOL CLIMATE   WARM CLIMATE

REGIONS

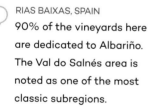

RIAS BAIXAS, SPAIN
90% of the vineyards here are dedicated to Albariño. The Val do Salnés area is noted as one of the most classic subregions.

MINHO, PORTUGAL
Alvarinho is one of the grapes in Vinho Verde, which is a crisp, aromatic white wine that often has some spritz.

AROMAS

The melon and grapefruit aromas found in Albariño come from a group of aroma compounds called thiols. Thiols are commonly found in light white wines from cooler-climate growing regions, such as Sauvignon Blanc from New Zealand and France and Pinot Grigio from northern Italy.

Albariño is particularly well suited to Thai, Moroccan, and Indian cuisine.

THAI

MOROCCAN

INDIAN

57

GRÜNER VELTLINER

◀ "GREW-ner FELT-lee-ner"

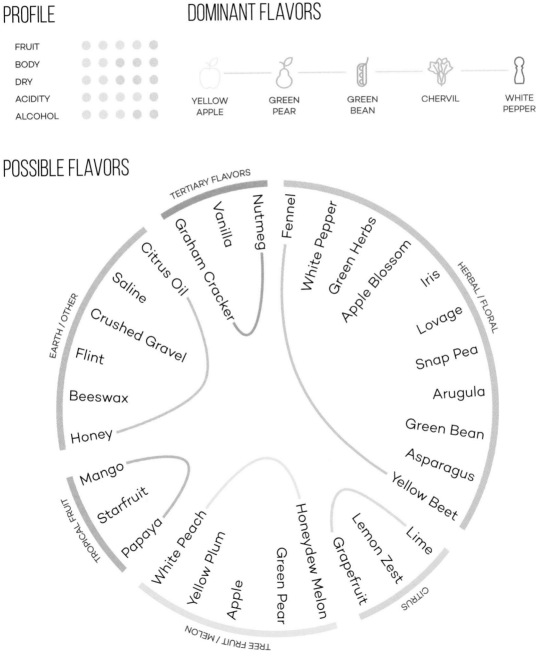

PROFILE

FRUIT
BODY
DRY
ACIDITY
ALCOHOL

DOMINANT FLAVORS

YELLOW APPLE — GREEN PEAR — GREEN BEAN — CHERVIL — WHITE PEPPER

POSSIBLE FLAVORS

TERTIARY FLAVORS

Nutmeg
Vanilla
Graham Cracker
Citrus Oil
Saline
Crushed Gravel
Flint
Beeswax
Honey

EARTH / OTHER

Mango
Starfruit
Papaya

TROPICAL FRUIT

White Peach
Yellow Plum
Apple
Green Pear
Honeydew Melon

TREE FRUIT / MELON

Grapefruit
Lemon Zest
Lime

CITRUS

Yellow Beet
Asparagus
Green Bean
Arugula
Snap Pea
Lovage
Iris

HERBAL / FLORAL

Apple Blossom
Green Herbs
White Pepper
Fennel

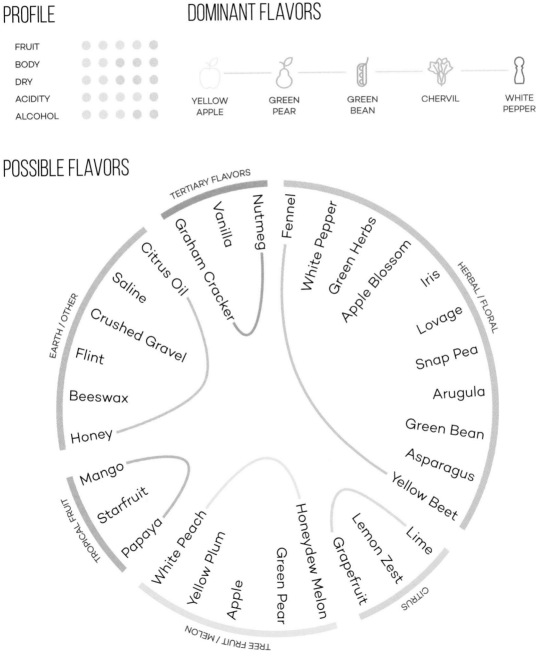

◉ Origin: Austria

WHERE IT GROWS

50,000
ACRES

~20,200
HA

◀ AUSTRIA
◀ SLOVAKIA
◀ CZECH REPUBLIC
◀ HUNGARY
◀ ELSEWHERE

WHITE

ICE-COLD

UP TO 2 YRS

$ $ $ $ $
$15–$20

Lime   Green Pear   Yellow Apple   Peach

COOL VINTAGE   WARM VINTAGE

QUALITY: There are 3 main quality levels of Austrian Grüner Veltliner:

LANDWEIN
Typically low alcohol wines made in bulk

QUALITÄTSWEIN
Austria's mark of quality for Grüner Veltliner

DAC
DAC
Subregional Qualitätswein with a light style, Classic, and a rich style, Reserve

COMMON STYLES

LIGHT & ZESTY
The most common and affordable style, known for tingling acidity and simple melon/lime flavors. DAC wines are labeled "Classic."

RICH, FRUITY, AND PEPPERY
A richer style often labeled "Reserve (DAC)" or "Smaragd (from Wachau)" in Austria. Wines are dry and taste of honey, apple, smoke, mango, and white pepper.

Grüner Veltliner pairs particularly well with aromatic vegetables, tofu, and Japanese cuisine.

GINGER

YUZU

WASABI

GREEN ONION

winefolly.com / learn / variety / gruner-veltliner

MUSCADET

🔊 "muss-kuh-day"
aka: Melon de Bourgogne

PROFILE

FRUIT
BODY
BONE-DRY
ACIDITY
ALCOHOL

DOMINANT FLAVORS

LIME — LEMON — GREEN APPLE — PEAR — SEASHELL

POSSIBLE FLAVORS

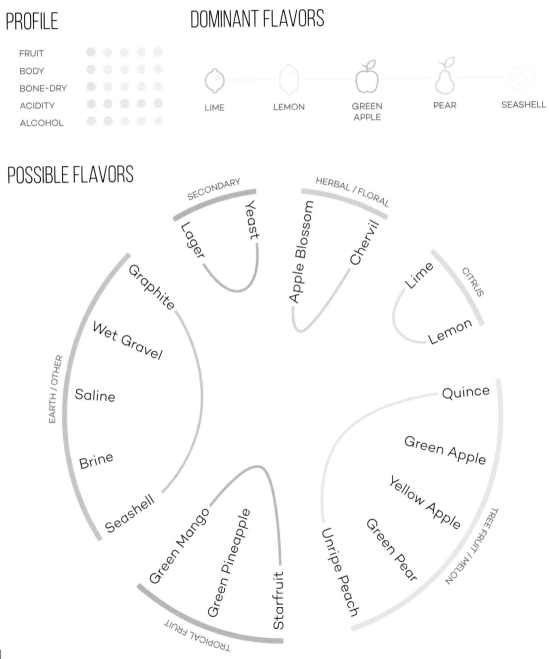

SECONDARY
- Lager
- Yeast

HERBAL / FLORAL
- Apple Blossom
- Chervil

CITRUS
- Lime
- Lemon

TREE FRUIT / MELON
- Quince
- Green Apple
- Yellow Apple
- Green Pear
- Unripe Peach

TROPICAL FRUIT
- Green Mango
- Green Pineapple
- Starfruit

EARTH / OTHER
- Graphite
- Wet Gravel
- Saline
- Brine
- Seashell

📍 Origin: Loire, France

WHERE IT'S MADE

◀ LOIRE, FRANCE

31,000
ACRES

~12,500
HA

WHITE

ICE-COLD

UP TO 2 YRS

$ $ $ $ $
$10–$15

Lime   Lemon   Yellow Apple   Starfruit

COOL VINTAGE   WARM VINTAGE

MUSCADET GRAPE: Melon de Bourgogne or just Melon is the grape of the Muscadet region in France. Two regions make up over 90% of Muscadet wine:

MUSCADET SÈVRE-ET-MAINE
This appellation produces over 70% of Muscadet wine.

MUSCADET
This appellation has lower quality standards than Muscadet Sèvre-et-Maine.

ON THE LABEL: It's common to see the words "sur lie" on a bottle of Muscadet. "Sur lie" means "on the lees," which is a term used to describe a process where wine is aged on the dead yeast particles for a period of time.

Lees aging adds an oily mouthfeel as well as yeasty bread-like flavors to wine. It's common to find it in white wines such as Muscadet, Viognier, and Marsanne, as well as many sparkling wines.

Muscadet is a classic match with shellfish, and fish and chips. Due to its high acidity, Muscadet pairs with pickled ingredients and vinegar-based sauces.

SHELLFISH

LEMON

FRIED FOOD

61

PINOT GRIS

🔊 "pee-no gree"
aka: Pinot Grigio, Grauburgunder

PROFILE

FRUIT
BODY
DRY
ACIDITY
ALCOHOL

DOMINANT FLAVORS

LEMON   YELLOW   MELON   NECTARINE   PEACH
          APPLE

POSSIBLE FLAVORS

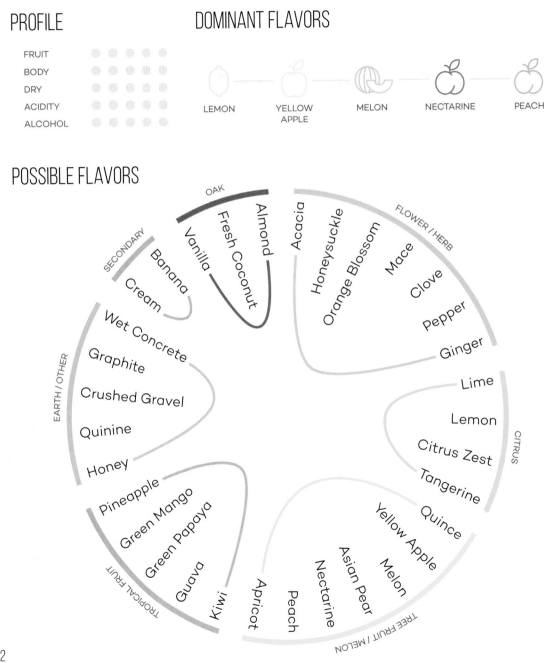

OAK

SECONDARY

FLOWER / HERB

Almond
Fresh Coconut
Vanilla
Banana
Cream
Wet Concrete
Graphite
Crushed Gravel
Quinine
Honey
Pineapple
Green Mango
Green Papaya
Guava
Kiwi
Apricot
Peach
Nectarine
Asian Pear
Yellow Apple
Melon
Quince
Tangerine
Citrus Zest
Lemon
Lime
Ginger
Pepper
Clove
Mace
Orange Blossom
Honeysuckle
Acacia

EARTH / OTHER

TROPICAL FRUIT

TREE FRUIT / MELON

CITRUS

🍷 Origin: France and Italy

WHERE IT GROWS

108,000
ACRES

~43,700
HA

◀ ITALY
◀ USA
◀ GERMANY
◀ AUSTRALIA
◀ FRANCE
◀ MOLDOVA
◀ HUNGARY
◀ ELSEWHERE

WHITE

ICE-COLD

UP TO 5 YRS

$ $
$10–$15

Lime   Lemon   Nectarine   Apricot

COOL CLIMATE   WARM CLIMATE

winefolly.com / learn / variety / pinot-gris

PINOT GRIS: Pinot Gris is 1 of 4 common types of Pinot:

PINOT BLANC
A white wine grape

PINOT GRIS
A gray-purple grape used for white and rosé wine

PINOT NOIR
A black grape for red and rosé wine

PINOT MEUNIER
A black grape used mainly in Champagne

COMMON STYLES

MINERALLY & DRY
Mostly known as Pinot Grigio, from northern Italy, with citrus notes and salinity.

FRUITY & DRY
This style is found in USA, Australia, and other warmer climate regions.

FRUITY & SWEET
This style is found mostly in Alsace, France, and offers flavors of lemon, peach, and honey.

In the Friuli-Venezia Giulia region of Italy there is a unique style of Pinot Grigio called Ramato in which the juice macerates on the grape skins for about 2–3 days to make a pale-copper-hued rosé.

Try pairing Pinot Gris with light flaky fish dishes, crab, and softer cow's milk cheeses such as a triple-cream cheese.

63

SAUVIGNON BLANC

PROFILE

FRUIT
BODY
DRY
ACIDITY
ALCOHOL

DOMINANT FLAVORS

GOOSEBERRY — GREEN MELON — GRAPEFRUIT — WHITE PEACH — PASSION FRUIT

POSSIBLE FLAVORS

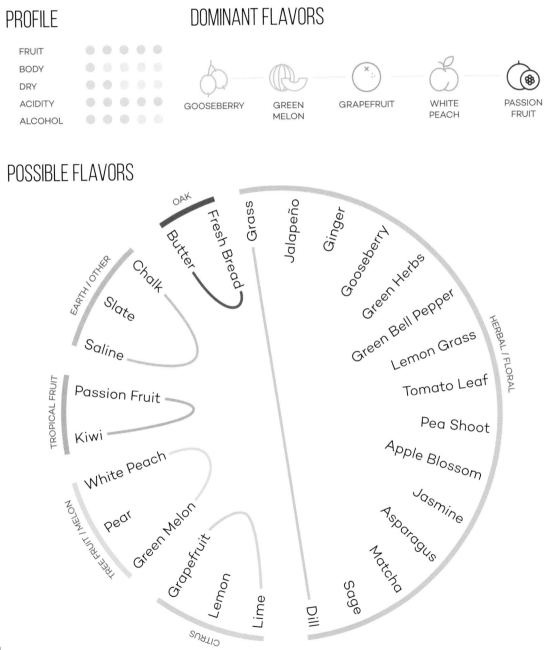

OAK
Butter
Fresh Bread
Grass
Jalapeño
Ginger
Gooseberry
Green Herbs
Green Bell Pepper
Lemon Grass
Tomato Leaf
Pea Shoot
Apple Blossom
Jasmine
Asparagus
Matcha
Sage
Dill
HERBAL / FLORAL

EARTH / OTHER
Chalk
Slate
Saline

TROPICAL FRUIT
Passion Fruit
Kiwi

White Peach
Pear
Green Melon
Grapefruit
Lemon
Lime
TREE FRUIT / MELON
CITRUS

📍 Origin: France

272,000
ACRES

~110,000
HA

WHERE IT GROWS

◄ FRANCE
◄ NEW ZEALAND
◄ CHILE
◄ SOUTH AFRICA
◄ MOLDOVA
◄ USA
◄ AUSTRALIA
◄ ROMANIA
◄ SPAIN

◄ ITALY
◄ UKRAINE
◄ ARGENTINA
◄ ELSEWHERE

WHITE

ICE-COLD

UP TO 2 YRS

$
$5–$10

Lime
Gooseberry
Melon
White Peach

COOL CLIMATE
WARM CLIMATE

REGIONAL DIFFERENCES: Every region produces a different taste of Sauvignon Blanc. Here are a few examples of dominant fruit flavors by region:

WHITE PEACH
North Coast, CA, USA

LIME
Loire Valley, FR

PASSION FRUIT
Marlborough, NZ

BARREL-AGED: A style made famous by Robert Mondavi in the 1970s when he renamed his barrel-aged Sauvignon Blanc to Fumé Blanc ("foom-aye blonk"). Barrel-aged Sauvignon Blanc tastes creamy while still exhibiting the variety's trademark "green" notes.

PEAR
TARRAGON
CREAM

Like Sauvignon Blanc? You'll find similar flavors in Austrian Grüner Veltliner, Spanish Verdejo, French Gros Manseng and Colombard, and Italian Vermentino.

Sauvignon Blanc is a parent of Cabernet Sauvignon. The cross happened naturally between Cabernet Franc and Sauvignon Blanc sometime during the 17th century in western France.

SOAVE

PROFILE

FRUIT	●	●	●	●	●
BODY	●	●	●	●	●
BONE-DRY	●	●	●	●	●
ACIDITY	●	●	●	●	●
ALCOHOL	●	●	●	●	●

DOMINANT FLAVORS

PRESERVED LEMON — HONEYDEW MELON — SALINE — GREEN ALMOND — CHERVIL

POSSIBLE FLAVORS

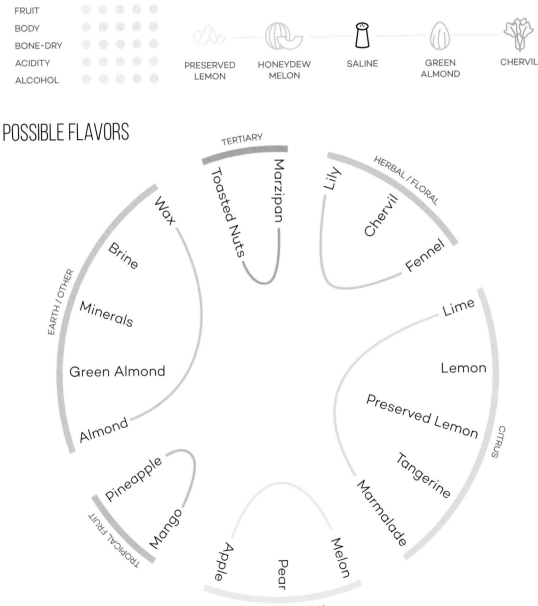

TERTIARY
- Marzipan
- Toasted Nuts

HERBAL / FLORAL
- Lily
- Chervil
- Fennel

CITRUS
- Lime
- Lemon
- Preserved Lemon
- Tangerine
- Marmalade

TREE FRUIT / MELON
- Apple
- Pear
- Melon

TROPICAL FRUIT
- Pineapple
- Mango

EARTH / OTHER
- Wax
- Brine
- Minerals
- Green Almond
- Almond

♀ Made in Veneto, Italy

WHERE IT GROWS

◀ VENETO, ITALY

20,000
ACRES

~8,000
HA

WHITE

ICE COLD

UP TO 2 YRS

$ $ $ $ $

$10–$15

Lemon Rind | Crisp Pear | Honeydew Melon | Mango

COOL VINTAGE   WARM VINTAGE

SOAVE GRAPE: Garganega ("gar-GAN-neh-gah") is the grape of Soave. The best vineyards are located on slopes in the hills above the walled city of Soave.

SOAVE & SOAVE SUPERIORE
A larger production zone. Soave Superiore has longer aging reqs.

SOAVE CLASSICO
The original classic growing zone located in the hills.

SOAVE COLLI SCALIGERI
Wines from hillside vineyards outside the classic zone.

COMMON STYLES

LIGHT & ZESTY
Young Soave wines taste of honeydew melon, saline, marmalade, and white peach, often with a subtle note of green almond.

RICH, HONEYED & FLORAL
Older vintage Soave wines taste of candied fennel, saffron, honey, baked apple, and preserved lemon. Look for Soave aged for 4 or more years.

Soave pairs very well with shellfish, chicken, tofu, and hard-to-pair foods including split peas, lentils, and asparagus.

Garganega is the same grape as Grecanico in Sicily. Grecanico wines tend to be bolder and more fruity, and Soave wines tend to be more lean and crisp.

67

VERMENTINO

🔊 "vur-men-tino"
aka: Rolle, Favorita, Pigato

PROFILE

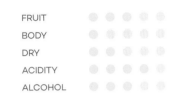

FRUIT
BODY
DRY
ACIDITY
ALCOHOL

DOMINANT FLAVORS

LIME　　GRAPEFRUIT　　GREEN APPLE　　ALMOND　　DAFFODIL

POSSIBLE FLAVORS

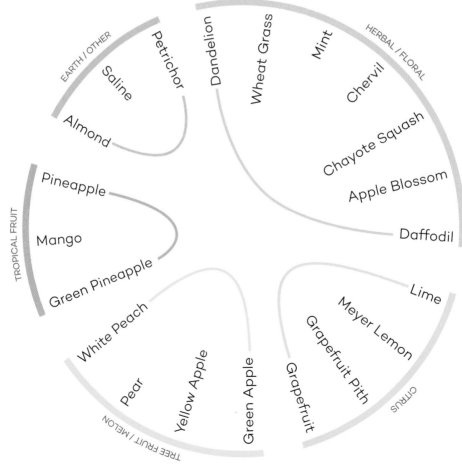

EARTH / OTHER
Saline
Petrichor
Almond

Dandelion
Wheat Grass
Mint

HERBAL / FLORAL
Chervil
Chayote Squash
Apple Blossom
Daffodil

TROPICAL FRUIT
Pineapple
Mango
Green Pineapple

White Peach
Pear
Yellow Apple
Green Apple

TREE FRUIT / MELON

Grapefruit
Grapefruit Pith
Meyer Lemon
Lime

CITRUS

Origin: Italy

22,000
ACRES

~8,900
HA

WHERE IT GROWS

◀ SOUTHERN FRANCE AND CORSICA
◀ CENTRAL ITALY AND SARDINIA
◀ ELSEWHERE

WHITE

ICE-COLD

UP TO 2 YRS

$ $ $ $ $
$10–$15

Lime | Grapefruit | Yellow Apple | Mango

COOL CLIMATE · WARM CLIMATE

REGIONS

SARDINIA, ITALY
Vermentino is the second most planted grape in Sardinia. Fine Vermentino wines come from the northern part of the island.

TUSCANY, ITALY
Vermentino grows primarily along the coast of Tuscany and extends up into Liguria.

BITTERNESS: Vermentino is often noted for having a bitter note on the finish that tastes similar to grapefruit pith. This type of flavor is referred to as phenolic bitterness, which is a common feature in several Italian white wines, including Verdicchio, Grechetto di Orvieto, and Vernaccia di San Gimignano.

Due to its complexity, Vermentino stands up well to richer foods, including seafood gumbo, fried calamari, and tomato-based sauces.

In Southern France, Vermentino is called Rolle and is a key blending grape in Provence Rosé.

Full-Bodied White Wine

CHARDONNAY

MARSANNE BLEND

SÉMILLON

VIOGNIER

Full bodied white wines are known for their rich, bold flavors. These wines are often aged on their lees or in oak barrels to add unctuous flavors of cream, vanilla, and butter.

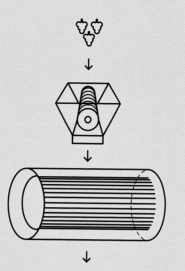

White or red wine grapes are collected and sorted.

↓

Grape bunches are destemmed.

↓

Grapes are pressed and separated from skins and seeds.

↓

Juice ferments into wine without skins.

↓

Wines are aged in barrels for a period of time.

↓

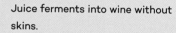

During aging, malolactic bacteria convert "green apple-y" malic acid into "creamy" lactic acid.

↓

Wines are clarified, bottled, and released shortly thereafter.

CHARDONNAY

PROFILE

FRUIT	●●●●○
BODY	●●●●○
DRY	●●●●○
ACIDITY	●●●●○
ALCOHOL	●●●●○

DOMINANT FLAVORS

YELLOW APPLE — STARFRUIT — PINEAPPLE — BUTTER — CHALK

POSSIBLE FLAVORS

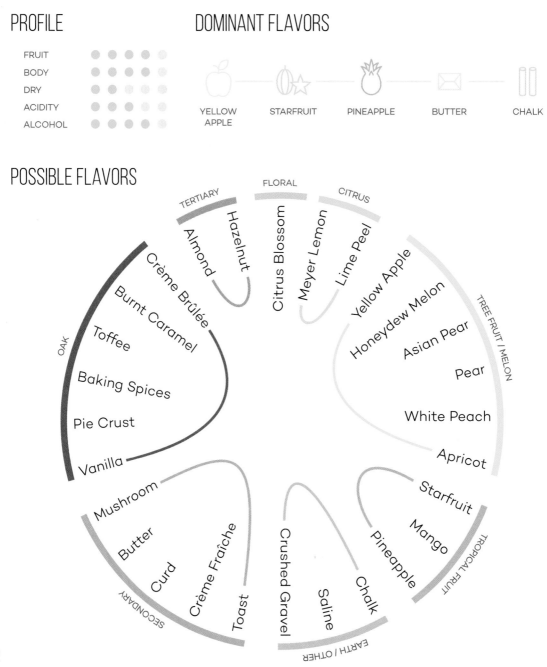

TERTIARY: Almond, Hazelnut

FLORAL: Citrus Blossom

CITRUS: Meyer Lemon, Lime Peel

OAK: Crème Brûlée, Burnt Caramel, Toffee, Baking Spices, Pie Crust, Vanilla

TREE FRUIT / MELON: Yellow Apple, Honeydew Melon, Asian Pear, Pear, White Peach, Apricot

SECONDARY: Mushroom, Butter, Curd, Crème Fraîche, Toast

EARTH / OTHER: Crushed Gravel, Saline, Chalk

TROPICAL FRUIT: Starfruit, Mango, Pineapple

72

Origin: France

WHERE IT GROWS

491,000 ACRES

~199,000 HA

◀ FRANCE
◀ USA
◀ AUSTRALIA
◀ ITALY
◀ CHILE
◀ SOUTH AFRICA
◀ SPAIN
◀ ARGENTINA
◀ MOLDOVA
◀ NEW ZEALAND
◀ ELSEWHERE

WHITE

COLD

UP TO 5 YRS

$ $ $ $ $
$15–$20

Quince — Lemon — Yellow Apple — Pineapple

COOL CLIMATE   WARM CLIMATE

REGIONAL DIFFERENCES

PINEAPPLE & YELLOW APPLE
- CALIFORNIA
- SOUTH AUSTRALIA
- SPAIN
- SOUTH AFRICA
- ARGENTINA
- SOUTHERN ITALY

QUINCE & STARFRUIT
- BURGUNDY, FRANCE
- NORTHERN ITALY
- COASTAL CHILE
- NEW ZEALAND
- WESTERN AUSTRALIA
- OREGON

COMMON STYLES

OAKED RICH & CREAMY
Found in California, Chile, Australia, Argentina, Spain, & Côte de Beaune, Burgundy.

UNOAKED LIGHT & ZESTY
Unoaked styles can be found in Mâconnais, Chablis, and western Australia.

SPARKLING
"Blanc de Blancs" labeled sparkling wines are made with Chardonnay.

Try serving a rich creamy Chardonnay warmer at 55°F (13°C). Warming it slightly will release more aromas into the bowl of the glass and make the wine bolder.

Chardonnay is the world's most planted white grape.

Bourgogne Blanc is normally 100% Chardonnay.

MARSANNE BLEND

🔊 "mar-sohn"
aka: Châteauneuf-du-Pape
Blanc, Côtes du Rhône Blanc

PROFILE

FRUIT
BODY
DRY
ACIDITY
ALCOHOL

DOMINANT FLAVORS

QUINCE — MANDARIN ORANGE — APRICOT — ACACIA — BEESWAX

POSSIBLE FLAVORS

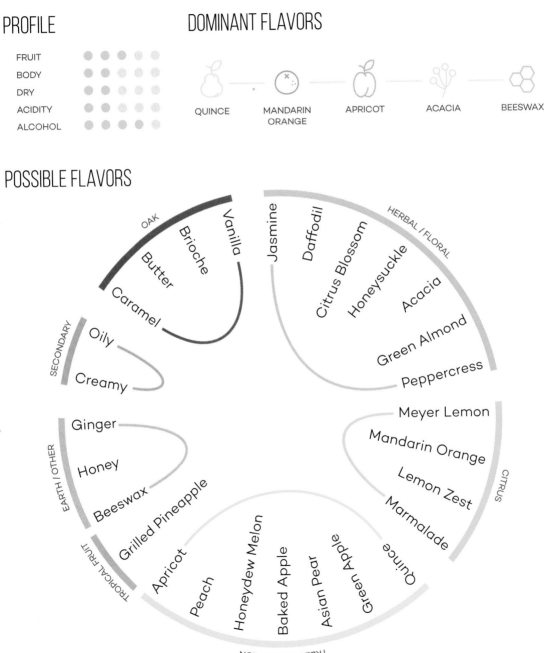

OAK: Vanilla, Brioche, Butter, Caramel

SECONDARY: Oily, Creamy

EARTH / OTHER: Ginger, Honey, Beeswax

TROPICAL FRUIT: Grilled Pineapple

TREE FRUIT / MELON: Apricot, Peach, Honeydew Melon, Baked Apple, Asian Pear, Green Apple, Quince

CITRUS: Meyer Lemon, Mandarin Orange, Lemon Zest, Marmalade

HERBAL / FLORAL: Jasmine, Daffodil, Citrus Blossom, Honeysuckle, Acacia, Green Almond, Peppercress

Origin: Rhône Valley, France

THE BLEND

◀ MARSANNE
◀ ROUSSANNE
◀ VIOGNIER
◀ GRENACHE BLANC
◀ CLAIRETTE
◀ BOURBOULENC
◀ PIQUEPOUL
◀ OTHERS

~120,000
ACRES

~48,600
HA

WHITE

COLD

UP TO 5 YRS

$ $ $ $ $
$15–$20

Quince   Lemon   Peach   Apricot

COOL CLIMATE   WARM CLIMATE

FRANCE: Generally, French white Rhône blends are light-bodied because they are a blend of many varieties, including Marsanne, Roussanne, Grenache Blanc, Clairette, Bourboulenc, and Viognier.

USA: Marsanne and other white Rhône varieties became popular in the US after Tablas Creek winery in Paso Robles imported cuttings from Château de Beaucastel in Châteauneuf-du-Pape.

THE BLEND: Because of the wide range of grape varieties that contribute to this blend, the secret to the flavor of a particular wine lies in its dominant grape.

PEACH & FLOWERS
Viognier

PEAR & BEESWAX
Marsanne & Roussanne

CITRUS FRUIT
Others

If you prefer a richer style, look for white Rhône blends with higher proportions of Viognier and Marsanne grapes in the blend.

As its name implies, the original white Rhône blend is from the Rhône in southern France, where today just 6% of the regional production is dedicated to white wine.

SÉMILLON

PROFILE

FRUIT
BODY
DRY
ACIDITY
ALCOHOL

DOMINANT FLAVORS

LEMON   BEESWAX   YELLOW PEACH   CHAMOMILE   SALINE

POSSIBLE FLAVORS

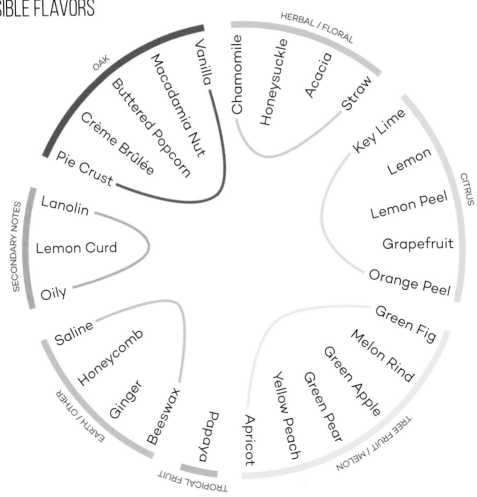

OAK
Vanilla
Macadamia Nut
Buttered Popcorn
Crème Brûlée
Pie Crust

HERBAL / FLORAL
Chamomile
Honeysuckle
Acacia
Straw

CITRUS
Key Lime
Lemon
Lemon Peel
Grapefruit
Orange Peel

SECONDARY NOTES
Lanolin
Lemon Curd
Oily

EARTH / OTHER
Saline
Honeycomb
Ginger
Beeswax

TROPICAL FRUIT
Papaya

TREE FRUIT / MELON
Green Fig
Melon Rind
Green Apple
Green Pear
Yellow Peach
Apricot

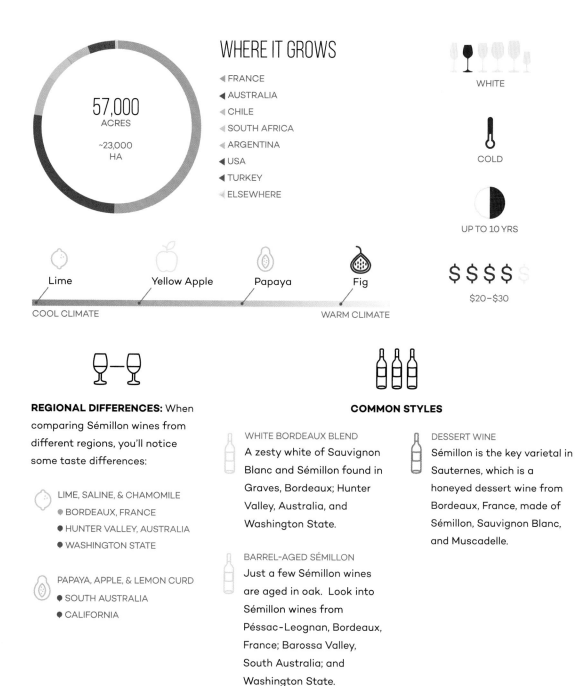

♀ Origin: France

57,000
ACRES

~23,000
HA

WHERE IT GROWS

◀ FRANCE
◀ AUSTRALIA
◀ CHILE
◀ SOUTH AFRICA
◀ ARGENTINA
◀ USA
◀ TURKEY
◀ ELSEWHERE

WHITE

COLD

UP TO 10 YRS

$ $ $ $ $
$20–$30

Lime   Yellow Apple   Papaya   Fig

COOL CLIMATE   WARM CLIMATE

REGIONAL DIFFERENCES: When comparing Sémillon wines from different regions, you'll notice some taste differences:

LIME, SALINE, & CHAMOMILE
● BORDEAUX, FRANCE
● HUNTER VALLEY, AUSTRALIA
● WASHINGTON STATE

PAPAYA, APPLE, & LEMON CURD
● SOUTH AUSTRALIA
● CALIFORNIA

COMMON STYLES

WHITE BORDEAUX BLEND
A zesty white of Sauvignon Blanc and Sémillon found in Graves, Bordeaux; Hunter Valley, Australia, and Washington State.

BARREL-AGED SÉMILLON
Just a few Sémillon wines are aged in oak. Look into Sémillon wines from Péssac-Leognan, Bordeaux, France; Barossa Valley, South Australia; and Washington State.

DESSERT WINE
Sémillon is the key varietal in Sauternes, which is a honeyed dessert wine from Bordeaux, France, made of Sémillon, Sauvignon Blanc, and Muscadelle.

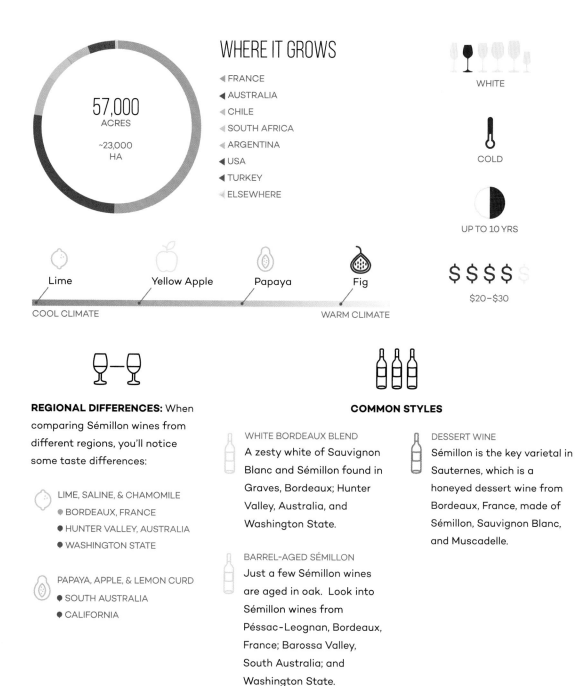

winefolly.com / learn / variety / semillon

77

VIOGNIER

PROFILE

FRUIT
BODY
OFF-DRY
ACIDITY
ALCOHOL

DOMINANT FLAVORS

TANGERINE   PEACH   MANGO   HONEYSUCKLE   ROSE

POSSIBLE FLAVORS

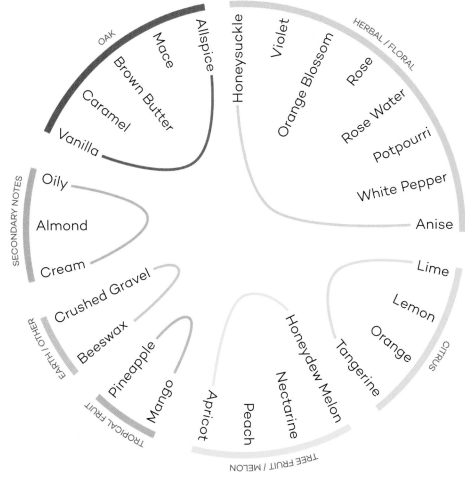

OAK
Allspice
Mace
Brown Butter
Caramel
Vanilla

Honeysuckle
Violet
Orange Blossom
Rose
Rose Water
Potpourri
White Pepper
Anise

HERBAL / FLORAL

SECONDARY NOTES
Oily
Almond
Cream

Crushed Gravel
Beeswax

EARTH / OTHER

Pineapple
Mango

TROPICAL FRUIT

Apricot
Peach
Nectarine
Honeydew Melon

TREE FRUIT / MELON

Tangerine
Orange
Lemon
Lime

CITRUS

📍 Origin: Southern France

winefolly.com / learn / variety / viognier

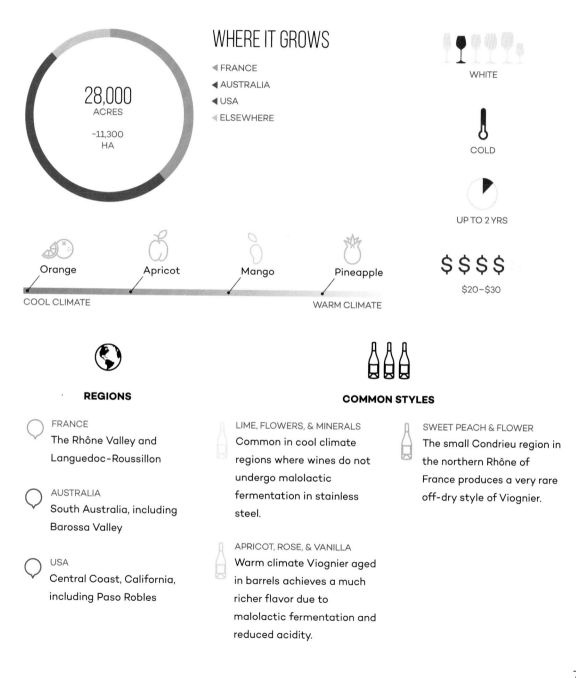

WHERE IT GROWS

28,000
ACRES

~11,300
HA

◀ FRANCE
◀ AUSTRALIA
◀ USA
◀ ELSEWHERE

WHITE

COLD

UP TO 2 YRS

$ $ $ $
$20–$30

Orange   Apricot   Mango   Pineapple

COOL CLIMATE   WARM CLIMATE

REGIONS

FRANCE
The Rhône Valley and Languedoc-Roussillon

AUSTRALIA
South Australia, including Barossa Valley

USA
Central Coast, California, including Paso Robles

COMMON STYLES

LIME, FLOWERS, & MINERALS
Common in cool climate regions where wines do not undergo malolactic fermentation in stainless steel.

APRICOT, ROSE, & VANILLA
Warm climate Viognier aged in barrels achieves a much richer flavor due to malolactic fermentation and reduced acidity.

SWEET PEACH & FLOWER
The small Condrieu region in the northern Rhône of France produces a very rare off-dry style of Viognier.

Aromatic White Wine

CHENIN BLANC

GEWÜRZTRAMINER

MUSCAT BLANC

RIESLING

TORRONTÉS

Aromatic white wines have highly perfumed and sweet-fruit aromas but can range from dry to sweet in taste. Aromatic whites are ideal pairing partners with Asian and Indian cuisine because they match well with sweet-and-sour flavors and quench spicy sauces.

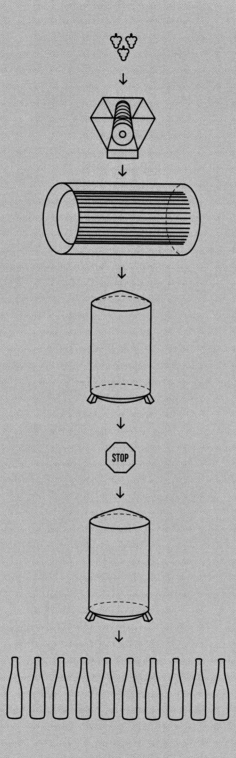

White wine grapes are collected and sorted.

Grape bunches are destemmed.

Grapes are pressed and separated from skins and seeds.

Juice begins to ferment without skins.

Fermentation is stopped before all the sugar has been fermented.

Wine is kept cool in storage tanks to settle and stabilize for a short period of time.

Wines are clarified, bottled, and released shortly thereafter.

CHENIN BLANC

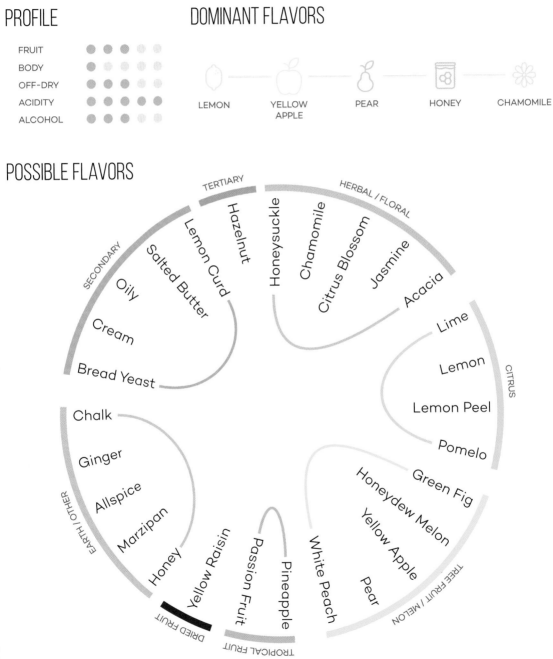

🔊 "shen-in blonk"
aka: Steen, Pineau, Vouvray

PROFILE

FRUIT
BODY
OFF-DRY
ACIDITY
ALCOHOL

DOMINANT FLAVORS

LEMON   YELLOW APPLE   PEAR   HONEY   CHAMOMILE

POSSIBLE FLAVORS

TERTIARY
Hazelnut
Lemon Curd
Salted Butter
Oily
Cream
Bread Yeast
SECONDARY

HERBAL / FLORAL
Honeysuckle
Chamomile
Citrus Blossom
Jasmine
Acacia

Lime
Lemon
Lemon Peel
Pomelo
CITRUS

Green Fig
Honeydew Melon
Yellow Apple
Pear
TREE FRUIT / MELON

White Peach

Chalk
Ginger
Allspice
Marzipan
Honey
EARTH / OTHER

Yellow Raisin
DRIED FRUIT

Passion Fruit
Pineapple
TROPICAL FRUIT

82

📍 Origin: France

WHERE IT GROWS

87,000
ACRES

35,200
HA

◀ SOUTH AFRICA
◀ FRANCE
◀ ARGENTINA
◀ USA
◀ ELSEWHERE

WHITE

COLD

UP TO 2 YRS

$ $$$$
$5–$10

Lemon   Pear   Pineapple   Honey

COOL CLIMATE   WARM CLIMATE

winefolly.com / learn / variety / chenin-blanc

COMMON STYLES

SPARKLING
Sparkling wines come from the Loire Valley in Vouvray, Saumur, and Montlouis, and in South Africa they are blended into Method Cap Classique.

LIGHT & ZESTY
Tasting of lime and tarragon, this dry style is common in value-priced South African Chenin and in Loire wines labeled "Sec."

PEACHES & FLOWERS
South Africa offers a rich style with nectarine, honey, and meringue notes. Also available on warm vintages in Anjou, Montlouis, and Vouvray in the Loire.

NOBLE ROT DESSERT WINE
In Anjou, close to the river where the fog collects on certain years, noble rot adds candied ginger notes.

Occasionally, you'll come across a Chenin Blanc with bruised apple flavors—a sign of oxidation. Some Chenin Blanc wines are made in an oxidative style on purpose, including a region in the Loire called Savennières.

Much of the Chenin Blanc grown in South Africa is used for brandy production.

GEWÜRZTRAMINER

PROFILE

FRUIT	●●●●●
BODY	●●●●○
OFF-DRY	●●●●○
ACIDITY	●●●○○
ALCOHOL	●●●●○

DOMINANT FLAVORS

LYCHEE · ROSE · PINK GRAPEFRUIT · TANGERINE · GUAVA

POSSIBLE FLAVORS

SECONDARY
Oily
Creamy

HERBAL / FLORAL
Rose
Acacia
Potpourri
True Cinnamon
Candied Ginger
Tarragon

EARTH / OTHER
Salt
Incense Smoke
Honey
Exotic Spices

CITRUS
Lemon Zest
Orange Zest
Pink Grapefruit
Tangerine

TROPICAL FRUIT
Guava
Lychee
Mango

TREE FRUIT / MELON
Mirabelle Plum
White Nectarine

84

📍 Origin: Germany and France

WHERE IT GROWS

35,000
ACRES

14,000
HA

◀ FRANCE
◀ MOLDOVA
◀ UKRAINE
◀ AUSTRALIA
◀ GERMANY
◀ USA
◀ HUNGARY
◀ ELSEWHERE

WHITE

COLD

UP TO 2 YRS

$ $ $ $ $
$10–$15

 Tangerine   Rose   Lychee   Guava

COOL CLIMATE   WARM CLIMATE

COMMON STYLES

DRY & OFF-DRY
There are several Gewürztraminer with sweet and floral aromas and a completely dry taste. This dry style can be found in Trento-Alto Adige, Italy; Alsace, France; and cooler areas in California including Mendocino and Monterey. Dry Gewürztraminer from Alsace, France, has rich, oily texture and subtle salinity.

DESSERT WINE
In Alsace, there are two very high-quality dessert wines produced with Gewürztraminer: Vendanges Tardives and Sélection de Grains Nobles (SGN). SGN is produced with noble rot grapes and Vendanges Tardives means "late harvest." These wines are generally rare and command high prices.

Try a dry Gewürztraminer with dim sum, Vietnamese cuisine, pot stickers, and dumpling soup.

As a general rule, Gewürztraminer tastes best within a year or two of release. This is to ensure it has the highest possible acidity, which gives Gewürztraminer a crisp, fresh flavor.

MUSCAT BLANC

"mus-kot blonk"
aka: Moscato d'Asti, Moscatel,
Muscat Blanc à Petit Grains,
Muscat Canelli, Muskateller

PROFILE

FRUIT
BODY
SWEET
ACIDITY
ALCOHOL

DOMINANT FLAVORS

MEYER LEMON · MANDARIN ORANGE · PEAR · ORANGE BLOSSOM · HONEYSUCKLE

POSSIBLE FLAVORS

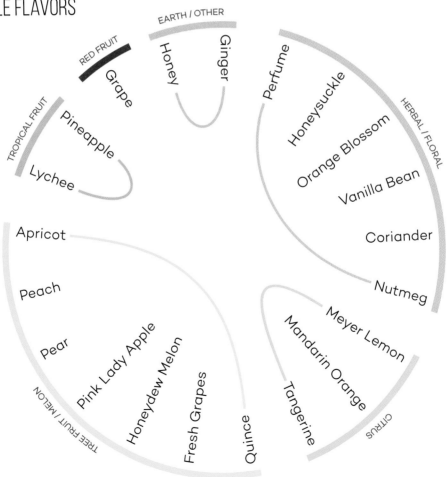

EARTH / OTHER
RED FRUIT
Grape
Honey
Ginger
Perfume
Honeysuckle
Orange Blossom
HERBAL / FLORAL
Vanilla Bean
Coriander
Nutmeg
TROPICAL FRUIT
Pineapple
Lychee
Apricot
Peach
Pear
Pink Lady Apple
Honeydew Melon
Fresh Grapes
Quince
TREE FRUIT / MELON
Meyer Lemon
Mandarin Orange
Tangerine
CITRUS

Origin: Ancient Greece and Italy

WHERE IT GROWS

77,000 ACRES

31,000 HA

- ◀ ITALY
- ◀ FRANCE
- ◀ GREECE
- ◀ SPAIN
- ◀ BRAZIL
- ◀ USA
- ◀ PORTUGAL
- ◀ ELSEWHERE

DEPENDS ON STYLE

COLD

UP TO 2 YRS

$ $ $ $ $
$10–$15

Lemon — Mandarin Orange — Ripe Melon — Lychee

COOL CLIMATE — WARM CLIMATE

MUSCAT: Muscat Blanc is an ancient grape with several closely related varieties:

MUSCAT OF ALEXANDRIA
The oldest—Cleopatra supposedly loved it

MUSCAT GIALLO
The Italian version from Roman times

MUSCAT OTTONEL
Hailing from the Ottoman Empire, a dry Muscat

COMMON STYLES

DRY & AROMATIC
This style is most classically associated with Alto Adige, Italy; Germany; and Alsace, France.

SWEET & LIGHTLY SPARKLING
The most famous Muscat Blanc is Moscato d'Asti, which comes from the Piedmont region in northern Italy.

SWEET DESSERT MUSCAT
Several regions produce Muscat-based dessert wines, which can have upward of 200 g/L of residual sugar with a viscosity like hot maple syrup.

winefolly.com / learn / variety / muscat-blanc

RIESLING

PROFILE

FRUIT	●●●●●
BODY	●○○○○
OFF-DRY	●●●○○
ACIDITY	●●●●●
ALCOHOL	●○○○○

DOMINANT FLAVORS

LIME   GREEN APPLE   BEESWAX   JASMINE   PETROLEUM

POSSIBLE FLAVORS

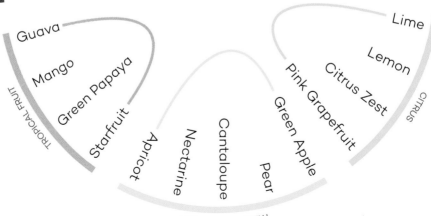

EARTH / OTHER
- Chalk
- Wet Slate
- Petroleum
- Ginger
- Beeswax

HERBAL / FLORAL
- Jasmine
- Honeysuckle
- Vanilla
- Nutmeg
- Cinnamon
- White Pepper
- Thai Basil
- Rosemary

RED FRUIT
- White Cherry
- Strawberry

CITRUS
- Lime
- Lemon
- Citrus Zest
- Pink Grapefruit
- Green Apple

TROPICAL FRUIT
- Guava
- Mango
- Green Papaya
- Starfruit

TREE FRUIT / MELON
- Apricot
- Nectarine
- Cantaloupe
- Pear

88

Origin: Germany

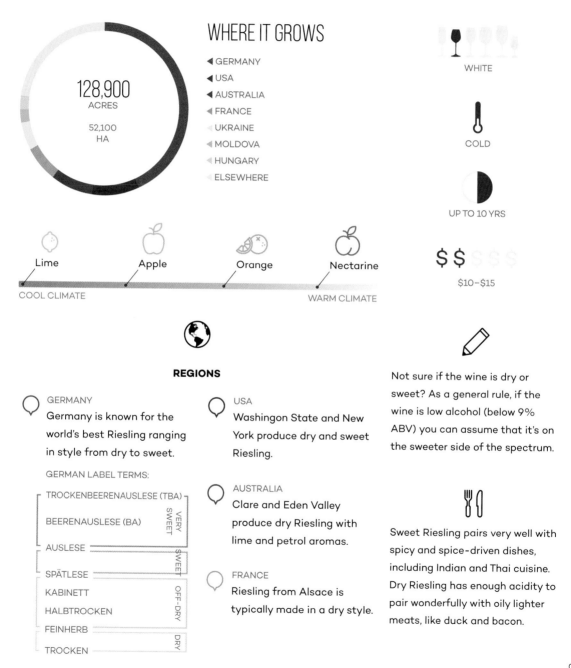

WHERE IT GROWS

128,900
ACRES

52,100
HA

◀ GERMANY
◀ USA
◀ AUSTRALIA
◀ FRANCE
◁ UKRAINE
◁ MOLDOVA
◀ HUNGARY
◁ ELSEWHERE

WHITE

COLD

UP TO 10 YRS

$ $ $ $ $
$10–$15

Lime · Apple · Orange · Nectarine

COOL CLIMATE — WARM CLIMATE

REGIONS

GERMANY
Germany is known for the world's best Riesling ranging in style from dry to sweet.

GERMAN LABEL TERMS:

TROCKENBEERENAUSLESE (TBA) — VERY SWEET

BEERENAUSLESE (BA)

AUSLESE — SWEET

SPÄTLESE

KABINETT — OFF-DRY

HALBTROCKEN

FEINHERB — DRY

TROCKEN

USA
Washingon State and New York produce dry and sweet Riesling.

AUSTRALIA
Clare and Eden Valley produce dry Riesling with lime and petrol aromas.

FRANCE
Riesling from Alsace is typically made in a dry style.

Not sure if the wine is dry or sweet? As a general rule, if the wine is low alcohol (below 9% ABV) you can assume that it's on the sweeter side of the spectrum.

Sweet Riesling pairs very well with spicy and spice-driven dishes, including Indian and Thai cuisine. Dry Riesling has enough acidity to pair wonderfully with oily lighter meats, like duck and bacon.

TORRONTÉS

◀ "torr-ron-TEZ"

PROFILE

FRUIT
BODY
DRY
ACIDITY
ALCOHOL

DOMINANT FLAVORS

MEYER LEMON — PEACH — LEMON PEEL — ROSE PETAL — GERANIUM

POSSIBLE FLAVORS

EARTH / OTHER
- Saline

TROPICAL FRUIT
- Guava
- Pineapple

HERBAL / FLORAL
- Jasmine
- Geranium
- Rose Petal
- Apple Blossom
- Fresh-Cut Grass
- Licorice
- Fennel

TREE FRUIT / MELON
- Apricot
- Canned Peach
- White Peach
- Asian Pear
- Pear
- Green Fig
- Honeydew Melon

CITRUS
- Meyer Lemon
- Lemon Peel
- Grapefruit
- Tangerine

📍 Origin: Argentina

WHERE IT GROWS

◁ ARGENTINA
◁ ELSEWHERE

21,000
ACRES

8,500
HA

WHITE

COLD

UP TO 2 YRS

$ $ $ $ $
$5–$10

Meyer Lemon   Honeydew Melon   Ripe Pear   Canned Peach

COOL VINTAGE   WARM VINTAGE

COMMON STYLES

DRY & ZESTY
The Argentine region of Salta is known for making dry Torrontés with flavors of grapefruit, lemon peel, nutmeg, and saline.

A TOUCH SWEET
The Torrontés from the warmer regions in Mendoza and San Juan taste sweeter, with flavors of peach and guava.

The high-altitude vineyards in Salta are known for producing high-quality Torrontés.

Torrontés is an indigenous Argentine grape that is a natural cross with Muscat of Alexandria and the Chilean grape called País.

Try Torrontés with delicately flavored meats and sweet-sour sauces such as miso-glazed sea bass or teriyaki-braised sesame tofu.

FISH & SUSHI

BRAISED TOFU

Rosé Wine

ROSÉ

Rosé wine is produced when red grape skins macerate in their juices for a period of time. Rosé is produced in every major country and is made of nearly every grape variety, both red and white. Rosé wines range in taste from dry to sweet. For example, a rosé of Tempranillo is usually always dry and savory. Whereas White Zinfandel is almost always sweet and fruity.

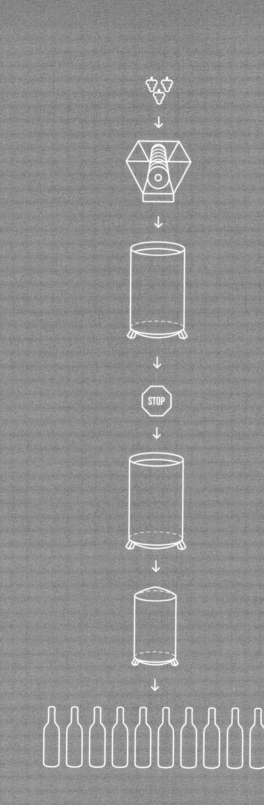

Red wine grapes are collected and sorted.

Grape bunches are destemmed.

Juice ferments with skins in a fermentation vessel for a short period of time.

STOP

Before wine becomes deep red, it's separated from the skins.

The fermentation completes without the skins.

Wine is kept cool in storage tanks to settle and stabilize for a short period of time.

Wines are clarified, bottled, and released shortly thereafter.

ROSÉ

🔊 "rose-aye"
aka: Rosado, Rosato, Vin Gris

PROFILE

FRUIT	●●●●●
BODY	●●●○○
DRY / SWEET	●●●○○
ACIDITY	●●●●○
ALCOHOL	●●○○○

DOMINANT FLAVORS

STRAWBERRY — HONEYDEW MELON — ROSE PETAL — CELERY — ORANGE PEEL

POSSIBLE FLAVORS

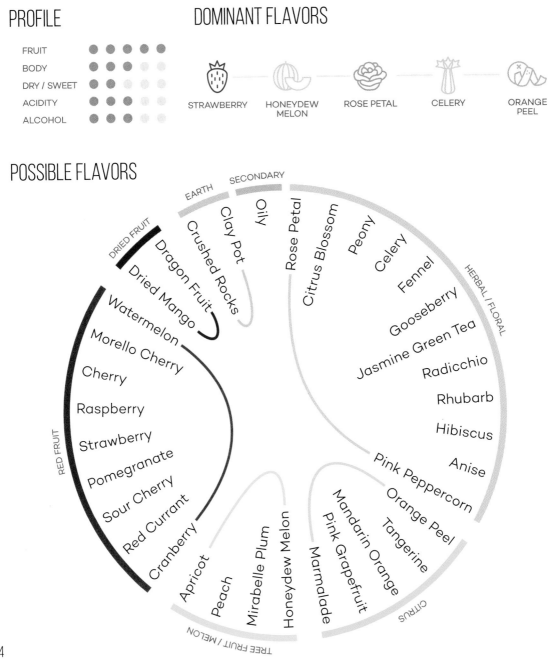

EARTH
- Crushed Rocks
- Clay Pot

SECONDARY
- Oily

DRIED FRUIT
- Dragon Fruit
- Dried Mango

RED FRUIT
- Watermelon
- Morello Cherry
- Cherry
- Raspberry
- Strawberry
- Pomegranate
- Sour Cherry
- Red Currant
- Cranberry

TREE FRUIT / MELON
- Apricot
- Peach
- Mirabelle Plum
- Honeydew Melon

HERBAL / FLORAL
- Rose Petal
- Citrus Blossom
- Peony
- Celery
- Fennel
- Gooseberry
- Jasmine Green Tea
- Radicchio
- Rhubarb
- Hibiscus
- Anise

CITRUS
- Pink Peppercorn
- Orange Peel
- Tangerine
- Mandarin Orange
- Pink Grapefruit
- Marmalade

📍 Origin: unknown

3 BILLION
BOTTLES

9% OF ALL WINE
(2012)

WHERE IT'S MADE

◀ FRANCE
◀ ITALY
◀ USA
◀ SPAIN
◀ ELSEWHERE

AROMA COLLECTOR

COLD

UP TO 2 YRS

$

$5–$10

◆ Cranberry   ◆ Red Currant   Morello Cherry   Raspberry

COOL CLIMATE   WARM CLIMATE

REGIONS

FRANCE
The rosé wines of France are dry and come mainly from Provence and Languedoc-Roussillon. The blend typically includes Grenache and Syrah.

ITALY
Rosato is made all over Italy using one or several of the country's indigenous grape varieties.

USA
Many new styles of rosé wine are introduced every year, but the largest rosé production is dedicated to White Zinfandel.

SPAIN
Spanish rosés include Tempranillo, with a meaty note; and Garnacha, with candied grapefruit flavors and a brilliant ruby hue.

An aroma collector glass will capture the subtle floral aromas that are harder to pick up in a regular white wine glass.

In the US, the majority of Zinfandel grapes go toward the production of White Zinfandel.

winefolly.com / learn / style / rose

95

Light-Bodied Red Wine

GAMAY

PINOT NOIR

Light bodied red wines are translucent in color and tend to have moderately high acidity. They are known for their perfumed aromas that are best collected in a large globe-shaped glass.

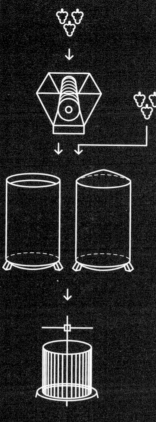

Red wine grapes are collected and sorted for quality and ripeness.

Grape bunches are destemmed or go into fermentation as a whole bunch.

Juice ferments with skins in fermentation vessels.

Wine is gently pressed off pomace (seeds, stems, skins, etc.).

Wine is aged in vessels for a period of time.

During aging, malolactic bacteria convert "green apple-y" malic acid into "creamy" lactic acid.

Wines are clarified, bottled, and released shortly thereafter.

GAMAY

PROFILE

FRUIT	●●● ○○
BODY	●●● ○○
TANNIN	●○○ ○○
ACIDITY	●●●● ○
ALCOHOL	●○○ ○○

DOMINANT FLAVORS

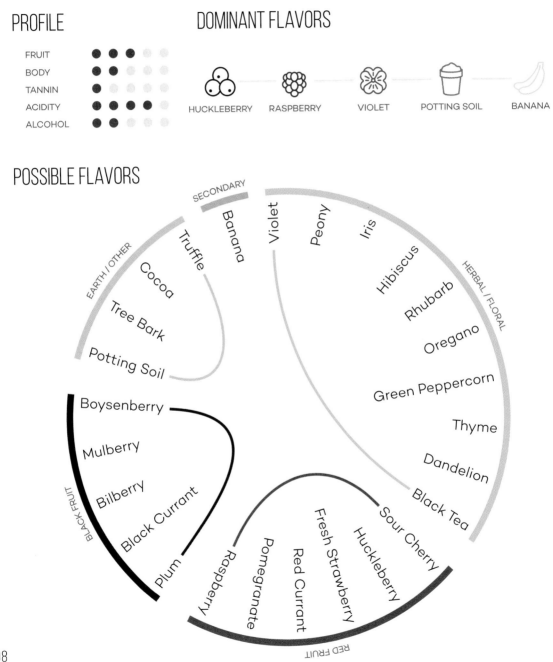

HUCKLEBERRY · RASPBERRY · VIOLET · POTTING SOIL · BANANA

POSSIBLE FLAVORS

SECONDARY
- Banana

EARTH / OTHER
- Truffle
- Cocoa
- Tree Bark
- Potting Soil

HERBAL / FLORAL
- Violet
- Peony
- Iris
- Hibiscus
- Rhubarb
- Oregano
- Green Peppercorn
- Thyme
- Dandelion
- Black Tea

BLACK FRUIT
- Boysenberry
- Mulberry
- Bilberry
- Black Currant
- Plum

RED FRUIT
- Raspberry
- Pomegranate
- Red Currant
- Fresh Strawberry
- Huckleberry
- Sour Cherry

Origin: France

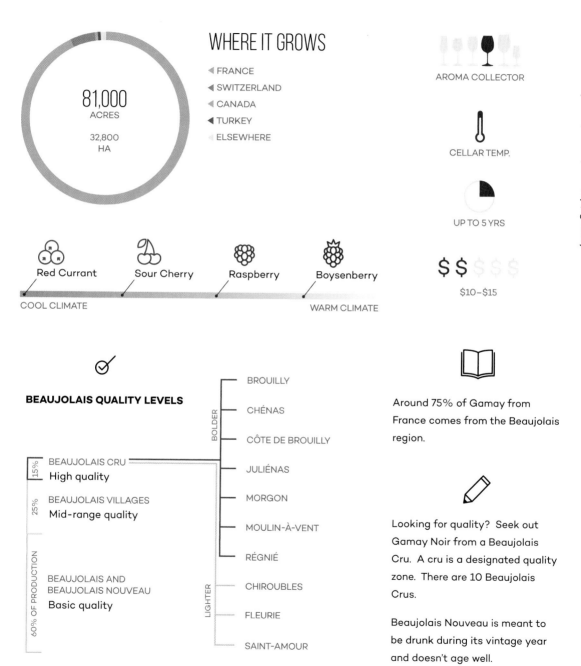

WHERE IT GROWS

81,000
ACRES

32,800
HA

◄ FRANCE
◄ SWITZERLAND
◄ CANADA
◄ TURKEY
◄ ELSEWHERE

AROMA COLLECTOR

CELLAR TEMP.

UP TO 5 YRS

$ $ $ $ $
$10–$15

winefolly.com / learn / variety / gamay

Red Currant   Sour Cherry   Raspberry   Boysenberry

COOL CLIMATE   WARM CLIMATE

BEAUJOLAIS QUALITY LEVELS

15% BEAUJOLAIS CRU
High quality

25% BEAUJOLAIS VILLAGES
Mid-range quality

60% OF PRODUCTION

BEAUJOLAIS AND
BEAUJOLAIS NOUVEAU
Basic quality

BOLDER
- BROUILLY
- CHÉNAS
- CÔTE DE BROUILLY
- JULIÉNAS
- MORGON
- MOULIN-À-VENT
- RÉGNIÉ

LIGHTER
- CHIROUBLES
- FLEURIE
- SAINT-AMOUR

Around 75% of Gamay from France comes from the Beaujolais region.

Looking for quality? Seek out Gamay Noir from a Beaujolais Cru. A cru is a designated quality zone. There are 10 Beaujolais Crus.

Beaujolais Nouveau is meant to be drunk during its vintage year and doesn't age well.

99

PINOT NOIR

🔊 "pee-no nwar"
aka: Spätburgunder

PROFILE

FRUIT
BODY
TANNIN
ACIDITY
ALCOHOL

DOMINANT FLAVORS

CRANBERRY   CHERRY   RASPBERRY   CLOVE   MUSHROOM

POSSIBLE FLAVORS

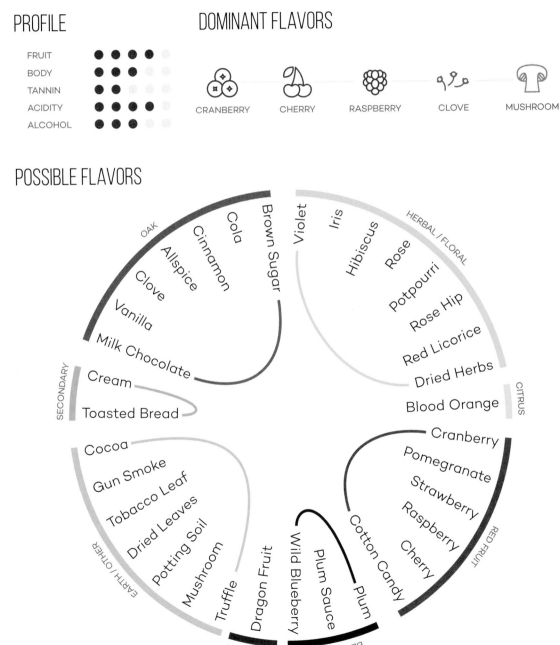

OAK
Brown Sugar
Cola
Cinnamon
Allspice
Clove
Vanilla
Milk Chocolate

SECONDARY
Cream
Toasted Bread

Cocoa
Gun Smoke
Tobacco Leaf
Dried Leaves
Potting Soil
Mushroom
Truffle
EARTH / OTHER

Dragon Fruit
DRIED FRUIT

Wild Blueberry
Plum Sauce
Plum
BLACK FRUIT

Cotton Candy

Violet
Iris
Hibiscus
Rose
Potpourri
Rose Hip
Red Licorice
Dried Herbs
HERBAL / FLORAL

Blood Orange
CITRUS

Cranberry
Pomegranate
Strawberry
Raspberry
Cherry
RED FRUIT

📍 Origin: France

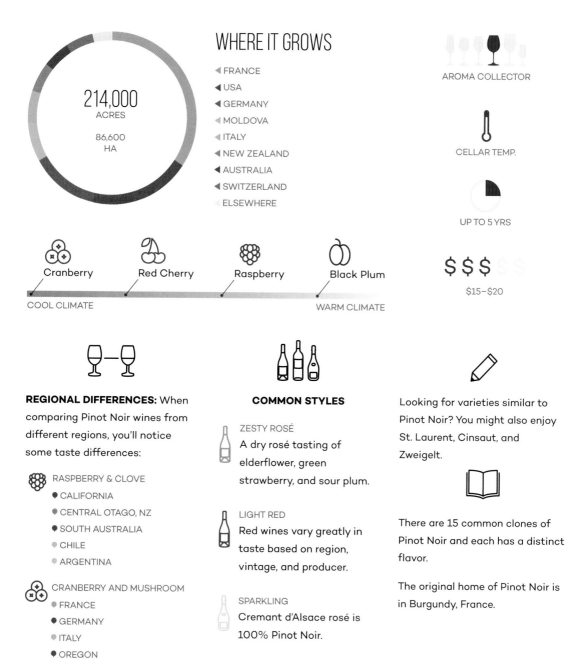

WHERE IT GROWS

214,000
ACRES

86,600
HA

◀ FRANCE
◀ USA
◀ GERMANY
◀ MOLDOVA
◀ ITALY
◀ NEW ZEALAND
◀ AUSTRALIA
◀ SWITZERLAND
◀ ELSEWHERE

AROMA COLLECTOR

CELLAR TEMP.

UP TO 5 YRS

$ $ $ $ $
$15–$20

Cranberry
Red Cherry
Raspberry
Black Plum

COOL CLIMATE
WARM CLIMATE

REGIONAL DIFFERENCES: When comparing Pinot Noir wines from different regions, you'll notice some taste differences:

RASPBERRY & CLOVE
● CALIFORNIA
● CENTRAL OTAGO, NZ
● SOUTH AUSTRALIA
● CHILE
● ARGENTINA

CRANBERRY AND MUSHROOM
● FRANCE
● GERMANY
● ITALY
● OREGON

COMMON STYLES

ZESTY ROSÉ
A dry rosé tasting of elderflower, green strawberry, and sour plum.

LIGHT RED
Red wines vary greatly in taste based on region, vintage, and producer.

SPARKLING
Cremant d'Alsace rosé is 100% Pinot Noir.

Looking for varieties similar to Pinot Noir? You might also enjoy St. Laurent, Cinsaut, and Zweigelt.

There are 15 common clones of Pinot Noir and each has a distinct flavor.

The original home of Pinot Noir is in Burgundy, France.

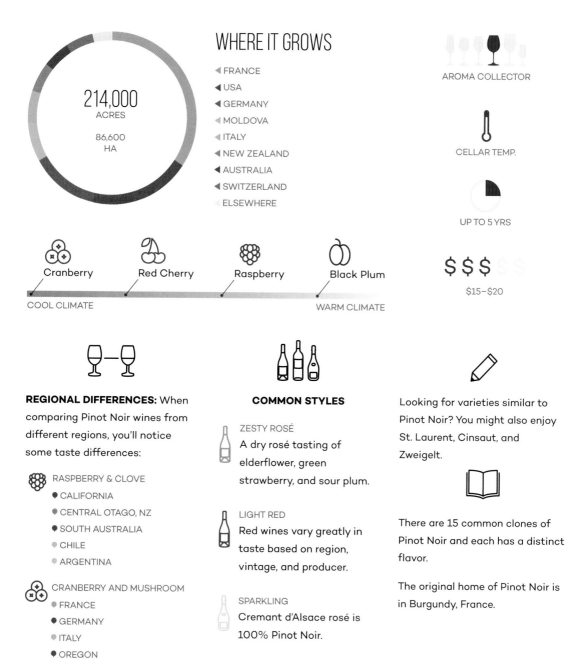
winefolly.com / learn / variety / pinot-noir

Medium-Bodied Red Wine

BARBERA

CABERNET FRANC

CARIGNAN

CARMÉNÈRE

GRENACHE

MENCÍA

MERLOT

MONTEPULCIANO

NEGROAMARO

RHÔNE/GSM BLEND

SANGIOVESE

VALPOLICELLA BLEND

ZINFANDEL

Medium-bodied red wines are often referred to as "food wines" because of their excellent ability to pair with a wide range of foods. Generally speaking, medium-bodied wines are characterized by dominant red-fruit flavors.

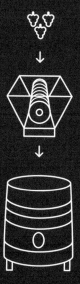

Red wine grapes are collected and sorted to remove leaves.

Grape bunches are destemmed.

Juice ferments with skins in fermentation vessels.

Wine is gently pressed off pomace (seeds, stems, skins, etc.).

Wine is aged in barrels or tanks for a period of time.

During aging, malolactic bacteria convert "green apple-y" malic acid into "creamy" lactic acid.

Wines are clarified, bottled, and released after a period of aging.

BARBERA

PROFILE

FRUIT
BODY
TANNIN
ACIDITY
ALCOHOL

DOMINANT FLAVORS

SOUR CHERRY

LICORICE

BLACKBERRY

DRIED HERBS

TAR

POSSIBLE FLAVORS

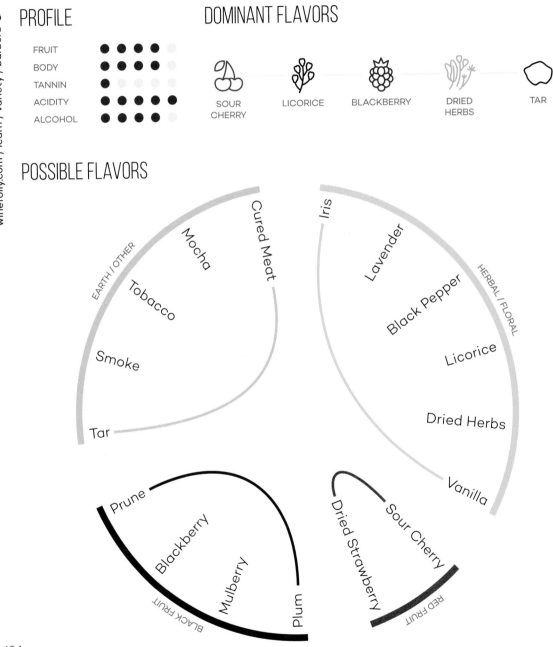

EARTH / OTHER
Cured Meat
Mocha
Tobacco
Smoke
Tar

HERBAL / FLORAL
Iris
Lavender
Black Pepper
Licorice
Dried Herbs
Vanilla

BLACK FRUIT
Prune
Blackberry
Mulberry
Plum

RED FRUIT
Dried Strawberry
Sour Cherry

104

◆ Origin: Italy

60,000
ACRES

24,300
HA

WHERE IT GROWS

◀ ITALY
◀ USA
◀ ARGENTINA
◀ ELSEWHERE

AROMA COLLECTOR

ROOM TEMP.

UP TO 5 YRS

$ $ $ $ $
$10–$15

Sour Cherry　　Plum　　Black Cherry　　Blackberry

COOL CLIMATE　　　　　　　　　　　　WARM CLIMATE

REGIONAL DIFFERENCES: When comparing Barbera wines from different regions, you'll notice some taste differences:

 BLACKBERRY JAM & LICORICE
Higher alcohol wines with more fruit flavors.
● CALIFORNIA
● ARGENTINA

 MULBERRY & HERBS
Lighter wines with tart fruit and herb flavors.
● PIEDMONT, ITALY

COMMON STYLES: Barbera is produced two ways that result in two different flavor profiles:

 UNOAKED = RED FRUIT
Aged in stainless steel, Barbera often has sour cherry, licorice, and herb aromas along with a brisk spicy taste.

 OAKED = CHOCOLATE
Aged in oak, Barbera loses a touch of its spicy acidity and develops richer fruit flavors along with chocolate.

Looking for a particular style? Pay attention to wine descriptions when seeking out Barbera. The color of the fruit (red vs. black) often helps to identify the style.

It's useful to note that many exceptional Piedmont Barbera wines have slightly higher alcohol levels, around 14% ABV.

CABERNET FRANC

🔊 "cab-err-nay fronk"
aka: Chinon, Bourgueil, Bouchet, Breton

PROFILE

FRUIT
BODY
TANNIN
ACIDITY
ALCOHOL

DOMINANT FLAVORS

STRAWBERRY ROASTED PEPPER RED PLUM CRUSHED GRAVEL CHILI PEPPER

POSSIBLE FLAVORS

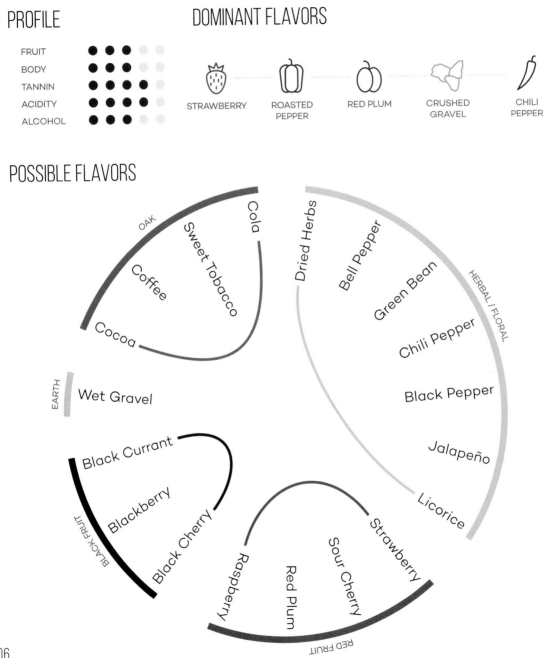

OAK
Cola
Sweet Tobacco
Coffee
Cocoa

Dried Herbs
Bell Pepper
Green Bean
HERBAL / FLORAL
Chili Pepper
Black Pepper
Jalapeño
Licorice

EARTH
Wet Gravel

BLACK FRUIT
Black Currant
Blackberry
Black Cherry

Raspberry
Red Plum
Sour Cherry
Strawberry
RED FRUIT

📍 Origin: France

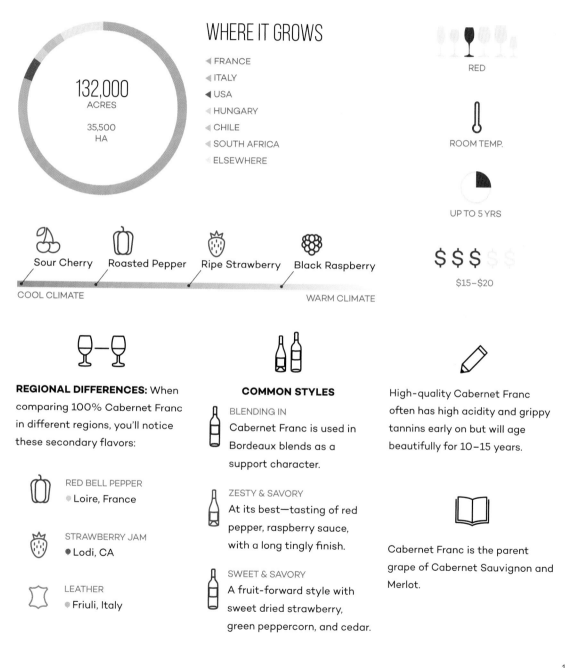

WHERE IT GROWS

132,000
ACRES

35,500
HA

◀ FRANCE
◀ ITALY
◀ USA
◀ HUNGARY
◀ CHILE
◀ SOUTH AFRICA
◀ ELSEWHERE

RED

ROOM TEMP.

UP TO 5 YRS

$ $ $ $ $
$15–$20

Sour Cherry Roasted Pepper Ripe Strawberry Black Raspberry

COOL CLIMATE   WARM CLIMATE

REGIONAL DIFFERENCES: When comparing 100% Cabernet Franc in different regions, you'll notice these secondary flavors:

RED BELL PEPPER
● Loire, France

STRAWBERRY JAM
● Lodi, CA

LEATHER
● Friuli, Italy

COMMON STYLES

BLENDING IN
Cabernet Franc is used in Bordeaux blends as a support character.

ZESTY & SAVORY
At its best—tasting of red pepper, raspberry sauce, with a long tingly finish.

SWEET & SAVORY
A fruit-forward style with sweet dried strawberry, green peppercorn, and cedar.

High-quality Cabernet Franc often has high acidity and grippy tannins early on but will age beautifully for 10–15 years.

Cabernet Franc is the parent grape of Cabernet Sauvignon and Merlot.

CARIGNAN

🔊 "care-in-yen"
aka: Mazuelo, Cariñena,
Carignano

PROFILE

FRUIT
BODY
TANNIN
ACIDITY
ALCOHOL

DOMINANT FLAVORS

DRIED CRANBERRY · RASPBERRY · LICORICE · BAKING SPICES · CURED MEAT

POSSIBLE FLAVORS

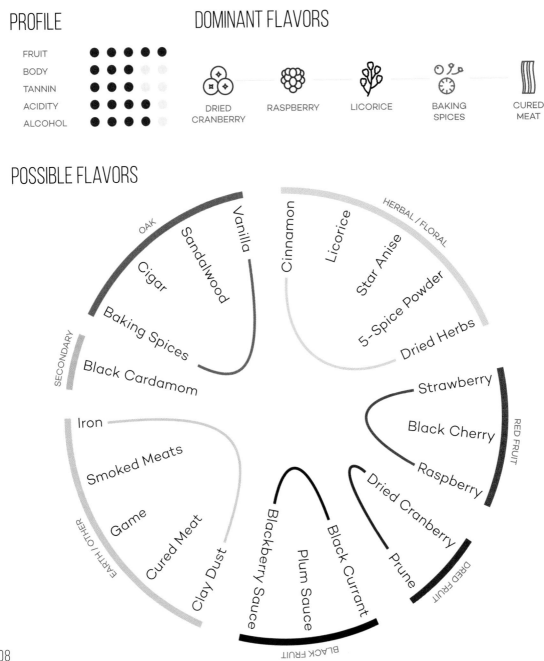

OAK: Vanilla, Sandalwood, Cigar

SECONDARY: Baking Spices, Black Cardamom

HERBAL / FLORAL: Cinnamon, Licorice, Star Anise, 5-Spice Powder, Dried Herbs

RED FRUIT: Strawberry, Black Cherry, Raspberry

DRIED FRUIT: Dried Cranberry, Prune

BLACK FRUIT: Blackberry Sauce, Plum Sauce, Black Currant

EARTH / OTHER: Iron, Smoked Meats, Game, Cured Meat, Clay Dust

winefolly.com / learn / variety / carignan

108

📍 Origin: Spain

198,000
ACRES

80,200
HA

WHERE IT GROWS

◀ FRANCE
◀ TUNISIA
◀ ALGERIA
◀ SPAIN
◀ ITALY
◀ MOROCCO
◀ USA
ELSEWHERE

RED

ROOM TEMP.

UP TO 5 YRS

$ $ $ $ $
$10–$15

Strawberry   Black Currant   Blackberry   Prune

COOL CLIMATE   WARM CLIMATE

Carignan is a highly productive, drought-resistant wine grape that grows well in desert conditions. Because of this, Carignan was historically over-cropped, which produced low-quality bulk wine.

Fortunately, several quality-minded producers in Languedoc-Roussillon, France, and central Chile have resurrected the variety and use the oldest vineyards to make highly concentrated Carignan-based wines.

Try Carignan as a Thanksgiving wine; it matches nicely with turkey, cranberries, roasted squash, and baking spices.

POULTRY

CRANBERRY

BAKING SPICES

Looking for value? Look for wines from Côtes Catalanes, Faugères, and Minervois appellations in Languedoc-Roussillon, France. Also, you'll find great buys from the Carignano del Sulcis region in Sardinia, Italy.

CARMÉNÈRE

PROFILE

FRUIT	●●●●● ○	
BODY	●●●● ○○	
TANNIN	●●●● ○○	
ACIDITY	●●● ○○○	
ALCOHOL	●●● ○○○	

DOMINANT FLAVORS

RASPBERRY   GREEN BELL PEPPER   BLACK PLUM   BLACKBERRY   VANILLA

POSSIBLE FLAVORS

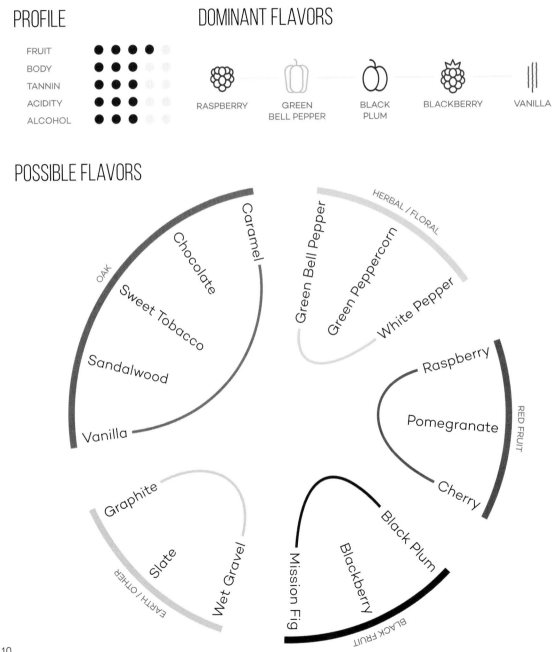

OAK: Caramel, Chocolate, Sweet Tobacco, Sandalwood, Vanilla

HERBAL / FLORAL: Green Bell Pepper, Green Peppercorn, White Pepper

RED FRUIT: Raspberry, Pomegranate, Cherry

BLACK FRUIT: Black Plum, Blackberry, Mission Fig

EARTH / OTHER: Graphite, Slate, Wet Gravel

📍 Origin: France

WHERE IT GROWS

28,000
ACRES

11,300
HA

◀ CHILE
◀ CHINA
◀ ITALY
◀ ELSEWHERE

RED

ROOM TEMP.

UP TO 2 YRS

$ $ $ $ $
$10–$15

Green Bell Pepper   Raspberry   Black Plum   Jam

COOL CLIMATE   WARM CLIMATE

Carménère is a very old variety from Bordeaux, France, that has many taste similarities to Merlot and Cabernet Sauvignon.

Carménère could have become extinct had it not been mistaken for Merlot and planted in Chile during the 19th century. It wasn't until 1994 that DNA research confirmed Carménère's true identity.

COMMON STYLES

RED FRUIT & GREEN PEPPER
A lighter style with very little oak aging offers notes of red fruits, green pepper, paprika, and cocoa powder.

BLUEBERRY & CHOCOLATE
A richer style that is made with extended barrel aging. Tastes of blueberry, black pepper, chocolate, green peppercorn, and caramel.

The region of Colchagua in Chile is well-known for fine Carménère. Keep your eyes peeled for the subregions of Los Lingues or Apalta on good vintages.

Today there are less than 20 acres of Carménère in France.

GRENACHE

PROFILE

FRUIT ●●●●●
BODY ●●●●○
TANNIN ●●●○○
ACIDITY ●●●●○
ALCOHOL ●●●●○

DOMINANT FLAVORS

DRIED STRAWBERRY · GRILLED PLUM · RUBY RED GRAPEFRUIT · LEATHER · LICORICE

POSSIBLE FLAVORS

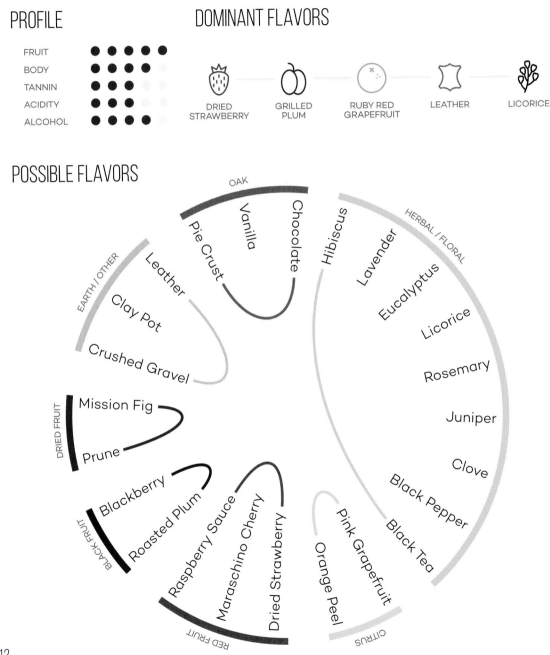

OAK: Pie Crust, Vanilla, Chocolate

HERBAL / FLORAL: Hibiscus, Lavender, Eucalyptus, Licorice, Rosemary, Juniper, Clove, Black Pepper, Black Tea

EARTH / OTHER: Leather, Clay Pot, Crushed Gravel

DRIED FRUIT: Mission Fig, Prune

BLACK FRUIT: Blackberry, Roasted Plum

RED FRUIT: Raspberry Sauce, Maraschino Cherry, Dried Strawberry

CITRUS: Orange Peel, Pink Grapefruit

Origin: Spain

456,000
ACRES

185,000
HA

WHERE IT GROWS

◄ FRANCE
◄ SPAIN
◄ ITALY
◄ ALGERIA
◄ USA
◄ AUSTRALIA
◄ ELSEWHERE

RED

ROOM TEMP.

UP TO 5 YRS

$
$5–$10

Dried Strawberry Raspberry Sauce Mission Fig Prune

COOL CLIMATE   WARM CLIMATE

REGIONAL DIFFERENCES: When comparing Grenache wines from different regions, you'll notice some taste differences:

RASPBERRY & CLOVE
Higher alcohol wines with more fruit flavors
● SPAIN
● AUSTRALIA
● USA

DRIED STRAWBERRY & HERBS
Lighter wines with more herb and tobacco flavors
● FRANCE
● ITALY

REGIONS

○ CÔTES DU RHÔNE & CHÂTEAUNEUF-DU-PAPE
○ LANGUEDOC-ROUSSILLON
○ CALATAYUD & PRIORAT
○ VINOS DE MADRID
○ CANNONAU, SARDINIA
○ PASO ROBLES, CA, USA
○ COLUMBIA VALLEY, WA, USA
○ SOUTH AUSTRALIA

In the glass, Grenache is a translucent violet-ruby hue that develops thick wine tears due to its naturally higher alcohol.

70% of the vineyards in the highly acclaimed Châteauneuf-du-Pape appellation in Rhône Valley, France, are Grenache. Quality Grenache easily ages 15–20 years.

winefolly.com / learn / variety / grenache

MENCÍA

PROFILE

FRUIT
BODY
TANNIN
ACIDITY
ALCOHOL

DOMINANT FLAVORS

SOUR CHERRY · POMEGRANATE · BLACKBERRY · BLACK LICORICE · CRUSHED GRAVEL

POSSIBLE FLAVORS

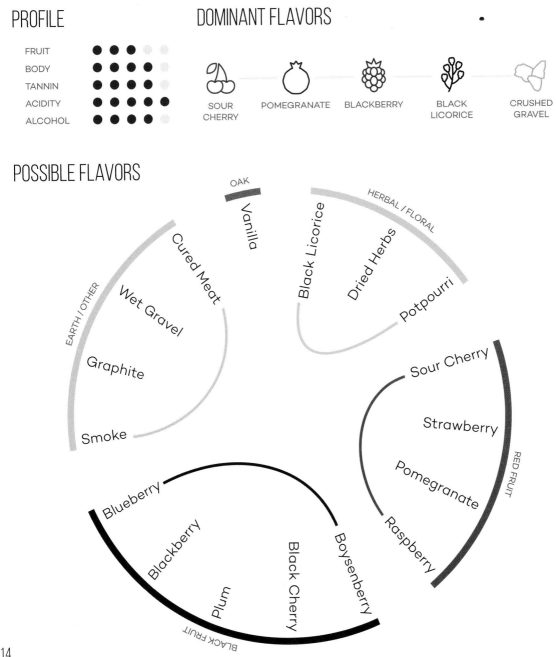

OAK
Vanilla

EARTH / OTHER
Cured Meat
Wet Gravel
Graphite
Smoke

HERBAL / FLORAL
Black Licorice
Dried Herbs
Potpourri

RED FRUIT
Sour Cherry
Strawberry
Pomegranate
Raspberry

BLACK FRUIT
Blueberry
Blackberry
Plum
Black Cherry
Boysenberry

📍 Origin: Spain

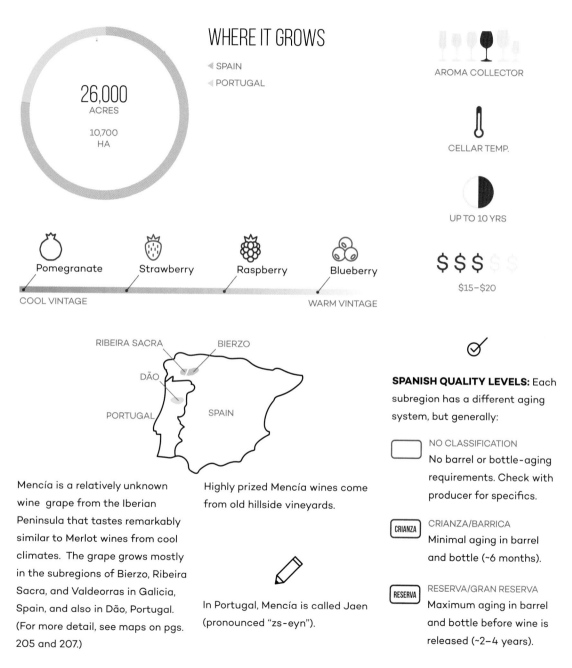

WHERE IT GROWS

26,000 ACRES

10,700 HA

◄ SPAIN
◄ PORTUGAL

Pomegranate   Strawberry   Raspberry   Blueberry

COOL VINTAGE   WARM VINTAGE

AROMA COLLECTOR

CELLAR TEMP.

UP TO 10 YRS

$ $ $

$15–$20

RIBEIRA SACRA   BIERZO
DÃO
PORTUGAL   SPAIN

Mencía is a relatively unknown wine grape from the Iberian Peninsula that tastes remarkably similar to Merlot wines from cool climates. The grape grows mostly in the subregions of Bierzo, Ribeira Sacra, and Valdeorras in Galicia, Spain, and also in Dão, Portugal. (For more detail, see maps on pgs. 205 and 207.)

Highly prized Mencía wines come from old hillside vineyards.

In Portugal, Mencía is called Jaen (pronounced "zs-eyn").

SPANISH QUALITY LEVELS: Each subregion has a different aging system, but generally:

NO CLASSIFICATION
No barrel or bottle-aging requirements. Check with producer for specifics.

CRIANZA — CRIANZA/BARRICA
Minimal aging in barrel and bottle (~6 months).

RESERVA — RESERVA/GRAN RESERVA
Maximum aging in barrel and bottle before wine is released (~2–4 years).

MERLOT

PROFILE

FRUIT
BODY
TANNIN
ACIDITY
ALCOHOL

DOMINANT FLAVORS

RASPBERRY   BLACK CHERRY   SUGAR PLUM   CHOCOLATE   CEDAR

POSSIBLE FLAVORS

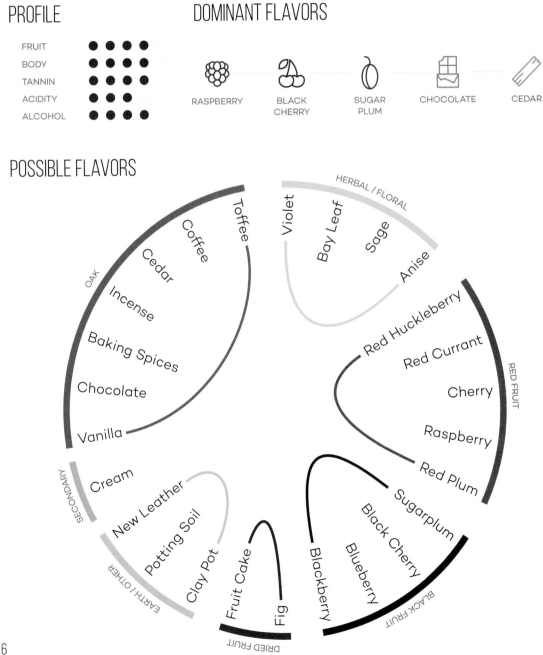

OAK: Toffee, Coffee, Cedar, Incense, Baking Spices, Chocolate, Vanilla

HERBAL / FLORAL: Violet, Bay Leaf, Sage, Anise

RED FRUIT: Red Huckleberry, Red Currant, Cherry, Raspberry, Red Plum

SECONDARY: Cream, New Leather

EARTH / OTHER: Potting Soil, Clay Pot

DRIED FRUIT: Fruit Cake, Fig

BLACK FRUIT: Sugarplum, Black Cherry, Blueberry, Blackberry

116

Origin: France

WHERE IT GROWS

660,000
ACRES

267,000
HA

◀ FRANCE
◀ USA
◀ SPAIN
◀ ITALY
◀ ROMANIA
◀ BULGARIA
◀ CHILE
◀ AUSTRALIA
◀ ELSEWHERE

OVERSIZED

ROOM TEMP.

UP TO 5 YRS

$ $ $
$15–$20

Red Currant   Red Plum   Sugarplum   Berry Jam

COOL CLIMATE   WARM CLIMATE

REGIONAL DIFFERENCES

When comparing Merlot wines from different regions, you'll notice some taste differences:

BLACKBERRY & VANILLA
- CALIFORNIA
- AUSTRALIA
- SOUTH AFRICA
- ARGENTINA

RED PLUM & CEDAR
- FRANCE
- ITALY
- WASHINGTON STATE
- CHILE

REGIONS

- BORDEAUX
- TUSCANY
- VENETO & FRIULI-VENEZIA GIULIA
- WASHINGTON STATE, USA
- SONOMA, CA, USA
- NAPA, CA, USA
- SOUTH AUSTRALIA
- WESTERN AUSTRALIA
- SOUTH AFRICA

Looking for quality? High-quality Merlot grapes grow in vineyards that struggle to concentrate the grapes. Look to hillside and high-elevation vineyards.

Merlot aged in American oak has rich herbaceous notes of dill and cedar.

Merlot is often misidentified as Cabernet Sauvignon in blind tasting because they're closely related (see Cabernet Franc, pgs. 106–107).

117

MONTEPULCIANO

PROFILE

FRUIT
BODY
TANNIN
ACIDITY
ALCOHOL

DOMINANT FLAVORS

RED PLUM · OREGANO · SOUR CHERRY · BOYSENBERRY · TAR

POSSIBLE FLAVORS

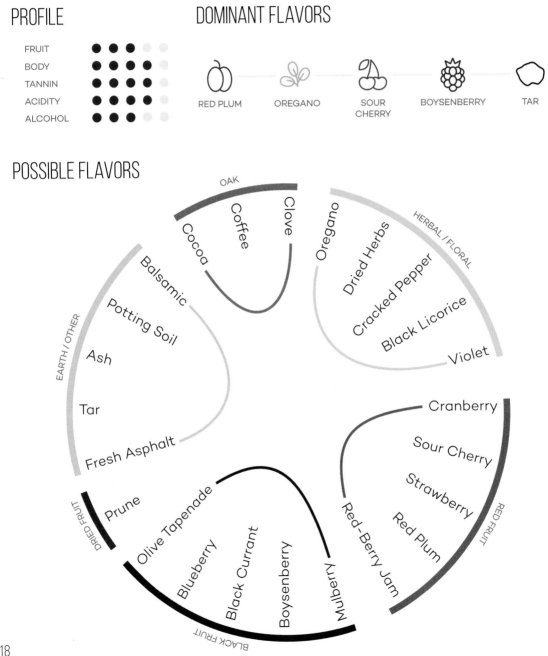

OAK
Cocoa
Coffee
Clove

HERBAL / FLORAL
Oregano
Dried Herbs
Cracked Pepper
Black Licorice
Violet

EARTH / OTHER
Balsamic
Potting Soil
Ash
Tar
Fresh Asphalt

RED FRUIT
Cranberry
Sour Cherry
Strawberry
Red Plum
Red-Berry Jam

DRIED FRUIT
Prune
Olive Tapenade

BLACK FRUIT
Blueberry
Black Currant
Boysenberry
Mulberry

📍 Origin: Southern Italy

86,000
ACRES

35,000
HA

WHERE IT GROWS

◀ ITALY
◀ ARGENTINA
◀ ELSEWHERE

OVERSIZED

ROOM TEMP.

UP TO 5 YRS

$ $ $ $ $
$5–$10

Sour Cherry · Boysenberry · Red-Berry Jam · Prune

COOL VINTAGE   WARM VINTAGE

Montepulciano is the second most planted red grape in Italy. The majority of wines made from this grape are labeled "Montepulciano d'Abruzzo" and are from Abruzzo, Italy.

Typically Montepulciano wines have red-fruit flavors similar to Merlot. High-quality producers, on the other hand, make dark-fruit full-bodied versions that will age 10+ years.

REGIONAL WINES: Montepulciano is labeled by its regional name:

● Abruzzo
  MONTEPULCIANO D'ABRUZZO
  CONTROGUERRA

● Marche
  ROSSO CONERO
  OFFIDA ROSSO DOCG
  ROSSO PICENO

● Molise
  BIFERNO

● Puglia
  SAN SEVERO

Looking for quality? Look for a wine with at least 4 years of age and expect to spend between $20–$30 a bottle.

Montepulciano is commonly confused with Vino Nobile di Montepulciano—a wine from Tuscany made with Sangiovese.

119

NEGROAMARO

PROFILE

FRUIT	●●●●●
BODY	●●●●○
TANNIN	●●●●○
ACIDITY	●●●○○
ALCOHOL	●●●●○

DOMINANT FLAVORS

BLACK CHERRY · BLACK PLUM · BLACKBERRY · PRUNE · DRIED HERBS

POSSIBLE FLAVORS

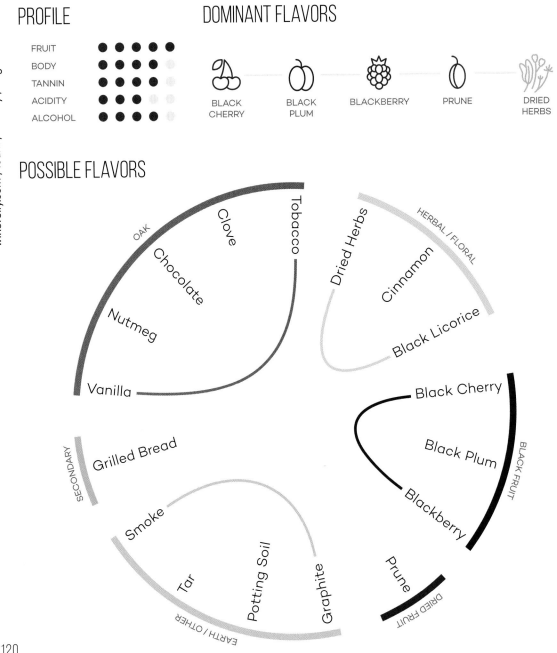

OAK: Tobacco, Clove, Chocolate, Nutmeg, Vanilla

HERBAL / FLORAL: Dried Herbs, Cinnamon, Black Licorice

BLACK FRUIT: Black Cherry, Black Plum, Blackberry

DRIED FRUIT: Prune

SECONDARY: Grilled Bread

EARTH / OTHER: Smoke, Tar, Potting Soil, Graphite

Origin: Puglia, Italy

WHERE IT GROWS

28,000
ACRES

11,400
HA

◀ ITALY

Black Cherry · Black Plum · Blackberry · Prune

COOL VINTAGE — WARM VINTAGE

OVERSIZED

ROOM TEMP.

UP TO 5 YRS

$ $ $ $ $
$5–$10

Negroamaro or "black bitter" is a native grape in Puglia, Italy. It grows mostly toward the very point of the "heel" of Puglia, Italy, along the Ionian Sea. The region is hot, so the best vineyards tend to be adjacent to the sea, where cooler nighttime temperatures produce grapes with higher natural acidity and longer life.

PUGLIA

REGIONAL WINES
Negroamaro is labeled by its regional name. The following regions contain 70–100% Negroamaro:

• Puglia
  SALICE SALENTO
  ALEZIO
  NARDO
  BRINDISI
  SQUINZANO
  MATINO
  COPERTINO

Negroamaro is often blended with Primitivo (aka Zinfandel), where it complements the sweet red fruit flavors of Primitivo with tannin structure, black fruit, and a smoky herbaceous quality.

Try Negroamaro with barbecued chicken and caramelized onion pizza, pulled pork sandwiches, fried mushrooms, or teriyaki.

RHÔNE/GSM BLEND

🔊 "roan"
aka: Grenache-Syrah-Mourvèdre,
Côtes du Rhône

PROFILE

FRUIT
BODY
TANNIN
ACIDITY
ALCOHOL

DOMINANT FLAVORS

RASPBERRY BLACKBERRY DRIED GREEN HERBS BAKING SPICES LAVENDER

POSSIBLE FLAVORS

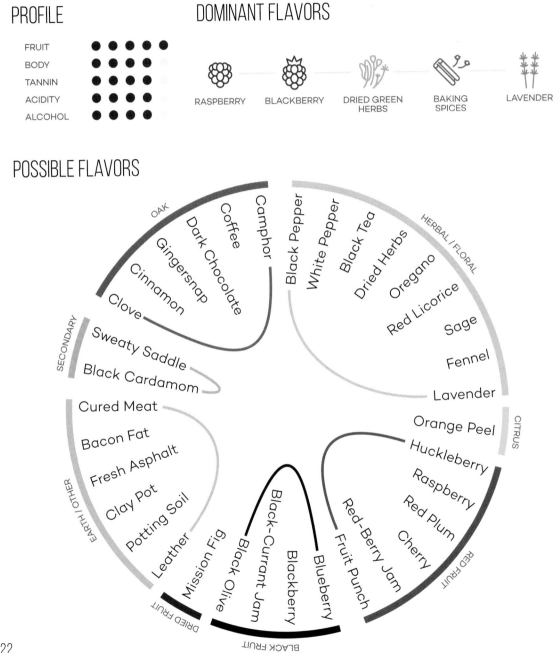

OAK
Camphor
Coffee
Dark Chocolate
Gingersnap
Cinnamon
Clove

SECONDARY
Sweaty Saddle
Black Cardamom

EARTH / OTHER
Cured Meat
Bacon Fat
Fresh Asphalt
Clay Pot
Potting Soil
Leather

DRIED FRUIT
Mission Fig

BLACK FRUIT
Black Olive
Black-Currant Jam
Blackberry
Blueberry
Fruit Punch

RED FRUIT
Red-Berry Jam
Cherry
Red Plum
Raspberry
Huckleberry

CITRUS
Orange Peel
Lavender

HERBAL / FLORAL
Black Pepper
White Pepper
Black Tea
Dried Herbs
Oregano
Red Licorice
Sage
Fennel

Production Regions: France, Spain, Australia, USA, South Africa

~1 MILLION ACRES

~440,000 HA

THE BLEND

◀ GRENACHE
◀ SYRAH
◀ MOURVÈDRE
◀ CINSAUT
◀ CARIGNAN
◀ OTHERS

OVERSIZED

ROOM TEMP.

UP TO 5 YRS

$ $ $
$15–$20

Red Currant — Red Plum — Blackberry — Mission Fig

COOL CLIMATE — WARM CLIMATE

REGIONAL DIFFERENCES

When comparing Rhône blends from different regions, you'll notice some taste differences:

BLACKBERRY & CLOVE
- SPAIN
- SOUTH AUSTRALIA
- SOUTH AFRICA
- CALIFORNIA, USA

DRIED STAWBERRY & HERBS
- FRANCE
- WASHINGTON STATE, USA

REGIONS

CÔTES DU RHÔNE (FR)

LANGUEDOC-ROUSSILLON (FR)

CATALONIA (ESP)

ARAGON (ESP)

LA MANCHA & MADRID (ESP)

CENTRAL COAST, CA (USA)

COLUMBIA VALLEY, WA (USA)

SOUTH AUSTRALIA

SOUTH AFRICA

Looking for value? Languedoc-Roussillon, France, and La Mancha, Spain, offer good values. Look for wines with high proportions of Grenache.

The highest quality GSMs come from Priorat and Méntrida, Spain; Châteauneuf-du-Pape, France; Barossa Valley, Australia; and Santa Barbara, CA, USA.

SANGIOVESE

◀ "san-jo vay-zay"
aka: Chianti, Brunello, Nielluccio,
Morellino

PROFILE

FRUIT
BODY
TANNIN
ACIDITY
ALCOHOL

DOMINANT FLAVORS

RED
CURRANT

ROASTED
TOMATO

RASPBERRY

POTPOURRI

CLAY POT

POSSIBLE FLAVORS

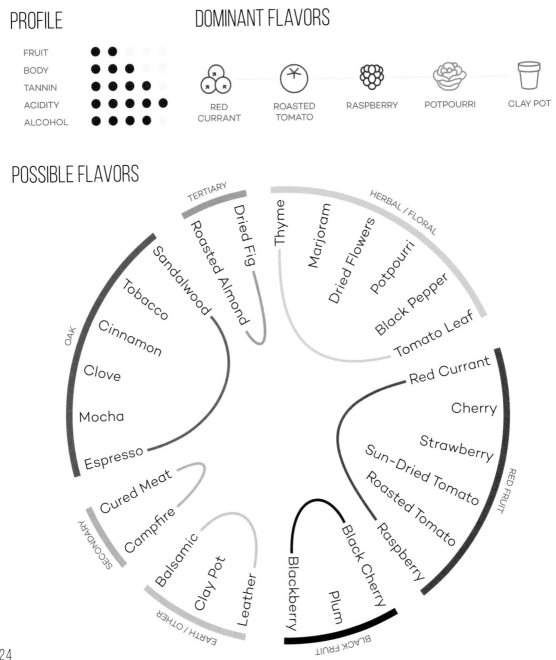

TERTIARY

Roasted Almond
Dried Fig
Thyme

HERBAL / FLORAL

Marjoram
Dried Flowers
Potpourri
Black Pepper
Tomato Leaf

Sandalwood
Tobacco
Cinnamon
Clove
Mocha
Espresso

OAK

Red Currant
Cherry
Strawberry
Sun-Dried Tomato
Roasted Tomato
Raspberry

RED FRUIT

Cured Meat
Campfire
Balsamic
Clay Pot
Leather

SECONDARY

EARTH / OTHER

Blackberry
Plum
Black Cherry

BLACK FRUIT

📍 Origin: Italy

192,000
ACRES

78,000
HA

WHERE IT GROWS

◄ ITALY
◄ ARGENTINA
◄ FRANCE
◄ TUNISIA
◄ USA
◄ AUSTRALIA
◄ ELSEWHERE

RED

CELLAR TEMP.

UP TO 5 YRS

$ $ $
$15–$20

Red Currant

Roasted Tomato

Raspberry

Blackberry

COOL CLIMATE   WARM CLIMATE

COMMON STYLES

RUSTIC TOMATO & LEATHER
Traditional production maintains Sangiovese's herbaceous flavors and high acidity by aging wines in well-used barrels that don't impart vanilla-like flavors.

MODERN CHERRY & CLOVE
The modern style of Sangiovese wines employs oak aging to produce sweet vanilla-like flavors and also smoother acidity.

REGIONAL WINES: Sangiovese is commonly labeled by its regional name. The following regions contain 60–100% Sangiovese:

- Tuscany
  CHIANTI
  BRUNELLO DI MONTALCINO
  ROSSO DI MONTALCINO
  VINO NOBILE DI MONTEPULCIANO
  MORELLINO DI SCANSANO
  CARMIGNANO
  MONTECUCCO

- Umbria
  MONTEFALCO ROSSO

Sangiovese pairs with rich meats and tomato-based dishes such as lasagna, pasta Bolognese, and pizza.

Sangiovese is Italy's top wine. It is produced primarily in Tuscany, Campania, and Umbria.

Sangiovese was first introduced to California in the 1980s.

VALPOLICELLA BLEND

🔊 "val-polla-chellah"
aka: Amarone

PROFILE

FRUIT
BODY
TANNIN
ACIDITY
ALCOHOL

DOMINANT FLAVORS

SOUR CHERRY · CINNAMON · GREEN PEPPERCORN · CAROB · GREEN ALMOND

POSSIBLE FLAVORS

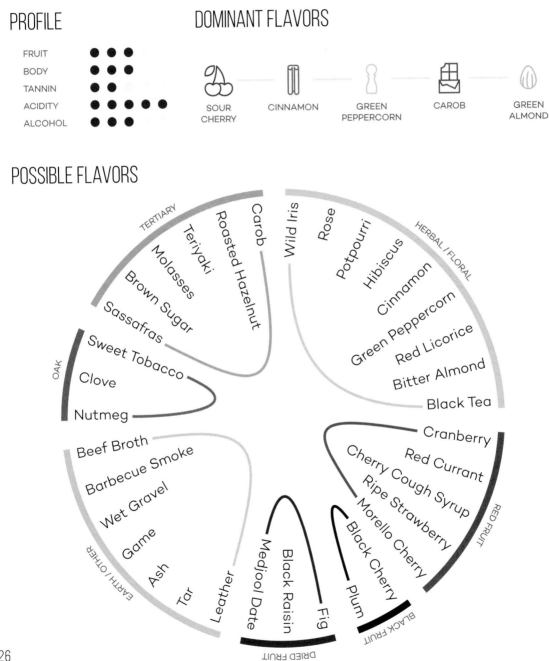

TERTIARY
Carob
Roasted Hazelnut
Teriyaki
Molasses
Brown Sugar
Sassafras

OAK
Sweet Tobacco
Clove
Nutmeg

Wild Iris
Rose
Potpourri
Hibiscus
Cinnamon
Green Peppercorn
Red Licorice
Bitter Almond
Black Tea

HERBAL / FLORAL

Cranberry
Red Currant
Cherry Cough Syrup
Ripe Strawberry
Morello Cherry
Black Cherry
Plum

RED FRUIT

Beef Broth
Barbecue Smoke
Wet Gravel
Game
Ash
Tar
Leather

EARTH / OTHER

Medjool Date
Black Raisin
Fig

DRIED FRUIT

BLACK FRUIT

● Origin: Veneto, Italy

THE BLEND

20,000 ACRES

8,000 HA

◄ CORVINA
◄ RONDINELLA
◄ CORVINONE
◄ MOLINARA
◄ OTHERS

RED

CELLAR TEMP.

UP TO 5 YRS

$ $ $

$15–$20

Cranberry

Black Cherry

Ripe Strawberry

Black Raisin

COOL VINTAGE

WARM VINTAGE

There are 4 main grapes of Valpolicella. The Corvina and Corvinone grapes are known to produce the highest quality wines.

CORVINA & CORVINONE
Spicy red fruit and green almond flavors

RONDINELLA
Adds floral aromas and has low tannin

MOLINARA
Known for high acidity

QUALITY LEVELS

$ VALPOLICELLA CLASSICO
tart cherry and ash

$$ VALPOLICELLA SUPERIORE
dark berries and high acidity

$$$ VALPOLICELLA SUPERIORE RIPASSO
cherry sauce, green peppercorn, and carob

$$$$$ AMARONE DELLA VALPOLICELLA
black cherry, fig, sassafras, chocolate, and brown sugar

$$$$$ RECIOTO DELLA VALPOLICELLA
sweet black raisin, black cherry, clove, and roasted hazelnut

Looking for value? Some Ripasso taste very similar to Amarone at a fraction of the price.

Amarone and Recioto are made with the *apassimento* method. Grapes are dried on straw mats over the winter to concentrate sugars and then pressed and fermented very slowly. The resulting wines are light in color but rich in body and flavor.

ZINFANDEL

PROFILE

FRUIT ●●●●●
BODY ●●●●●
TANNIN ●●●○○
ACIDITY ●●●○○
ALCOHOL ●●●●●

DOMINANT FLAVORS

BLACKBERRY STRAWBERRY PEACH PRESERVES 5-SPICE POWDER SWEET TOBACCO

POSSIBLE FLAVORS

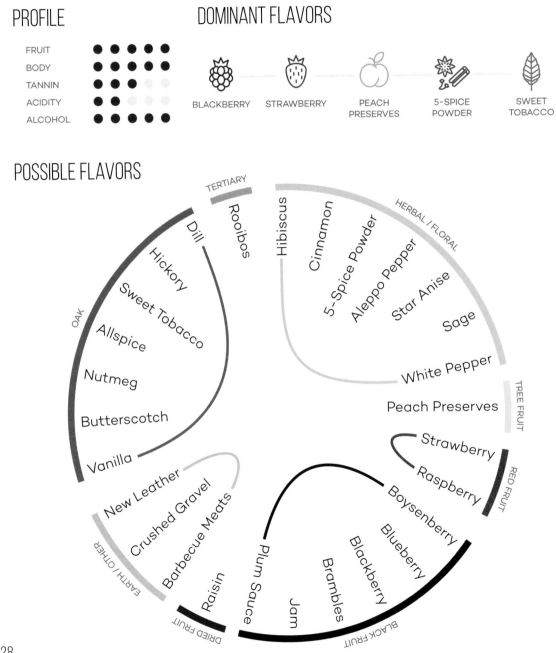

TERTIARY

Rooibos · Dill · Hickory · Sweet Tobacco · Allspice · Nutmeg · Butterscotch · Vanilla

OAK

New Leather · Crushed Gravel · Barbecue Meats

EARTH / OTHER

Raisin · Plum Sauce

DRIED FRUIT

Jam · Brambles · Blackberry · Blueberry · Boysenberry

BLACK FRUIT

Raspberry · Strawberry

RED FRUIT

Peach Preserves

TREE FRUIT

White Pepper · Sage · Star Anise · Aleppo Pepper · 5-Spice Powder · Cinnamon · Hibiscus

HERBAL / FLORAL

128

📍 Origin: Croatia

WHERE IT GROWS

81,000
ACRES

32,800
HA

◀ USA
◀ ITALY
◀ OTHERS

RED

ROOM TEMP.

UP TO 2 YRS

$ $ $ $ $
$10–$15

winefolly.com / learn / variety / zinfandel

Boysenberry   Strawberry   Blackberry   Raisin

COOL CLIMATE   WARM CLIMATE

The origin of Zinfandel remained a mystery until DNA testing showed it was identical to Primitivo in Italy and Tribidrag in Croatia, where the grape originated. Zinfandel used to be prized and traded in Venice during the 1400s.

Zinfandel naturally produces a rich red wine; however, only about 15% of the US production is dedicated to this style. The rest goes into sappy-sweet rosé called White Zinfandel.

REGIONS

CALIFORNIA, USA
The best Zinfandel grows in the hills of Napa, Sonoma, Paso Robles, and the Sierra Foothills. Exceptional old vineyards can be found in Lodi.

ITALY
In Puglia, most Primitivo is lighter in style but can reach incredible depth in and around Manduria. It's often blended with Negroamaro.

COMMON STYLES

RED FRUITS & SPICE
A lighter style with lower alcohol (~13.5%) has raspberry, rose petal, spice cake, sage, and black pepper flavors.

JAM & SMOKED CARAMEL
A rich style with higher alcohol (~15%) offers blackberry, cinnamon, caramel, jam, chocolate, and smoky tobacco flavors.

Full-Bodied Red Wine

AGLIANICO

BORDEAUX BLEND

CABERNET SAUVIGNON

MALBEC

MOURVÈDRE

NEBBIOLO

NERO D'AVOLA

PETIT VERDOT

PETITE SIRAH

PINOTAGE

SYRAH

TEMPRANILLO

TOURIGA NACIONAL

Full-bodied red wines typically have high tannin, opaque ruby color from high anthocyanin content, and rich fruit flavors. Wines that are bold such as these can be enjoyed on their own or with equally bold-flavored foods.

Red wine grapes are collected and sorted.

Grape bunches are destemmed.

Juice ferments with skins in fermentation vessels.

Wine is gently pressed off pomace (seeds, stems, skins, etc.).

Wine is aged in barrels for a period of time.

During aging, malolactic bacteria convert "green apple-y" malic acid into "creamy" lactic acid.

Wines are clarified, bottled, and released after a period of aging.

AGLIANICO

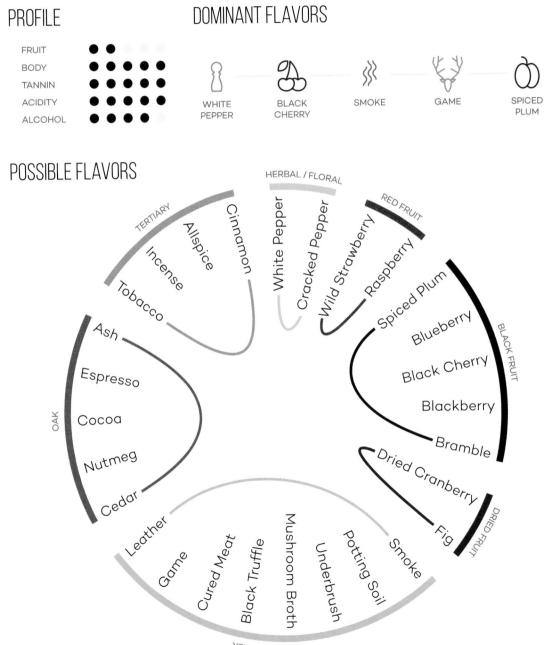

"alli-yawn-nico"
aka: Taurasi

PROFILE

FRUIT
BODY
TANNIN
ACIDITY
ALCOHOL

DOMINANT FLAVORS

WHITE PEPPER · BLACK CHERRY · SMOKE · GAME · SPICED PLUM

POSSIBLE FLAVORS

HERBAL / FLORAL

RED FRUIT

TERTIARY
Cinnamon
Allspice
Incense
Tobacco

White Pepper
Cracked Pepper
Wild Strawberry
Raspberry
Spiced Plum
Blueberry
Black Cherry
Blackberry
Bramble

BLACK FRUIT

Ash
Espresso
Cocoa
Nutmeg
Cedar

OAK

Dried Cranberry
Fig

DRIED FRUIT

Leather
Game
Cured Meat
Black Truffle
Mushroom Broth
Underbrush
Potting Soil
Smoke

EARTH / OTHER

132

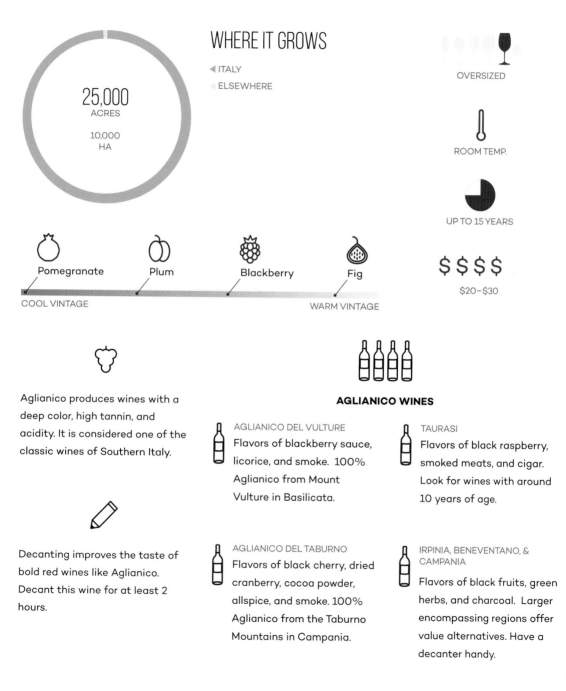

📍 Origin: Southern Italy

25,000 ACRES

10,000 HA

WHERE IT GROWS

◀ ITALY
◀ ELSEWHERE

OVERSIZED

ROOM TEMP.

UP TO 15 YEARS

$ $ $ $
$20–$30

Pomegranate   Plum   Blackberry   Fig

COOL VINTAGE   WARM VINTAGE

Aglianico produces wines with a deep color, high tannin, and acidity. It is considered one of the classic wines of Southern Italy.

Decanting improves the taste of bold red wines like Aglianico. Decant this wine for at least 2 hours.

AGLIANICO WINES

AGLIANICO DEL VULTURE
Flavors of blackberry sauce, licorice, and smoke. 100% Aglianico from Mount Vulture in Basilicata.

TAURASI
Flavors of black raspberry, smoked meats, and cigar. Look for wines with around 10 years of age.

AGLIANICO DEL TABURNO
Flavors of black cherry, dried cranberry, cocoa powder, allspice, and smoke. 100% Aglianico from the Taburno Mountains in Campania.

IRPINIA, BENEVENTANO, & CAMPANIA
Flavors of black fruits, green herbs, and charcoal. Larger encompassing regions offer value alternatives. Have a decanter handy.

winefolly.com / learn / variety / aglianico

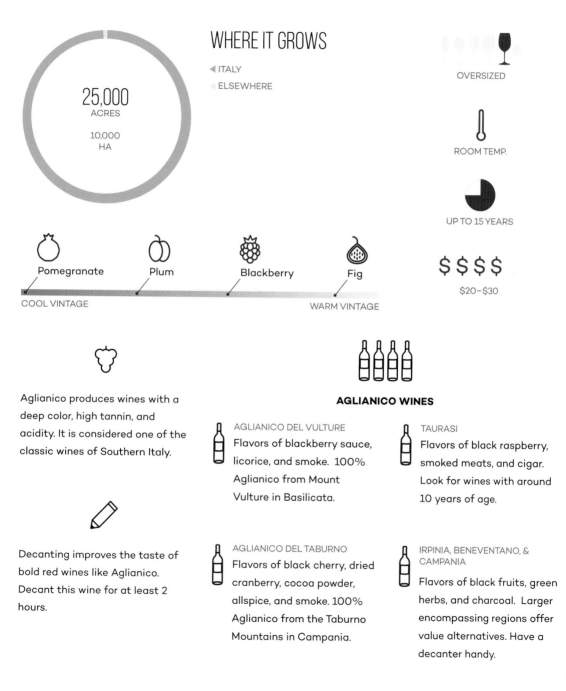

133

BORDEAUX BLEND

🔊 "bore-doe"
aka: Meritage, Cabernet-Merlot

PROFILE

FRUIT
BODY
TANNIN
ACIDITY
ALCOHOL

DOMINANT FLAVORS

PLUM · BLACK CURRANT · VIOLET · GRAPHITE · CEDAR

POSSIBLE FLAVORS

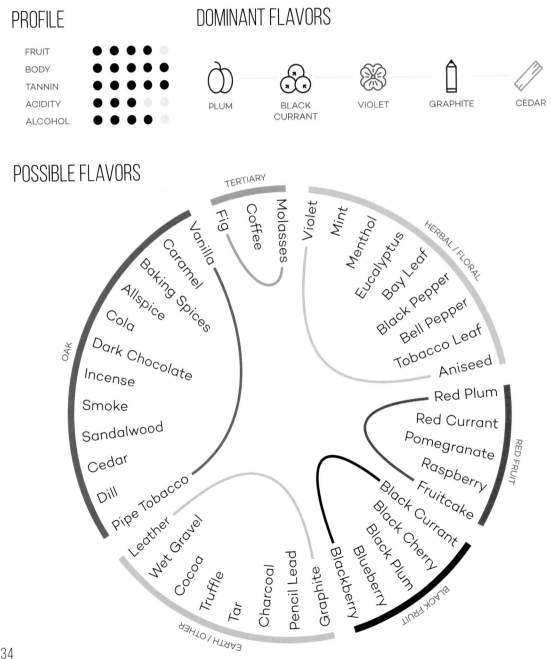

TERTIARY
Fig
Vanilla
Caramel
Baking Spices
Allspice
Cola
Dark Chocolate
Incense
Smoke
Sandalwood
Cedar
Dill
Pipe Tobacco
OAK

Coffee
Molasses

Violet
Mint
Menthol
Eucalyptus
Bay Leaf
Black Pepper
Bell Pepper
Tobacco Leaf
Aniseed
HERBAL / FLORAL

Red Plum
Red Currant
Pomegranate
Raspberry
Fruitcake
RED FRUIT

Black Currant
Black Cherry
Black Plum
Blueberry
Blackberry
BLACK FRUIT

Leather
Wet Gravel
Cocoa
Truffle
Tar
Charcoal
Pencil Lead
Graphite
EARTH / OTHER

THE BLEND

◄ CABERNET SAUVIGNON
◄ MERLOT
◄ CABERNET FRANC
◄ PETIT VERDOT
◄ MALBEC
◄ CARMÉNÈRE
◄ OTHERS

1.7 MILLION
ACRES

671,000
HA

OVERSIZED

ROOM TEMP.

UP TO 10 YRS

$ $ $ $ $
$15–$20

Graphite   Black Cherry   Blackberry   Blueberry

COOL CLIMATE   WARM CLIMATE

REGIONAL DIFFERENCES: When comparing Bordeaux blends from different regions, you'll notice some taste differences:

BLACKBERRY, MENTHOL, & CEDAR
Expect ripe black fruit with undertones of menthol, chocolate, and allspice. Wines may be bolder with riper-tasting tannin.

● PASO ROBLES & NAPA, CA, USA
● AUSTRALIA
● MENDOZA, ARGENTINA
● SOUTH AFRICA
● TUSCANY, ITALY
● SPAIN

BLACK CHERRY, VIOLET, & BAY LEAF
Expect tart black and red fruit flavors with undertones of violet, black pepper, and bay leaf. Wines may taste lighter due to higher acidity.

● BORDEAUX, FRANCE
● SOUTH WEST FRANCE
● CHILE
● VENETO, ITALY
● WASHINGTON STATE, USA
● COASTAL SONOMA, CA, USA
● MENDOCINO, CA, USA

Blends dominated by Cabernet Sauvignon typically have grippier tannin and green peppercorn notes, whereas Merlot blends have smoother tannins and more red fruit notes.

The first Bordeaux blend to become popular was not a red wine but a brilliant red rosé called Claret ("Clair-ette"). Today, Claret is rare but can still be found under the basic Bordeaux appellation.

135

CABERNET SAUVIGNON

PROFILE

FRUIT
BODY
TANNIN
ACIDITY
ALCOHOL

DOMINANT FLAVORS

BLACK CHERRY

BLACK CURRANT

RED BELL PEPPER

BAKING SPICES

CEDAR

POSSIBLE FLAVORS

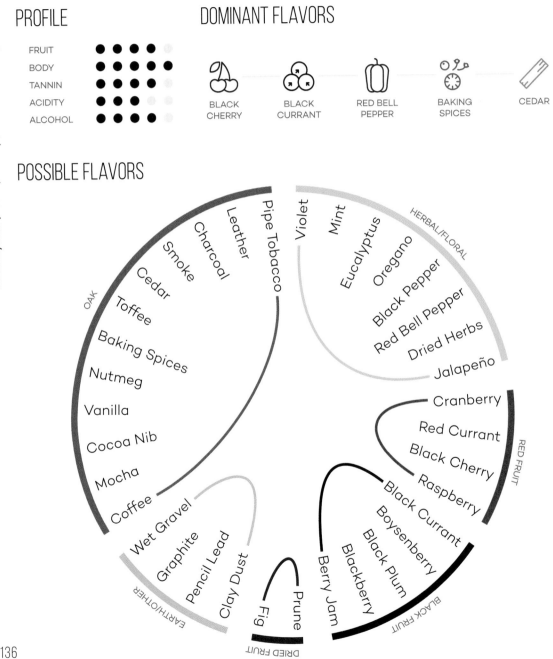

OAK
Pipe Tobacco
Leather
Charcoal
Smoke
Cedar
Toffee
Baking Spices
Nutmeg
Vanilla
Cocoa Nib
Mocha
Coffee

HERBAL/FLORAL
Violet
Mint
Eucalyptus
Oregano
Black Pepper
Red Bell Pepper
Dried Herbs
Jalapeño

RED FRUIT
Cranberry
Red Currant
Black Cherry
Raspberry

BLACK FRUIT
Black Currant
Boysenberry
Black Plum
Blackberry
Berry Jam

EARTH/OTHER
Wet Gravel
Graphite
Pencil Lead
Clay Dust

DRIED FRUIT
Fig
Prune

136

Origin: France

WHERE IT GROWS

717,000
ACRES

290,000
HA

◀ FRANCE   ◀ ITALY
◀ CHILE   ◀ SOUTH AFRICA
◀ USA   ◀ ELSEWHERE
◀ AUSTRALIA
◀ SPAIN
◀ CHINA
◀ ARGENTINA

Red Currant   Black Currant   Black Cherry   Blackberry

COOL CLIMATE   WARM CLIMATE

OVERSIZED

ROOM TEMP.

UP TO 10 YRS

$ $ $ $ $
$20-$30

REGIONAL DIFFERENCES: When comparing Cabernet Sauvignon wines from different regions, you'll notice some taste differences:

 BLACK FRUITS, BLACK PEPPER, AND COCOA POWDER

Warm climate regions lend to more fruit-forward wines with higher alcohol and ripe-tasting tannin.

● CALIFORNIA, USA
● AUSTRALIA
● ARGENTINA
● SOUTH AFRICA
● CENTRAL AND SOUTHERN ITALY
● SPAIN

RED FRUITS, MINT, AND GREEN PEPPERCORN

Cool-climate Cabernet tends to exhibit red fruit flavors and a lighter body.

● BORDEAUX, FRANCE
● CHILE
● NORTHERN ITALY
● WASHINGTON STATE, USA
● NORTHERN CALIFORNIA, USA

Cabernet Sauvignon is a natural cross between Cabernet Franc and Sauvignon Blanc that first appeared in Bordeaux in the mid-1600s. Today, it is the most planted wine grape in the world.

MALBEC

◀ "mal-bek"
aka: Côt

PROFILE

FRUIT
BODY
TANNIN
ACIDITY
ALCOHOL

DOMINANT FLAVORS

RED PLUM   BLUEBERRY   VANILLA   SWEET TOBACCO   COCOA

POSSIBLE FLAVORS

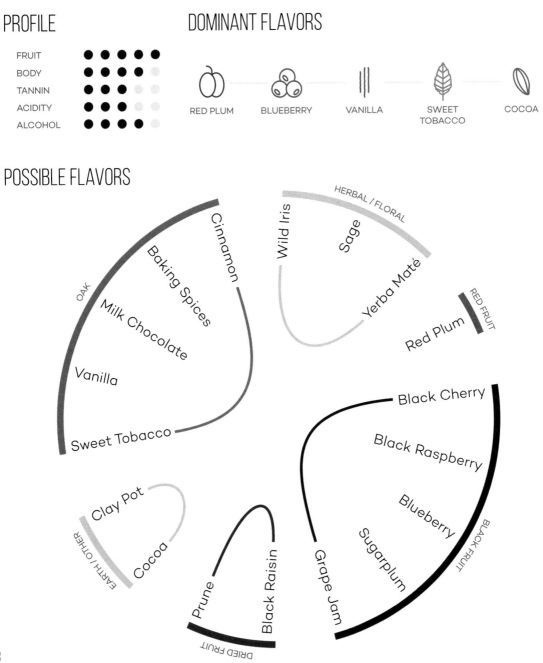

Cinnamon
Wild Iris
HERBAL / FLORAL
Sage
Yerba Maté
OAK
Baking Spices
Milk Chocolate
Vanilla
Red Plum
RED FRUIT
Sweet Tobacco
Black Cherry
Black Raspberry
Blueberry
Clay Pot
Cocoa
EARTH / OTHER
Sugarplum
BLACK FRUIT
Prune
Black Raisin
Grape Jam
DRIED FRUIT

♥ Origin: South West France

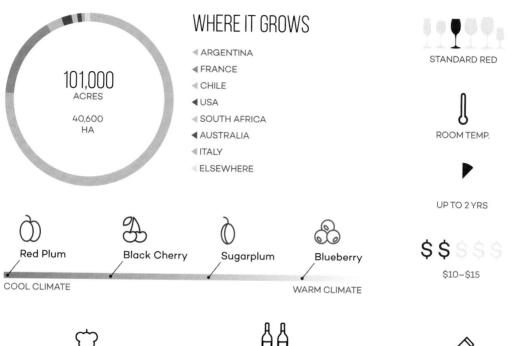

101,000
ACRES

40,600
HA

WHERE IT GROWS

◄ ARGENTINA
◄ FRANCE
◄ CHILE
◄ USA
◄ SOUTH AFRICA
◄ AUSTRALIA
◄ ITALY
◄ ELSEWHERE

Red Plum   Black Cherry   Sugarplum   Blueberry

COOL CLIMATE   WARM CLIMATE

STANDARD RED

ROOM TEMP.

UP TO 2 YRS

$ $ $ $ $
$10–$15

Malbec originated in South West France around Cahors but was never considered an important wine until Argentina revived the variety. Today, Argentina produces over 75% of the world's Malbec wines.

The majority of Malbec in Argentina comes from around Mendoza, with the best wines coming primarily from the high-elevation subregions of Uco Valley and Lujan de Cuyo.

COMMON STYLES

BASIC MALBEC
A juicy style of Malbec with dominant red fruit flavors and balanced tannin, and is made with little to no oak aging.

RESERVA MALBEC
Higher-end Malbec wines tend to age in oak longer and offer black fruit, chocolate, sweet tobacco, and subtle notes of wild iris.

In Argentina, altitude is a key quality indicator for Malbec. Higher-elevation Malbec will have higher acidity, more tannin, and additional flower and herb notes.

In France, Malbec is mostly from Cahors in the South West region. This wine, with a more earthy profile, is much different than Argentine Malbec. Expect higher tannin and flavors of red and black currant, smoke, and licorice.

139

MOURVÈDRE

🔊 "moore-ved"

aka: Monastrell, Mataro

PROFILE

FRUIT
BODY
TANNIN
ACIDITY
ALCOHOL

DOMINANT FLAVORS

BLACKBERRY

BLACK PEPPER

COCOA

SWEET TOBACCO

ROASTED MEAT

POSSIBLE FLAVORS

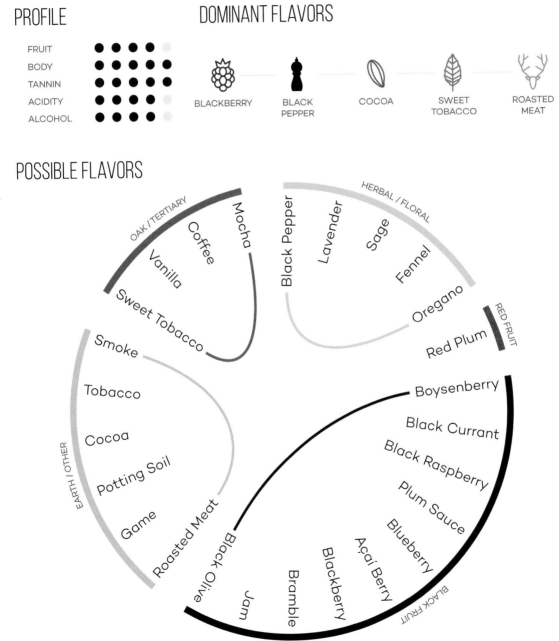

OAK / TERTIARY
- Mocha
- Coffee
- Vanilla
- Sweet Tobacco

HERBAL / FLORAL
- Black Pepper
- Lavender
- Sage
- Fennel
- Oregano

RED FRUIT
- Red Plum

EARTH / OTHER
- Smoke
- Tobacco
- Cocoa
- Potting Soil
- Game
- Roasted Meat

BLACK FRUIT
- Boysenberry
- Black Currant
- Black Raspberry
- Plum Sauce
- Blueberry
- Açaí Berry
- Blackberry
- Bramble
- Jam
- Black Olive

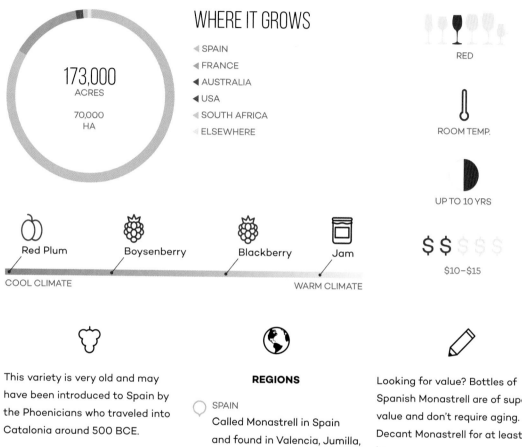

173,000
ACRES

70,000
HA

WHERE IT GROWS

◀ SPAIN
◀ FRANCE
◀ AUSTRALIA
◀ USA
◀ SOUTH AFRICA
◀ ELSEWHERE

RED

ROOM TEMP.

UP TO 10 YRS

$ $ $ $ $
$10–$15

Red Plum — Boysenberry — Blackberry — Jam

COOL CLIMATE   WARM CLIMATE

This variety is very old and may have been introduced to Spain by the Phoenicians who traveled into Catalonia around 500 BCE.

Mourvèdre is most commonly used as a blending grape, and is the "M" in the Rhône/GSM blend. It adds color, tannin structure, and black fruit flavors.

REGIONS

SPAIN
Called Monastrell in Spain and found in Valencia, Jumilla, Yecla, Almansa, and Alicante.

FRANCE
Single-varietal Mourvèdre wines are labeled "Bandol," an appellation in Provence.

AUSTRALIA
Called Mataro and found in South Australia, where it's used in GSM blends.

Looking for value? Bottles of Spanish Monastrell are of superb value and don't require aging. Decant Monastrell for at least 1 hour.

In Spain, Monastrell is used in Cava to make sparkling rosé.

In France, Mourvèdre is also made into a non-sparkling rosé. You can find this style in Bandol, Provence.

NEBBIOLO

🔊 "nebby-oh-low"
aka: Barolo, Barbaresco, Spanna, Chiavennasca

PROFILE

FRUIT	●●●○○
BODY	●●●●○
TANNIN	●●●●●
ACIDITY	●●●●●
ALCOHOL	●●●●○

DOMINANT FLAVORS

ROSE · CHERRY · LEATHER · CLAY POT · ANISE

POSSIBLE FLAVORS

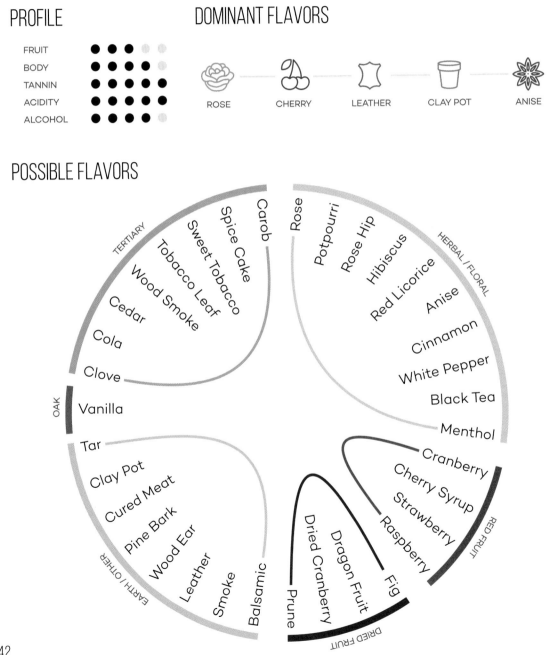

TERTIARY: Carob, Spice Cake, Sweet Tobacco, Tobacco Leaf, Wood Smoke, Cedar, Cola, Clove

OAK: Vanilla, Tar

EARTH / OTHER: Clay Pot, Cured Meat, Pine Bark, Wood Ear, Leather, Smoke, Balsamic

DRIED FRUIT: Prune, Dried Cranberry, Dragon Fruit, Fig

RED FRUIT: Raspberry, Strawberry, Cherry Syrup, Cranberry

HERBAL / FLORAL: Rose, Potpourri, Rose Hip, Hibiscus, Red Licorice, Anise, Cinnamon, White Pepper, Black Tea, Menthol

📍 Origin: northern Italy

14,800
ACRES

6,000
HA

WHERE IT GROWS

◀ ITALY
◀ MEXICO
◀ ARGENTINA
◀ AUSTRALIA
◀ USA
◀ OTHERS

AROMA COLLECTOR

CELLAR TEMP.

15+ YRS

$ $ $ $ $
$30+

Cranberry   Cherry   Dried Dragon Fruit   Fruitcake

COOL VINTAGE   WARM VINTAGE

winefolly.com / learn / variety / nebbiolo

Nebbiolo is considered one of Italy's top red wines. It is perhaps more famously known by the names of its two top regions: Barolo and Barbaresco. Nebbiolo wines are pale-colored and aromatic—*features of a light-bodied wine*—however, since Nebbiolo is naturally high in tannin, it can be characterized as a full-bodied red.

Nebbiolo wines improve with age and reveal subtle molasses, fig, and leather flavors.

REGIONAL WINES: Nebbiolo is commonly labeled by its regional name. The following regions contain 70–100% Nebbiolo:

● Piedmont
  BAROLO
  BARBARESCO
  NEBBIOLO D'ALBA
  LANGHE NEBBIOLO
  ROERO
  GATTINARA
  CAREMA
  GHEMME

● Lombardy
  VALTELLINA & SFORZATO

Love Nebbiolo? Wines labeled as "Langhe Nebbiolo" offer exceptional value on good vintages.

During the mid-1800s Barolo was a sweet red wine.

Barolo Chinato is a richly spiced red vermouth made with Nebbiolo.

NERO D'AVOLA

🔊 "nair-oh davo-la"
aka: Calabrese

PROFILE

FRUIT
BODY
TANNIN
ACIDITY
ALCOHOL

DOMINANT FLAVORS

BLACK CHERRY

BLACK PLUM

LICORICE

TOBACCO

CHILI PEPPER

POSSIBLE FLAVORS

OAK
Wood Smoke
Cedar
Carob
Vanilla

HERBAL / FLORAL
Eucalyptus
Dried Herbs
Bay Leaf
Chili Pepper
Licorice
Menthol
Mint

Leather
Desert Dust
Clay Dust
Tar
Grilled Meat
Chewing Tobacco
Dark Chocolate
Cocoa

EARTH / OTHER

CITRUS
Orange Rind

RED FRUIT
Cherry
Raspberry
Fruit Roll-Up
Mulberry

Black Raisin
Prune
Dried Strawberry

DRIED FRUIT

Plum Sauce
Blueberry
Blackberry Jam
Black Plum

BLACK FRUIT

📍 Origin: Sicily, Italy

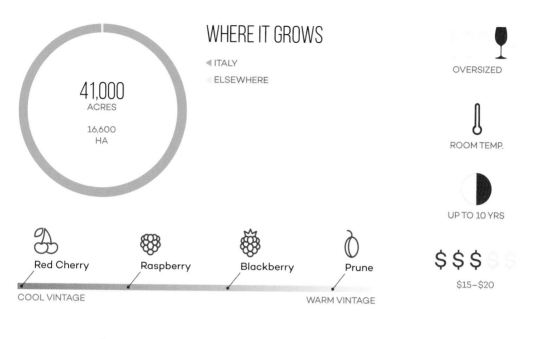

41,000
ACRES

16,600
HA

WHERE IT GROWS

◄ ITALY
◄ ELSEWHERE

OVERSIZED

ROOM TEMP.

UP TO 10 YRS

$ $ $ $ $
$15–$20

Red Cherry　　Raspberry　　Blackberry　　Prune

COOL VINTAGE　　　　　　　　　　WARM VINTAGE

Nero d'Avola is the most planted red variety on the Island of Sicily. The wines have very bold sweet fruit flavors and often a subtly sweet smoky finish.

Quality Nero d'Avola wines are often described as having red fruit, black pepper, licorice, and spice cake flavors.

The spicy pepper flavors in Nero d'Avola become smoother with an hour of decanting.

If you like the candied red fruit flavors of Nero d'Avola, you might also enjoy other Sicilian red wines:

🍷 FRAPPATO
🍷 NERELLO MASCALESE

Try pairing Nero d'Avola with oxtail soup, beef and barley stew, or bacon burgers. Dishes with gamy and meaty flavors will bring out the wine's bright, sweet fruit flavors.

OXTAIL SOUP

BEEF AND BARLEY STEW

BACON BURGER

145

PETIT VERDOT

◀ "peh-tee vur-doe"

PROFILE

FRUIT
BODY
TANNIN
ACIDITY
ALCOHOL

DOMINANT FLAVORS

BLACK CHERRY

PLUM

VIOLET

LILAC

SAGE

POSSIBLE FLAVORS

Clove
Nutmeg
Vanilla
Dark Chocolate
Mocha
Hazelnut

OAK

Violet
Iris
Lilac
Lavender
Dried Herbs
Thyme
Sage
Matcha Powder

HERBAL / FLORAL

Potting Soil
Smoked Meats
Charcoal
Smoke

EARTH / OTHER

Marionberry
Boysenberry
Black Cherry
Blackberry Jam
Blueberry
Plum

BLACK FRUIT

146

Origin: France

WHERE IT GROWS

17,800
ACRES

7,200
HA

◀ SPAIN
◀ FRANCE
◀ AUSTRALIA
◀ USA
◀ SOUTH AFRICA
◀ CHILE
◀ ARGENTINA
◀ ELSEWHERE

Dried Herbs   Black Cherry   Blueberry   Blackberry Jam

COOL CLIMATE   WARM CLIMATE

OVERSIZED

ROOM TEMP.

UP TO 5 YRS

$ $ $ $ $
$15–$20

winefolly.com / learn / variety / petit-verdot

Petit Verdot is highly desired as a blending grape because of its deep purple color, high tannin, and floral aromas. You'll find this grape most commonly used in Bordeaux blends.

If you would like to taste a single-varietal Petit Verdot, look in Washington State, California, Spain, and Australia, where conditions are sunny enough to properly ripen the grape.

REGIONS

○ SPAIN
Found in Castilla-La Mancha where it adds dark fruit flavors to Bordeaux blends.

○ BORDEAUX, FRANCE
The classic "Left Bank" Bordeaux blend has about 1–2% Petit Verdot.

○ AUSTRALIA & USA
Single-varietal Petit Verdot wines taste of blueberry, vanilla, and violets.

Looking for a bolder Bordeaux blend? Seek wines with a higher proportion of Petit Verdot and/or Petite Sirah.

The most famous Chilean Carménère, called "Purple Angel," adds 10% Petit Verdot to embolden the wine with notes of dark fruit, chocolate, and sage.

PETITE SIRAH

◀ "peh-teet sear-ah"
aka: Durif, Petite Syrah

PROFILE

FRUIT
BODY
TANNIN
ACIDITY
ALCOHOL

DOMINANT FLAVORS

SUGAR-PLUM

BLUEBERRY

DARK CHOCOLATE

BLACK PEPPER

BLACK TEA

POSSIBLE FLAVORS

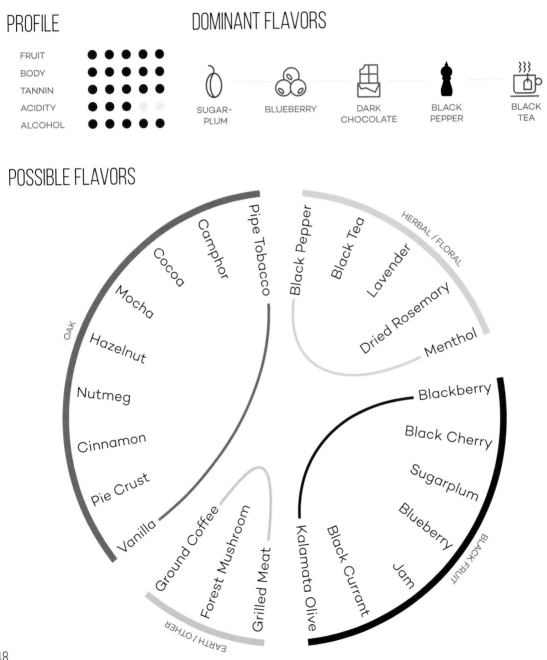

OAK
Pipe Tobacco
Camphor
Cocoa
Mocha
Hazelnut
Nutmeg
Cinnamon
Pie Crust
Vanilla

HERBAL / FLORAL
Black Pepper
Black Tea
Lavender
Dried Rosemary
Menthol

BLACK FRUIT
Blackberry
Black Cherry
Sugarplum
Blueberry
Jam
Black Currant
Kalamata Olive

EARTH / OTHER
Ground Coffee
Forest Mushroom
Grilled Meat

📍 Origin: France

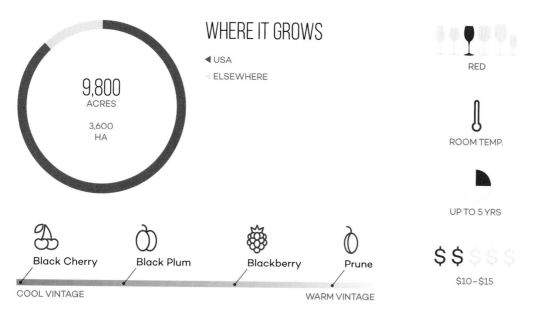

9,800
ACRES

3,600
HA

WHERE IT GROWS

◀ USA
◀ ELSEWHERE

RED

ROOM TEMP.

UP TO 5 YRS

$ $ $ $ $
$10–$15

Black Cherry   Black Plum   Blackberry   Prune

COOL VINTAGE   WARM VINTAGE

Petite Sirah is the offspring grape of Syrah and a rare black grape from South West France called Peloursin.

Today, Petite Sirah grows primarily in California, where it's often used to add body to Cabernet Sauvignon and Zinfandel.

Petite Sirah is one of the best values for full-bodied red wine. Look for wines with extended oak aging or a small percentage of Zinfandel, which acts to soften the high tannin.

Petite Sirah and other opaque, high-tannin red wines contain 2–3 times as many antioxidants as light, translucent red wines like Zinfandel and Gamay.

Petite Sirah will taste great alongside rich braised meats, barbecue, casseroles, and meaty pasta dishes.

BARBECUE

MEATY PASTA DISHES

CASSEROLE

winefolly.com / learn / variety / petite-sirah

PINOTAGE

PROFILE

FRUIT ● ● ● ● ○
BODY ● ● ● ● ●
TANNIN ● ● ● ● ○
ACIDITY ● ● ○ ○ ○
ALCOHOL ● ● ● ● ●

DOMINANT FLAVORS

BLACK CHERRY — BLACKBERRY — FIG — MENTHOL — ROASTED MEAT

POSSIBLE FLAVORS

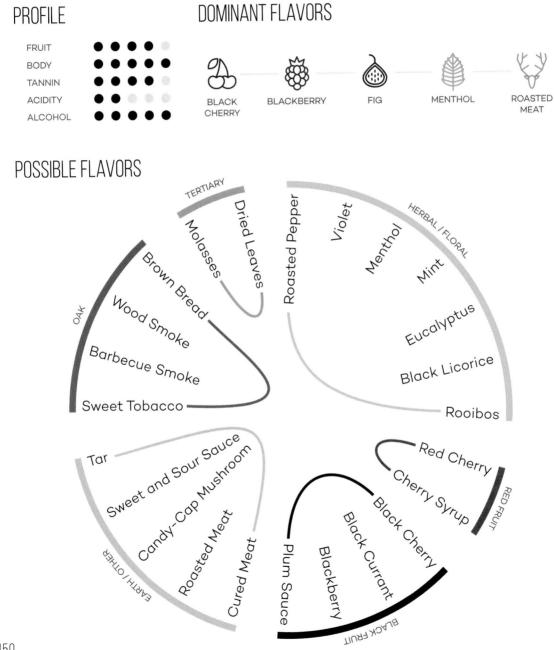

TERTIARY
Dried Leaves
Molasses

OAK
Brown Bread
Wood Smoke
Barbecue Smoke
Sweet Tobacco

Roasted Pepper
Violet
Menthol
Mint
HERBAL / FLORAL
Eucalyptus
Black Licorice
Rooibos

Tar
Sweet and Sour Sauce
Candy-Cap Mushroom
Roasted Meat
Cured Meat
EARTH / OTHER

Red Cherry
Cherry Syrup
RED FRUIT
Black Cherry
Black Currant
Blackberry
Plum Sauce
BLACK FRUIT

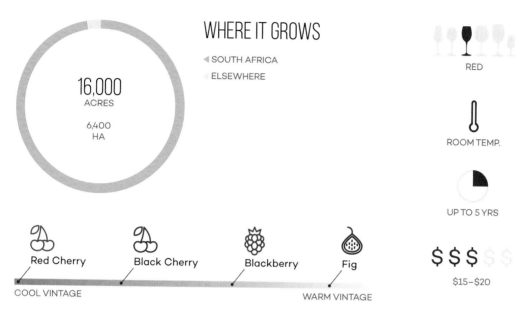

WHERE IT GROWS

16,000 ACRES

6,400 HA

◀ SOUTH AFRICA

◀ ELSEWHERE

RED

ROOM TEMP.

UP TO 5 YRS

Red Cherry · Black Cherry · Blackberry · Fig

COOL VINTAGE — WARM VINTAGE

$ $ $ $ $
$15–$20

Pinotage is the fourth most planted red grape in South Africa. It was created by a scientist who crossed Cinsaut with Pinot Noir in 1925. The scientist, Abraham Perold, was attempting to create a wine that tasted like Pinot Noir but was hardy enough to thrive in South Africa's climate.

Oddly enough, Pinotage tastes nothing like either of its progenitors. It is an enigma.

Look for Pinotage wines with descriptions of both red and black fruit flavors, a hint that suggests a wine with more balance and complexity.

Avoid low-quality bulk Pinotage. The wines can have a pungent note of tar and nail polish remover—a sign of volatile acidity.

SIMILAR WINES: If you like Australian Shiraz or American Petite Sirah, you will enjoy the black fruit flavors and sweet tobacco notes in South African Pinotage.

SOUTH AFRICAN PINOTAGE

AMERICAN PETITE SIRAH

AUSTRALIAN SHIRAZ

SYRAH

🔊 "sear-ah"

aka: Shiraz

PROFILE

FRUIT
BODY
TANNIN
ACIDITY
ALCOHOL

DOMINANT FLAVORS

BLUEBERRY · PLUM · MILK CHOCOLATE · TOBACCO · GREEN PEPPERCORN

POSSIBLE FLAVORS

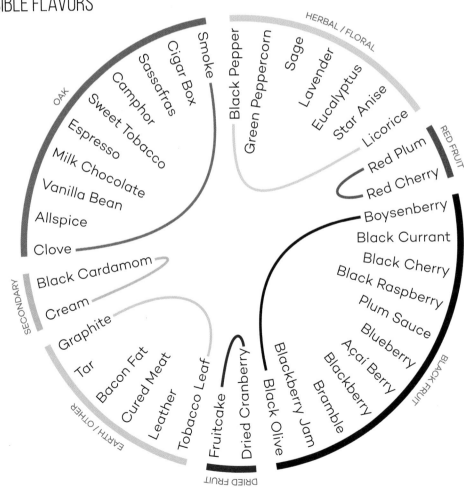

HERBAL / FLORAL
Black Pepper · Green Peppercorn · Sage · Lavender · Eucalyptus · Star Anise · Licorice

OAK
Smoke · Cigar Box · Sassafras · Camphor · Sweet Tobacco · Espresso · Milk Chocolate · Vanilla Bean · Allspice · Clove

RED FRUIT
Red Plum · Red Cherry

BLACK FRUIT
Boysenberry · Black Currant · Black Cherry · Black Raspberry · Plum Sauce · Blueberry · Açaí Berry · Blackberry · Bramble · Blackberry Jam · Black Olive

SECONDARY
Black Cardamom · Cream · Graphite

EARTH / OTHER
Tar · Bacon Fat · Cured Meat · Leather · Tobacco Leaf

DRIED FRUIT
Fruitcake · Dried Cranberry

Origin: France

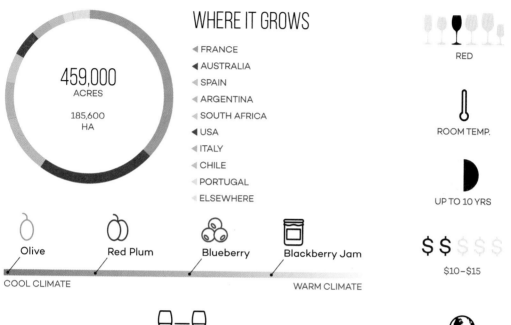

WHERE IT GROWS

459,000
ACRES

185,600
HA

◀ FRANCE
◀ AUSTRALIA
◀ SPAIN
◀ ARGENTINA
◀ SOUTH AFRICA
◀ USA
◀ ITALY
◀ CHILE
◀ PORTUGAL
◀ ELSEWHERE

RED

ROOM TEMP.

UP TO 10 YRS

$ $ $ $
$10–$15

Olive   Red Plum   Blueberry   Blackberry Jam

COOL CLIMATE   WARM CLIMATE

REGIONAL DIFFERENCES: When comparing Syrah wines from different regions, you'll notice some taste differences:

FRUIT-FORWARD BLACKBERRY, BLUEBERRY, & SWEET TOBACCO

Full-bodied wines with fruit-forward flavors of blackberry, blueberry, sweet tobacco smoke, chocolate, baking spices, and vanilla

● CALIFORNIA, USA
● SOUTH AUSTRALIA
● SPAIN
● ARGENTINA
● SOUTH AFRICA

SAVORY PLUM, OLIVE, & GREEN PEPPERCORN

Medium- to full-bodied wines with savory flavors of plum, olive, boysenberry, leather, green peppercorn, bacon fat, and cocoa powder

● RHÔNE, FRANCE
● COLUMBIA VALLEY, WA, USA
● VICTORIA, AUSTRALIA
● WESTERN AUSTRALIA
● CHILE

 Regions where Syrah is a single-varietal wine:

● SOUTH AUSTRALIA
● NORTHERN RHÔNE
● CALIFORNIA, USA
● COLUMBIA VALLEY, WA, USA

Regions where Syrah is blended with other varieties:

● CÔTES DU RHÔNE, FRANCE
● LANGUEDOC-ROUSSILLON, FRANCE
● CASTILLA-LA MANCHA, SPAIN
● EXTREMADURA, SPAIN
● CATALONIA, SPAIN
● VALENCIA, SPAIN
● ARAGON, SPAIN

winefolly.com / learn / variety / syrah

153

TEMPRANILLO

PROFILE

FRUIT	●●○○○
BODY	●●●●○
TANNIN	●●●●●
ACIDITY	●●●●○
ALCOHOL	●●●○○

DOMINANT FLAVORS

CHERRY — DRIED FIG — CEDAR — TOBACCO — DILL

POSSIBLE FLAVORS

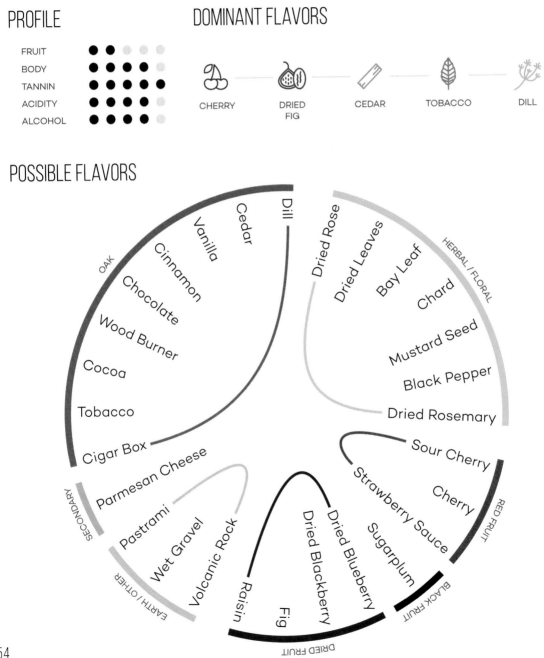

OAK: Dill, Cedar, Vanilla, Cinnamon, Chocolate, Wood Burner, Cocoa, Tobacco, Cigar Box

HERBAL / FLORAL: Dried Rose, Dried Leaves, Bay Leaf, Chard, Mustard Seed, Black Pepper, Dried Rosemary

RED FRUIT: Sour Cherry, Cherry

BLACK FRUIT: Strawberry Sauce, Sugarplum

DRIED FRUIT: Dried Blueberry, Dried Blackberry, Fig, Raisin

SECONDARY: Parmesan Cheese, Pastrami

EARTH / OTHER: Wet Gravel, Volcanic Rock

📍 Origin: Spain

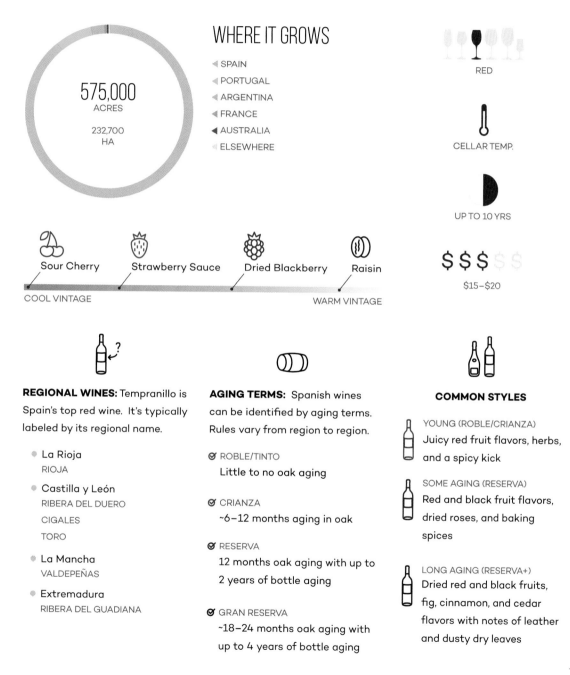

WHERE IT GROWS

575,000 ACRES

232,700 HA

◄ SPAIN
◄ PORTUGAL
◄ ARGENTINA
◄ FRANCE
◄ AUSTRALIA
◄ ELSEWHERE

RED

CELLAR TEMP.

UP TO 10 YRS

$ $ $ $ $
$15–$20

Sour Cherry   Strawberry Sauce   Dried Blackberry   Raisin

COOL VINTAGE   WARM VINTAGE

REGIONAL WINES: Tempranillo is Spain's top red wine. It's typically labeled by its regional name.

- **La Rioja**
  RIOJA
- **Castilla y León**
  RIBERA DEL DUERO
  CIGALES
  TORO
- **La Mancha**
  VALDEPEÑAS
- **Extremadura**
  RIBERA DEL GUADIANA

AGING TERMS: Spanish wines can be identified by aging terms. Rules vary from region to region.

☑ ROBLE/TINTO
  Little to no oak aging

☑ CRIANZA
  ~6–12 months aging in oak

☑ RESERVA
  12 months oak aging with up to 2 years of bottle aging

☑ GRAN RESERVA
  ~18–24 months oak aging with up to 4 years of bottle aging

COMMON STYLES

YOUNG (ROBLE/CRIANZA)
Juicy red fruit flavors, herbs, and a spicy kick

SOME AGING (RESERVA)
Red and black fruit flavors, dried roses, and baking spices

LONG AGING (RESERVA+)
Dried red and black fruits, fig, cinnamon, and cedar flavors with notes of leather and dusty dry leaves

155

TOURIGA NACIONAL

◀ "tor-ee-gah nah-see-un-nall"

PROFILE

FRUIT
BODY
TANNIN
ACIDITY
ALCOHOL

DOMINANT FLAVORS

VIOLET · BLUEBERRY · PLUM · MINT · WET SLATE

POSSIBLE FLAVORS

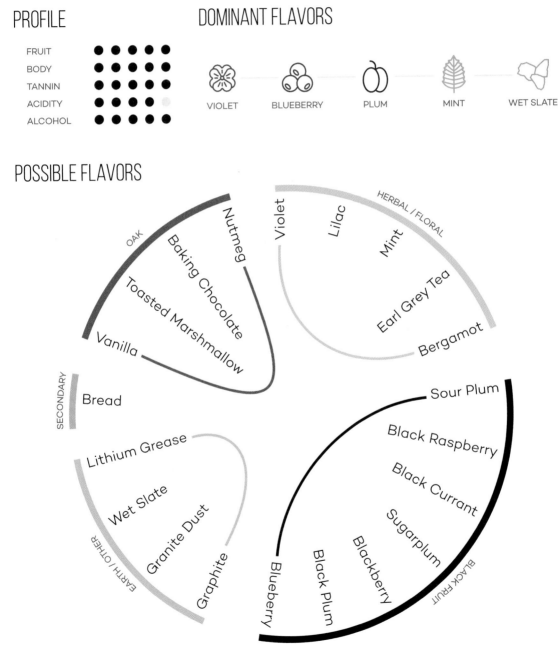

OAK
Nutmeg
Baking Chocolate
Toasted Marshmallow
Vanilla

SECONDARY
Bread

EARTH / OTHER
Lithium Grease
Wet Slate
Granite Dust
Graphite

HERBAL / FLORAL
Violet
Lilac
Mint
Earl Grey Tea
Bergamot

BLACK FRUIT
Sour Plum
Black Raspberry
Black Currant
Sugarplum
Blackberry
Black Plum
Blueberry

📍 Origin: Portugal

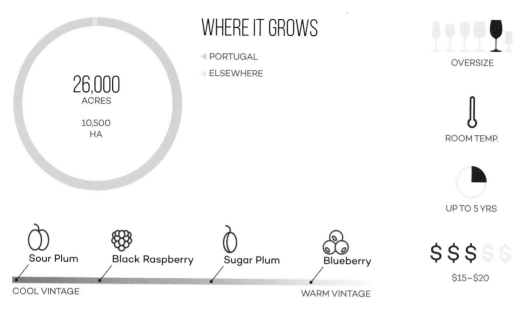

26,000
ACRES

10,500
HA

WHERE IT GROWS

◄ PORTUGAL
◄ ELSEWHERE

OVERSIZE

ROOM TEMP.

UP TO 5 YRS

$ $ $ $ $
$15–$20

Sour Plum | Black Raspberry | Sugar Plum | Blueberry

COOL VINTAGE — WARM VINTAGE

Touriga Nacional is a deeply colored red wine grape that originated in the Douro Valley of Portugal. It has been traditionally used for Port wine, although several Portuguese winemakers have started to create dry red wines with Touriga Nacional and the other primary Port varieties.

Touriga Nacional wines are characterized by lush black fruit flavors, bold tannin, and a subtle floral aroma of violets.

REGIONS

DOURO
Expect flavors of blueberry, black currant, violets, vanilla, and subtle notes of roasted meat. Wine is structured with fine gravelly tannins.

DÃO
The Dão is cooler and higher elevation than Douro and produces wines with more red fruit flavors, bergamot, and violet supported by spicy acidity.

ALENTEJO
Alentejo produces a rich but juicy style with black and red fruit, violet, licorice, and usually a touch of vanilla from oak aging.

There are just under 100 acres of Touriga Nacional in the US, found mostly in Lodi, CA.

157

Dessert Wine

MADEIRA

MARSALA

PORT

SAUTERNAIS

SHERRY

VIN SANTO

Dessert wines range in style from off-dry to very sweet. The sweetest and highest acidity of these dessert wines can be cellared for many years to develop subtle nutty flavors.

Some dessert wines are stabilized with the addition of brandy in a process called fortification. Fortified wines have high alcohol and can store open for up to a month.

This book includes to examples of common dessert wines but there are many more variations found throughout the world.

TYPES OF DESSERT WINE

FORTIFIED WINE

Wines are preserved with the addition of spirits usually before all the grape sugar is fermented.

LATE-HARVEST WINE

Grapes are harvested late in the growing season when the sugar content is highest.

DRIED GRAPE WINE

Also known as Passito in Italy. Grapes are laid out to raisinate and lose up to 70% of their moisture content.

ICE WINE / EISWEIN

Grapes freeze while still on the vine and are picked and pressed before they thaw, making a very sweet wine.

"NOBLE ROT" WINE

Botrytis cinerea (aka "noble rot") is a fungal rot that causes grapes to shrivel and sweeten with honey and ginger-like flavors.

MADEIRA

🔊 "mad-deer-uh"
Style: Fortified Wine

PROFILE

FRUIT	●●●○○
BODY	●●●●●
SWEET	●●●●○
ACIDITY	●●●●○
ALCOHOL	●●●●●

DOMINANT FLAVORS

BURNT CARAMEL — WALNUT OIL — PEACH — HAZELNUT — ORANGE PEEL

POSSIBLE FLAVORS

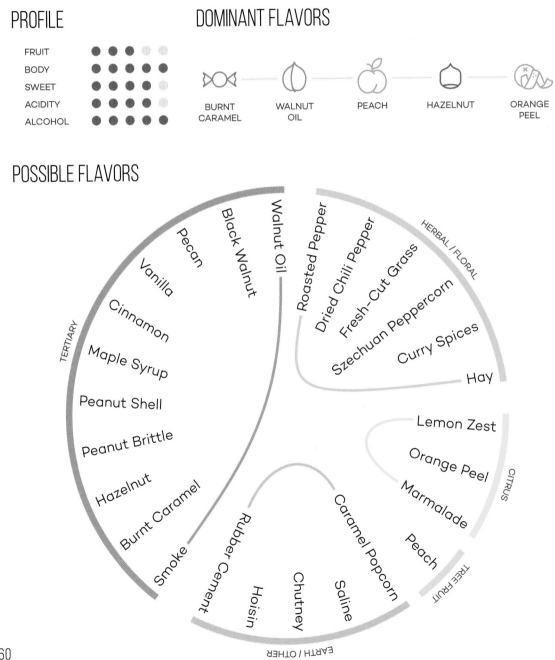

TERTIARY: Walnut Oil · Black Walnut · Pecan · Vanilla · Cinnamon · Maple Syrup · Peanut Shell · Peanut Brittle · Hazelnut · Burnt Caramel · Smoke

HERBAL / FLORAL: Roasted Pepper · Dried Chili Pepper · Fresh-Cut Grass · Szechuan Peppercorn · Curry Spices · Hay

CITRUS: Lemon Zest · Orange Peel · Marmalade

TREE FRUIT: Peach

EARTH / OTHER: Rubber Cement · Hoisin · Chutney · Saline · Caramel Popcorn

Origin: Madeira Island, Portugal

WHERE IT'S MADE

◀ MADEIRA, PORTUGAL

1,000
ACRES

400
HA

GUARANTEE

PRODUCER

STYLE

SWEETNESS

QUALITY &
AGING

W. FOLLY
MADEIRA
BUAL
MEDIUM RICH
1990
COLHEITA

SWEETNESS LEVELS

- EXTRA DRY: 0–50 g/L RS
- DRY: 50–65 g/L RS
- MEDIUM DRY: 65–80 g/L RS
- MEDIUM RICH/SWEET: 80–96 g/L RS
- RICH/SWEET: 96+ g/L RS

QUALITY LEVELS & AGING

NON-VINTAGE MADEIRA

FINEST/CHOICE/SELECT
Aged 3 yrs by Estufa & made with Tinta Negramoll.

RAINWATER
Medium-dry style aged 3 yrs and typically blended w/ T. Negramoll.

5-YEAR/RESERVE/MATURE
Aged 5–10 years and typically blended with Tinta Negramoll.

10-YEAR/SPECIAL RESERVE
Aged 10–15 years by Canteiro. Often a single variety.

15-YEAR/EXTRA RESERVE
Aged 15–20 years by Canteiro. Often a single variety.

VINTAGE MADEIRA

COLHEITA/HARVEST
A single vintage aged 5+ years by Canteiro. Often a single variety.

SOLERA
Multi-vintage blend by Canteiro. First year of solera is listed on the bottle but is no longer made.

FRASQUEIRA/GARRAFEIRA
Single vintage aged 20+ years by Canteiro method. Very rare.

WHITE OR DESSERT (3 OZ)

CELLAR TEMP.

UP TO 2 YRS

$ $ $ $ $
$10–$15

ESTUFA METHOD
Wine is heated in tanks for a short period of time.

CANTEIRO METHOD
Wines age naturally in barrels in warm rooms or under the sun.

TYPES OF MADEIRA

TINTA NEGRAMOLL / RAINWATER
Dry–sweet and basic quality

SERCIAL
The lightest, extra-dry style (serve chilled)

VERDELHO
Light, aromatic, & dry to med. dry wines (serve chilled)

BUAL / BOAL
Medium-sweet nutty wines

MALMSEY
The sweetest style

winefolly.com / learn / wine / madeira

161

MARSALA

◀ "mar-sal-uh"
Style: Fortified Wine

PROFILE

FRUIT	● ● ● ◐ ○
BODY	● ● ● ● ○
SWEET	● ● ● ● ◐
ACIDITY	● ● ● ◐ ○
ALCOHOL	● ● ● ● ●

DOMINANT FLAVORS

STEWED APRICOT — VANILLA — TAMARIND — BROWN SUGAR — TOBACCO

POSSIBLE FLAVORS

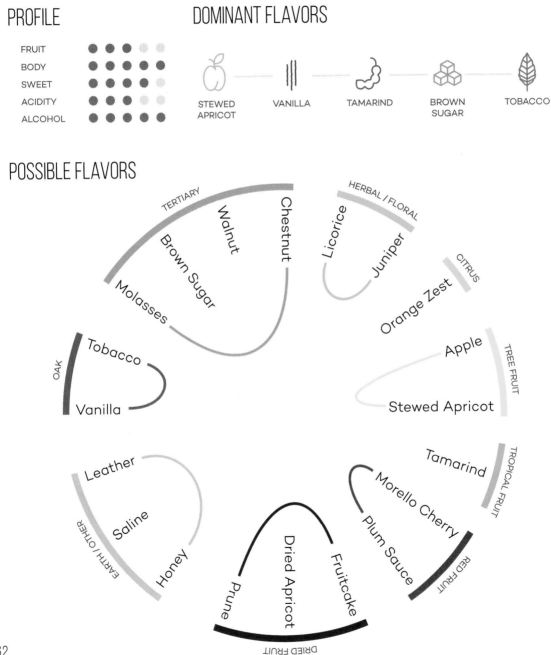

TERTIARY: Chestnut, Walnut, Brown Sugar, Molasses

HERBAL / FLORAL: Licorice, Juniper

CITRUS: Orange Zest

TREE FRUIT: Apple, Stewed Apricot

TROPICAL FRUIT: Tamarind

RED FRUIT: Morello Cherry, Plum Sauce

DRIED FRUIT: Fruitcake, Dried Apricot, Prune

OAK: Tobacco, Vanilla

EARTH / OTHER: Leather, Saline, Honey

162

◉ Origin: Italy

~100,000
ACRES

45,500
HA

WHERE IT'S MADE

◀ SICILY, ITALY

DESSERT (3 OZ)

CELLAR TEMP.

UP TO 2 YRS

$ $ $ $ $
$10–$15

winefolly.com / learn / wine / marsala

STYLES OF MARSALA

GOLD (ORO)
Made with white grapes.

AMBER (AMBRA)
Made with white grapes and cooked wine must.

ROSSO (RUBINO)
Rare. A red Marsala with up to 30% white grapes.

MARSALA WINE GRAPES

GRILLO
CATTARATO
INZOLIA
GRECIANO

NERO D'AVOLA
PIGNATELLO
NERELLO MASCALESE

AGING TERMS & STYLES

COOKING

FINE/FINE IP
All styles. Aged 1 year.

SUPERIOR
All styles. Aged 2 years.

DRINKING

SUPERIOR RESERVE
Dry to semisweet. Aged 4+ years.

VIRGIN/VIRGIN SOLERA
Dry. Aged 5+ years.

VIRGIN STRAVECCHIO/ VIRGIN RESERVE
Dry. Aged 10+ years.

SWEETNESS LEVELS

⬡ DRY (SECCO): 0–40 g/L RS

⬡⬡ SEMISWEET (SEMISECCO): 40–100 g/L RS

⬡⬡⬡ SWEET/GD (DOLCE): 100+ g/L RS

MARSALA FOR COOKING

SWEET MARSALA
Use for sweet sauces with pork and chicken or in desserts such as zabaglione.

DRY MARSALA
Use for savory entrées, to add nutty flavors in beef tenderloin, mushrooms, turkey, or veal. Dry Marsala tends to be the more versatile choice to have on hand.

PORT

PROFILE

FRUIT
BODY
TANNIN
ACIDITY
ALCOHOL

DOMINANT FLAVORS

RIPE BLACKBERRY

RASPBERRY SAUCE

CINNAMON

CANDY APPLE

STAR ANISE

POSSIBLE FLAVORS

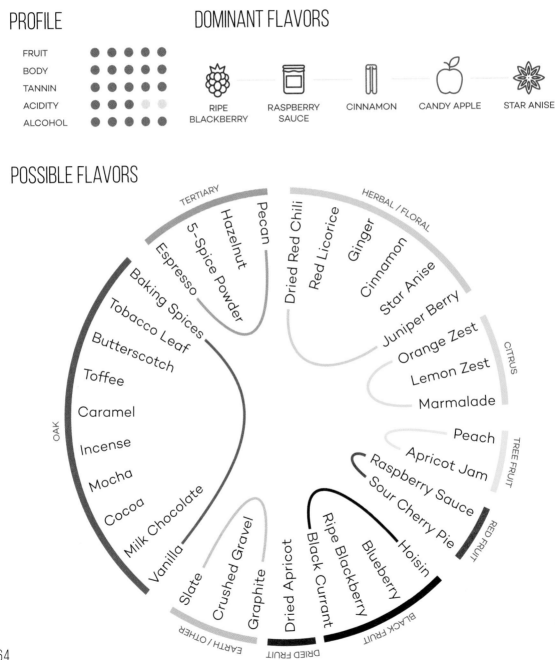

TERTIARY
Pecan
Hazelnut
5-Spice Powder
Espresso
Baking Spices
Tobacco Leaf
Butterscotch
Toffee
Caramel
Incense
Mocha
Cocoa
Milk Chocolate
Vanilla

OAK

HERBAL / FLORAL
Dried Red Chili
Red Licorice
Ginger
Cinnamon
Star Anise
Juniper Berry
Orange Zest
Lemon Zest
Marmalade

CITRUS

Peach
Apricot Jam

TREE FRUIT

Raspberry Sauce
Sour Cherry Pie
Hoisin

RED FRUIT

Ripe Blackberry
Black Currant
Blueberry

BLACK FRUIT

Dried Apricot

DRIED FRUIT

Slate
Crushed Gravel
Graphite

EARTH / OTHER

164

111,000
ACRES

45,000
HA

WHERE IT'S MADE

◀ DOURO, PORTUGAL

DESSERT (3 OZ)

ROOM TEMP.

15+ YRS

$ $ $ $ $

$20–$30

YOUNG PORT

A youthful style of Port wine that's aged for a short time and designed to be drunk immediately. Wines tend to have more spice notes and tannin.

🍷 **RUBY**
Red fruit and chocolate flavors with spicy acidity

🍷 **LBV (LATE BOTTLED VINTAGE)**
Red and black fruit flavors, spice, and cocoa with high tannin and acidity

🍷 **WHITE**
Dried peach, white pepper, tangerine zest, and incense

🍷 **ROSÉ**
Notes of strawberry, honey, cinnamon, and framboise liqueur

TAWNY PORT

Oak-aged Port wines that age for several years develop nutty flavors from oxidation. Since they are aged by the winery, they can be enjoyed immediately.

🍷 **10-YEAR**
Raspberry, dried blueberry, cinnamon, clove, and caramel

🍷 **20-YEAR**
Fig, raisin, caramel, orange zest, and cinnamon

🍷 **40-YEAR**
Dried apricot, orange zest, caramel, and toffee

🍷 **COLHEITA**
Single-vintage tawny port. Flavors vary depending on the age of the wine.

AGE-WORTHY PORT

Stoppered with a standard cork and designed to age 40+ years.

🍷 **VINTAGE PORT**
Single-vintage Ports from exceptional years. Expect to age for a minimum of 10 years and ideally 30–50 years.

🍷 **CRUSTED PORT**
A multi-vintage Port designed to age just like vintage Port. Wines often develop a "crust" and need to be decanted with a filter screen.

SAUTERNAIS

◀ "sow-turn-aye"
Style: Noble Rot

PROFILE

FRUIT	●●●●●
BODY	●●●○○
VERY SWEET	●●●●●
ACIDITY	●●●●●
ALCOHOL	●●●○○

DOMINANT FLAVORS

LEMON CURD — APRICOT — QUINCE — HONEY — GINGER

POSSIBLE FLAVORS

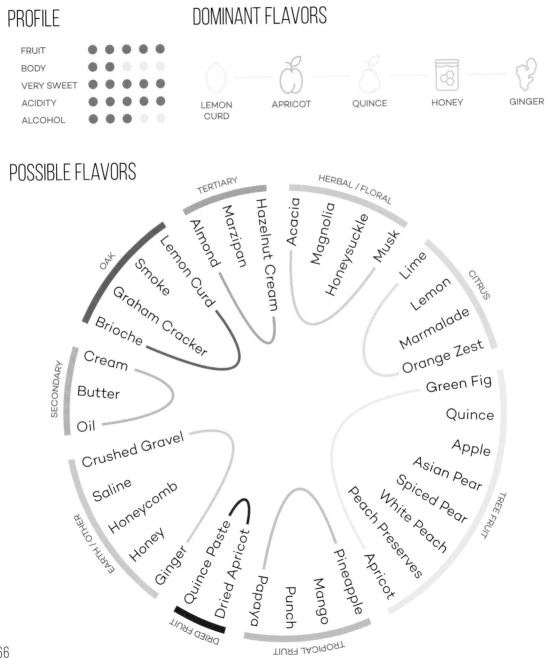

TERTIARY
Hazelnut Cream
Marzipan
Almond
Lemon Curd
Smoke
Graham Cracker
Brioche

OAK

SECONDARY
Cream
Butter
Oil

EARTH / OTHER
Crushed Gravel
Saline
Honeycomb
Honey
Ginger

DRIED FRUIT
Quince Paste
Dried Apricot

TROPICAL FRUIT
Papaya
Punch
Mango
Pineapple
Apricot

Peach Preserves
White Peach
Spiced Pear
Asian Pear
Apple
Quince
Green Fig

TREE FRUIT

CITRUS
Orange Zest
Marmalade
Lemon
Lime

HERBAL / FLORAL
Acacia
Magnolia
Honeysuckle
Musk

📍 Origin: France

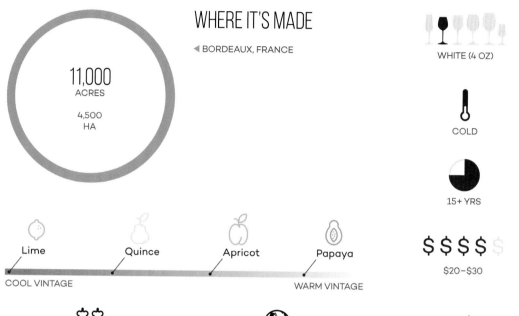

WHERE IT'S MADE

◄ BORDEAUX, FRANCE

11,000 ACRES

4,500 HA

WHITE (4 OZ)

COLD

15+ YRS

$ $ $ $ $

$20–$30

Lime — Quince — Apricot — Papaya

COOL VINTAGE   WARM VINTAGE

GRAPES: The sweet wines of Bordeaux are made exclusively with white grapes.

🍇 **SÉMILLON**
The popular choice. Sémillon adds body and tropical fruit notes.

🍇 **SAUVIGNON BLANC**
Adds lime and grapefruit notes with tingling acidity.

🍇 **MUSCADELLE**
Typically only a small portion of the blend.

MAIN REGIONS: The name Sauternais refers to the dessert-wine-producing areas in Bordeaux that are typically found close to the river where grapes often develop noble rot (see Glossary).

- SAUTERNES
- BORDEAUX MOELLEUX
- BARSAC
- SAINTE-CROIX-DU-MONT
- LOUPIAC
- GRAVES SUPÉRIEURES
- PREMIÈRES CÔTES DE BORDEAUX
- CADILLAC

Some producers only produce sweet wines on vintages when white grapes develop noble rot.

An average glass of Sauternes has nearly 17 grams of sugar per 4 oz serving. However, due to the wine's high natural acidity, the sugar level tastes balanced.

167

SHERRY

winefolly.com / learn / wine / sherry

PROFILE

FRUIT
BODY
OFF-DRY
ACIDITY
ALCOHOL

DOMINANT FLAVORS

JACKFRUIT — SALINE — PRESERVED LEMON — BRAZIL NUT — ALMOND

POSSIBLE FLAVORS

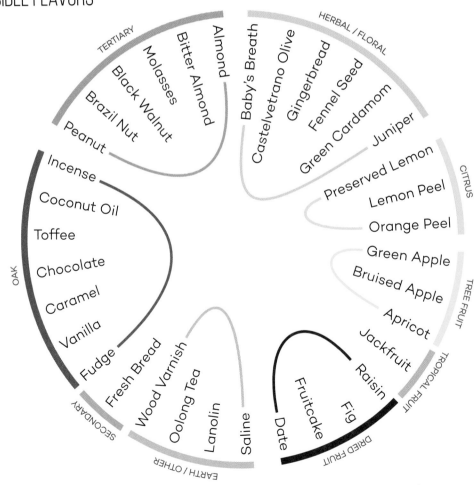

TERTIARY
Almond
Bitter Almond
Molasses
Black Walnut
Brazil Nut
Peanut

HERBAL / FLORAL
Baby's Breath
Castelvetrano Olive
Gingerbread
Fennel Seed
Green Cardamom
Juniper

CITRUS
Preserved Lemon
Lemon Peel
Orange Peel

TREE FRUIT
Green Apple
Bruised Apple
Apricot

TROPICAL FRUIT
Jackfruit

DRIED FRUIT
Raisin
Fig
Fruitcake
Date

OAK
Incense
Coconut Oil
Toffee
Chocolate
Caramel
Vanilla
Fudge

SECONDARY
Fresh Bread
Wood Varnish
Oolong Tea
Lanolin
Saline

EARTH / OTHER

168

78,000
ACRES

31,600
HA

WHERE IT'S MADE

◀ ANDALUCÍA, SPAIN

WHITE OR
DESSERT (3 OZ)

CELLAR TEMP.

UP TO 2 YRS

$15–$20

DRY SHERRY STYLES

These Sherry wines are made with Palomino Fino grapes and come in a range of styles depending on the winemaking method.

🍷 FINO & MANZANILLA
Very light styles with salty fruit flavors. Serve chilled.

🍷 AMONTILLADO
Slightly bolder nutty style in between Fino and Oloroso.

🍷 PALO CORTADO
Rich with roasted flavors of coffee and molasses.

🍷 OLOROSO
Dark nutty style from long-term oxidative aging.

SWEET SHERRY STYLES

Sweet Sherries are typically produced with Pedro Ximénez or Moscatel grapes.

🍷 PX (PEDRO XIMÉNEZ)
The sweetest style made of Pedro Ximénez with fig and date flavors.

🍷 MOSCATEL
A very sweet style made of Muscat of Alexandria with caramel flavors.

🍷 SWEETENED SHERRY
Typically made by blending Oloroso Sherry with PX.

⬡ DRY: 5–45 g/L RS
⬡ MEDIUM: 5–115 g/L RS
⬡ PALE CREAM: 45–115 g/L RS
⬡ CREAM: 115–140 g/L RS
⬡ DULCE: 160+ g/L RS

SOLERA AGING

Sherry wines employ a unique multi-vintage aging technique called a solera. Soleras are tiers of barrels with 3 to 9 steps called criaderas, or scales:

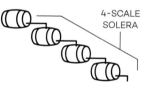

4-SCALE
SOLERA

New wine goes into the top scale, and finished wine is taken in small portions from the bottom scale. Wines "run the scales" for at least 3 years up to 50 years (or more). There is also a rare vintage Sherry, Añada, that doesn't use a solera.

VIN SANTO

PROFILE

FRUIT	
BODY	
VERY SWEET	
ACIDITY	
ALCOHOL	

DOMINANT FLAVORS

PERFUME — FIG — RAISIN — ALMOND — TOFFEE

POSSIBLE FLAVORS

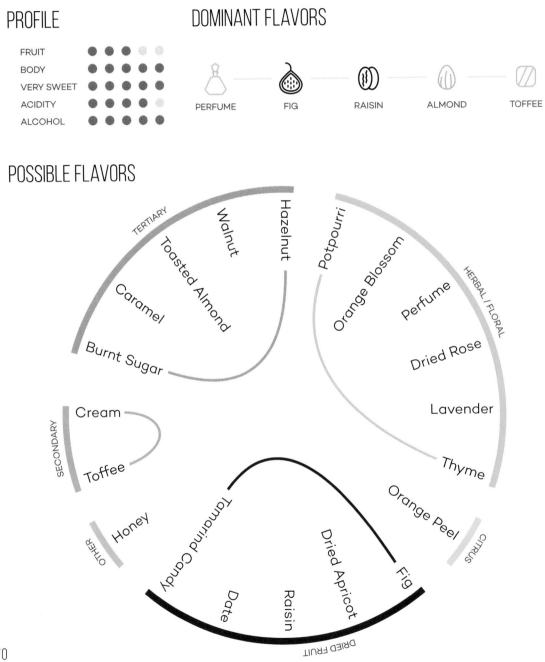

TERTIARY
Walnut
Hazelnut
Toasted Almond
Caramel
Burnt Sugar

Potpourri
Orange Blossom
Perfume
HERBAL / FLORAL
Dried Rose
Lavender
Thyme

SECONDARY
Cream
Toffee

OTHER
Honey

Tamarind Candy
Date
Raisin
Dried Apricot
Fig
Orange Peel
CITRUS
DRIED FRUIT

📍 Origin: Italy

58,000
ACRES

23,400
HA

WHERE IT'S MADE

◀ CENTRAL ITALY

WHITE (4 OZ)

CELLAR TEMP.

15+ YRS

$ $ $ $ $

$20–$30

Vin Santo is made with the *appassimento* method. Grapes are harvested and laid out on straw mats for up to 6 months where they will dry and lose about 70% of their water content.

GRAPES → STRAW MATS → RAISINS

Then, the raisinated grapes are squeezed and put into oak or chestnut barrels to vinify. The fermentation is very slow and can take 4 years to complete.

COMMON STYLES

WHITE VIN SANTO
The most common type of Vin Santo has dried fig, almond, and toffee flavors and is made primarily with Malvasia Bianca and Trebbiano.

RED VIN SANTO
A rare style of Vin Santo called Occhio di Pernice offers caramel, coffee, and hazelnut flavors and is made with Sangiovese grapes.

Tuscany and Umbria are the main regions that produce Vin Santo in Italy. You can also find excellent passito-style aged Malvasia wines from Sicily called Malvasia delle Lipari.

Vin Santo is traditionally enjoyed during Easter week and paired with almond biscotti.

171

Wine Regions

Wine Regions

WINE REGIONS OF THE WORLD

There are over 90 countries making wine in the world. The 12 countries included in this book account for 80% of the wine produced in the world.

WORLD WINE PRODUCTION

6.8 BILLION
GALLONS OF WINE
ANNUALLY (2012)

◀ ITALY
◀ FRANCE
◀ SPAIN
◀ UNITED STATES
◀ ARGENTINA
◀ AUSTRALIA
◀ SOUTH AFRICA

◀ CHILE
◀ GERMANY
◀ PORTUGAL
◀ AUSTRIA
◀ NEW ZEALAND
◀ OTHERS

6.8 billion gallons of wine is enough to fill the area of 99 city blocks of Manhattan with 40 feet of wine.

COOL VS. WARM CLIMATE WINE REGIONS

Climate affects the taste of wine. Generally, cool climates make wines with more tart flavors and hot climates make wines with more ripe flavors.

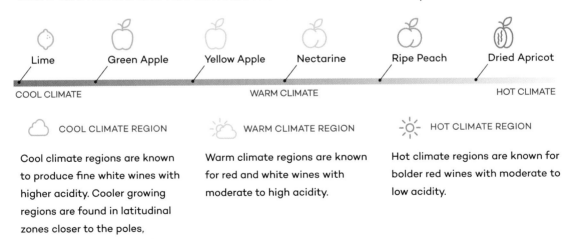

| Lime | Green Apple | Yellow Apple | Nectarine | Ripe Peach | Dried Apricot |

COOL CLIMATE   WARM CLIMATE   HOT CLIMATE

COOL CLIMATE REGION

Cool climate regions are known to produce fine white wines with higher acidity. Cooler growing regions are found in latitudinal zones closer to the poles, higher elevation areas, and areas affected by cooling breezes.

WARM CLIMATE REGION

Warm climate regions are known for red and white wines with moderate to high acidity.

HOT CLIMATE REGION

Hot climate regions are known for bolder red wines with moderate to low acidity.

WHERE WINE GROWS

LATITUDINAL ZONES WHERE
WINE GRAPES GROW

The latitudinal zones above
illustrate a general overview of
where wine grapes grow. It's useful
to note that some regions outside
of these zones, including parts of
Brazil, Mexico, and India, can also
make wine due to their unique
microclimates.

Argentina

Argentina is a New World region that is most known for a bold and fruity style of Malbec. The country accounts for over 75% of the world's Malbec wines.

497,000
ACRES

202,000
HA

WINE REGIONS BY SIZE

◀ MENDOZA
◀ SAN JUAN
◀ LA RIOJA
◀ PATAGONIA
◀ SALTA
◀ CATAMARCA
◀ TUCUMÁN

TOP WINES OF ARGENTINA

🍇 MALBEC

The country's top wine ranges in taste from juicy tart raspberry flavors to rich blueberry and sweet tobacco depending on vintage, quality, and oak program.

- MENDOZA — LUJÁN DE CUYO
- SALTA — UCO VALLEY

🍇 CABERNET SAUVIGNON

Argentine Cabernet Sauvignon offers rich black raspberry, mocha, and tobacco leaf flavors with medium tannin and peppery acidity.

- MENDOZA — LUJÁN DE CUYO
  MAIPÚ

🍇 BONARDA (DOUCE NOIR)

Also known as Charbono in California, Bonarda is the second most planted Argentine grape. Expect flavors of black currant, licorice, and dried green herbs.

- LA RIOJA
- MENDOZA

🍇 SYRAH

Argentine Syrah offers full-bodied flavors of boysenberry, licorice, plum, and cocoa. The best examples come from high elevation subregions.

- SAN JUAN
- UCO VALLEY (MENDOZA)

🍇 TORRONTÉS

Argentina's own variety ranges in taste from dry and citrusy, to off-dry with rich aromas of peach and guava.

- SALTA
- CATAMARCA
- LA RIOJA

🍇 PINOT NOIR

Argentine Pinot Noir offers flavors of ripe raspberries, rhubarb, minerals, and spiced plum.

- PATAGONIA
- UCO VALLEY (MENDOZA)

BOLIVIA

PARAGUAY

CHILE

Salta
▼ TORRONTÉS
♥ MALBEC

■
SALTA

Tucumán
♥ MALBEC

■
TUCUMÁN

Catamarca
▼ TORRONTÉS
♥ SYRAH

La Rioja
▼ TORRONTÉS
♥ BONARDA

BRAZIL

San Juan
♥ SYRAH
♥ MALBEC
♥ CABERNET SAUVIGNON
♥ BONARDA

Maipú
Luján de Cuyo
Uco Valley

■ MENDOZA

URUGUAY

Mendoza
♥ MALBEC
♥ CABERNET SAUVIGNON
▼ TORRONTÉS
▼ CHARDONNAY

■ BUENOS AIRES

Patagonia
♥ PINOT NOIR
SAUVIGNON BLANC

NEUQUEN ■

N

300km   300mi

179

Australia

Australia is most famous for Shiraz, a very rich, smoky, and fruit-forward style of Syrah. Australia has 3 distinct climate areas offering a range of wines.

376,000
ACRES

152,000
HA

WINE REGIONS BY SIZE

◀ SOUTH AUSTRALIA
◀ NEW SOUTH WALES
◀ VICTORIA
◀ WESTERN AUSTRALIA
◀ TASMANIA
◀ QUEENSLAND

WESTERN AUSTRALIA

☁ WARM CLIMATE

Western Australia is famous for unoaked Chardonnay. However, the region makes quite a bit of lighter-bodied Cabernet Sauvignon, tasting of ripe black fruit and violets with persistent acidity.

▼ UNOAKED CHARDONNAY
▽ SAUVIGNON BLANC
🍷 ELEGANT CABERNET & MERLOT BLENDS

SOUTH AND CENTRAL

☀ HOT CLIMATE

The largest area is famous for smoky and rich Shiraz, Sémillon, and Chardonnay. Cooler micro regions produce excellent petrol-driven dry Rieslings and peachy Sauvignon Blanc.

▼ BOLD SHIRAZ
▽ BUTTERY CHARDONNAY
▼ DRY RIESLING

VICTORIA AND TASMANIA

☁ COOL CLIMATE

A much cooler area produces Pinot Noir and Chardonnay with excellent acidity. This area tends to make leaner, more elegant red wines.

▼ PLUMMY PINOT NOIR
▼ CREAMY CHARDONNAY
▽ CITRUSY SAUVIGNON BLANC

180

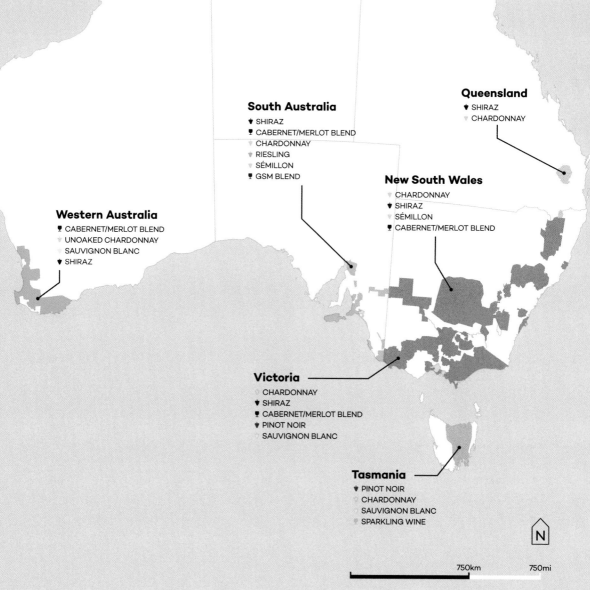

Queensland
- ♟ SHIRAZ
- ▽ CHARDONNAY

South Australia
- ♟ SHIRAZ
- ♟ CABERNET/MERLOT BLEND
- ▽ CHARDONNAY
- ▽ RIESLING
- ▽ SÉMILLON
- ♟ GSM BLEND

New South Wales
- ▽ CHARDONNAY
- ♟ SHIRAZ
- ▽ SÉMILLON
- ♟ CABERNET/MERLOT BLEND

Western Australia
- ♟ CABERNET/MERLOT BLEND
- ▽ UNOAKED CHARDONNAY
- ▽ SAUVIGNON BLANC
- ♟ SHIRAZ

Victoria
- ▽ CHARDONNAY
- ♟ SHIRAZ
- ♟ CABERNET/MERLOT BLEND
- ♟ PINOT NOIR
- ▽ SAUVIGNON BLANC

Tasmania
- ♟ PINOT NOIR
- ▽ CHARDONNAY
- ▽ SAUVIGNON BLANC
- ▽ SPARKLING WINE

750km   750mi

N

AUSTRALIA DETAIL

Western Australia

- 🍷 CABERNET/MERLOT BLEND
- 🍷 UNOAKED CHARDONNAY
- 🍷 SAUVIGNON BLANC
- 🍷 SHIRAZ

Swan District

Perth Hills

■ PERTH

Peel

Geographe

Blackwood Valley

Manjimup

Great Southern

Pemberton

Margaret River

Queensland
- ♥ SHIRAZ
- ▽ CHARDONNAY

South Burnett

Granite Belt

New England
Australia

BRISBANE ■

South Australia
- ♥ SHIRAZ
- ♟ CABERNET/MERLOT BLEND
- ▽ CHARDONNAY
- ▽ RIESLING
- ▽ SÉMILLON
- ♟ GSM BLEND

Southern
Flinders
Ranges

Clare Valley

Barossa Valley

Eden Valley

Riverland

New South Wales
- ▽ CHARDONNAY
- ♥ SHIRAZ
- ▽ SÉMILLON
- ♟ CABERNET/MERLOT BLEND

Hastings River

Adelaide
Plains

Mudgee

Orange

Cowra

Hunter Valley

ADELAIDE ■

Adelaide Hills

Murray Darling

Hilltops

SYDNEY ■

McLaren Vale

Swan Hill

Riverina

Gundagai

Langhorne Creek

Southern Highlands

Currency Creek

Heathcote

Pericoota

Shoalhaven Coast

Southern Fleurieu

Bendigo

Canberra District

Kangaroo Island

Macedon Ranges

Goulburn Valley

Tumbarumba

Mount Benson

Pyrenees

Rutherglen

Robe

Grampians

Glenrowan

Padthaway

Beechworth

Wrattonbully

MELBOURNE ■

Alpine Valleys

Henty

King Valley

Coonawarra

Geelong

Strathbogie Ranges

Mount Gambier

Sunbury

Gippsland

Mornington Peninsula

Upper Goulburn

Yarra Valley

Victoria
- ▽ CHARDONNAY
- ♥ SHIRAZ
- ♟ CABERNET/MERLOT BLEND
- ♥ PINOT NOIR
- ▽ SAUVIGNON BLANC

North West

Pipers River

Tamar Valley

Tasmania
- ♥ PINOT NOIR
- ▽ CHARDONNAY
- ▽ SAUVIGNON BLANC
- ▽ SPARKLING

East Coast

Coal River Valley

Derwent Valley

Huon Valley

N

300km   300mi

Austria

Austria is a cool climate growing region famous for Grüner Veltliner wines. Austria is known for its minerally white wines and spicy red wines.

113,000
ACRES

45,900
HA

WINE REGIONS BY SIZE

◀ NIEDERÖSTERREICH (LOWER AUSTRIA)
◀ BURGENLAND
◀ STEIERMARK (STYRIA)
◀ WIEN (VIENNA)
◀ OTHER

TOP WINES OF AUSTRIA

GRÜNER VELTLINER

The country's champion wine ranges from light peppery citrus flavors to richer Reserve level wines that are often oaked and have more tropical fruit flavors.

Peppery regions
└ ● NIEDERÖSTERREICH
    ├ ● WEINVIERTEL
    └ ● TRAISENTAL

Fruity regions
└ ● NIEDERÖSTERREICH
    ├ ● KREMSTAL
    ├ ● KAMPTAL
    ├ ● WAGRAM
    └ ● WACHAU

ZWEIGELT

("zz-Y-gelt") A light-bodied red with bold cherry flavors and a slight herbaceous bitter note on the finish. Rosé wines are fruity.

└ ● BURGENLAND
└ ● NIEDERÖSTERREICH
    ├ ● CARNUNTUM
    └ ● THERMENREGION

BLAUER PORTUGIESER

Simple light red wines tasting of red berries and woody herbs with lighter tannin and acidity.

└ ● NIEDERÖSTERREICH
    ├ ● THERMENREGION
    └ ● WEINVIERTEL

BLAUFRÄNKISCH

("blao-frankish") A spicy medium red wine with red forest-berry flavors and dry tannin.

└ ● BURGENLAND
└ ● NIEDERÖSTERREICH
    ├ ● CARNUNTUM
    └ ● THERMENREGION

PINOT BLANC

Known as Weissburgunder, this wine offers floral aromas with a dry herbal minerally taste.

└ ● NIEDERÖSTERREICH
└ ● LEITHABERG (BURGENLAND)

CZECH
REPUBLIC

SLOVAKIA

■ LINZ

Weinviertel

Kamptal
Kremstal
Wachau
Wagram
Traisental

Wien
GEMISCHTER SATZ (BLEND)

■ VIENNA

Carnuntum

Niederösterreich
GRÜNER VELTLINER
♥ BLAUER PORTUGIESER
♥ RIESLING

Thermenregion

Neusiedlersee

EISENSTADT

Neusiedlersee-Hügelland
(Leithaberg)

Burgenland
♥ BLAUFRANKISCH
♥ ZWEIGELT

Mittelburgenland

Südburgenland

Steiermark
PINOT BLANC
SAUVIGNON BLANC
♥ MÜLLER-THURGAU

Süd-Oststeiermark

Weststeiermark

Südsteiermark

N

50km   50mi

SLOVENIA

185

Chile

Chile is a cool climate region most known for its lean and fruity Bordeaux blends. Chile is divided into 3 areas from the coast to the Andes Mountains.

276,000
ACRES

111,500
HA

WINE REGIONS BY SIZE

◀ CENTRAL VALLEY
◀ ACONCAGUA
◀ SOUTH
◀ COQUIMBO
◀ AUSTRAL
◀ ATACAMA

COASTAL CHILE

☁ COOL CLIMATE

Coastal Chile is chilled by the frigid Humboldt current. Wines that thrive here include slightly saline citrus-driven white wines and juicy Pinot Noir.

⚲ CHARDONNAY
⚲ SAUVIGNON BLANC
⚲ PINOT NOIR

INLAND VALLEYS

⛅ WARM CLIMATE

The inland valleys include the Central Valley Region and are known for elegant red wines. The zone focuses on red Bordeaux blends with red fruit flavors and heightened acidity.

⚲ BORDEAUX BLEND
⚲ PETIT VERDOT
⚲ SYRAH
⚲ CARMÉNÈRE
⚲ CARIÑENA (CARIGNAN)

THE ANDES

⛅ WARM CLIMATE

The higher elevation vineyards in the foothills of the Andes produce red wines with tannin structure and, on good vintages, offer plentiful ripe fruit flavors along with heightened acidity.

⚲ SYRAH
⚲ CABERNET SAUVIGNON
⚲ CABERNET FRANC
⚲ CARMÉNÈRE

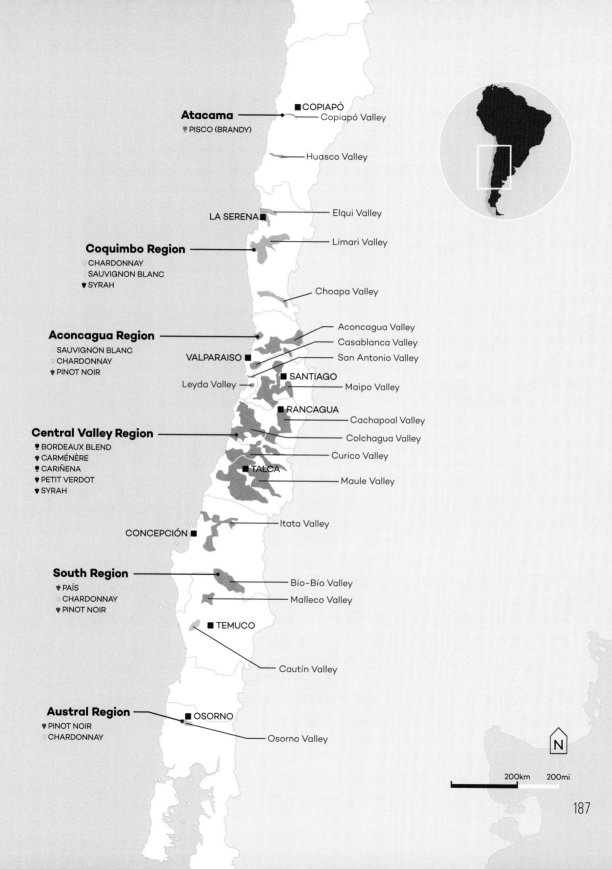

Atacama —————— ■ COPIAPÓ
                 —— Copiapó Valley
🍷 PISCO (BRANDY)

—— Huasco Valley

■ LA SERENA ————— Elqui Valley

Coquimbo Region ———— —— Limari Valley
▽ CHARDONNAY
▽ SAUVIGNON BLANC
♥ SYRAH

—— Choapa Valley

Aconcagua Region ———— —— Aconcagua Valley
▽ SAUVIGNON BLANC   —— Casablanca Valley
▽ CHARDONNAY
♥ PINOT NOIR   ■ VALPARAISO —— San Antonio Valley
                    ■ SANTIAGO
Leyda Valley ——   —— Maipo Valley

           ■ RANCAGUA
Central Valley Region ———— —— Cachapoal Valley
🍷 BORDEAUX BLEND
♥ CARMÉNÈRE   —— Colchagua Valley
🍷 CARIÑENA
♥ PETIT VERDOT   —— Curico Valley
♥ SYRAH   ■ TALCA
                 —— Maule Valley

—— Itata Valley
■ CONCEPCIÓN

South Region ———— —— Bío-Bío Valley
♥ PAÍS
▽ CHARDONNAY —— Malleco Valley
♥ PINOT NOIR

■ TEMUCO

—— Cautín Valley

Austral Region ———— ■ OSORNO
♥ PINOT NOIR
▽ CHARDONNAY —— Osorno Valley

N

200km   200mi

187

France

A wine region known for earthy and mineral-driven wines with heightened acidity. The country can be divided into three zones by the climate.

2 MILLION
ACRES

836,000
HA

WINE REGIONS BY SIZE

◀ LANGUEDOC-ROUSSILLON
◀ BORDEAUX
◀ RHÔNE VALLEY
◀ LOIRE VALLEY
◀ SOUTH WEST
◀ PROVENCE
◀ CHAMPAGNE

◀ BURGUNDY
◀ BEAUJOLAIS
◀ ALSACE
◀ CORSICA

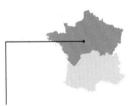

NORTHERN FRANCE

☁ COOL CLIMATE

Northern French wines have very high acidity, tart fruit, and mineral flavors.

REGIONAL PRODUCTION:

- CHAMPAGNE
- MUSCADET
- LOIRE SAUVIGNON BLANC
- BURGUNDY CHARDONNAY
- LOIRE CHENIN BLANC
- ALSACE RIESLING
- BURGUNDY PINOT NOIR

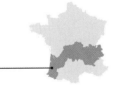

CENTRAL FRANCE

⛅ WARM CLIMATE

Central France wines have moderate acidity, tart fruit, and soil flavors.

REGIONAL PRODUCTION:

- BORDEAUX SÉMILLON
- BEAUJOLAIS GAMAY
- RED BORDEAUX BLEND
- NORTHERN RHÔNE SYRAH
- SAUTERNAIS

MEDITERRANEAN FRANCE

⛅ WARM CLIMATE

Mediterranean French wines have medium acidity, ripe fruit, and rustic earthy flavors.

REGIONAL PRODUCTION:

- LIMOUX SPARKLING
- PROVENCE ROSÉ
- RHÔNE/GSM BLEND
- CORBIERES CARIGNAN & GSM
- CAHORS MALBEC

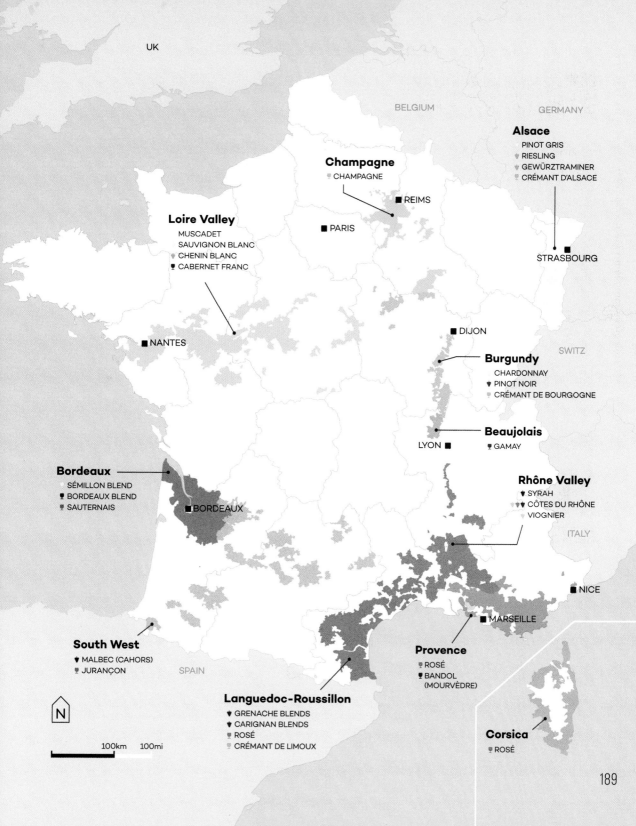

UK

BELGIUM

GERMANY

Alsace
PINOT GRIS
RIESLING
GEWÜRZTRAMINER
CRÉMANT D'ALSACE

Champagne
CHAMPAGNE

■ REIMS

■ PARIS

Loire Valley
MUSCADET
SAUVIGNON BLANC
CHENIN BLANC
CABERNET FRANC

■ DIJON

■ STRASBOURG

■ NANTES

Burgundy
CHARDONNAY
PINOT NOIR
CRÉMANT DE BOURGOGNE

SWITZ

Beaujolais
GAMAY

LYON ■

Bordeaux
SÉMILLON BLEND
BORDEAUX BLEND
SAUTERNAIS

■ BORDEAUX

Rhône Valley
SYRAH
CÔTES DU RHÔNE
VIOGNIER

ITALY

■ NICE

■ MARSEILLE

South West
MALBEC (CAHORS)
JURANÇON

SPAIN

Provence
ROSÉ
BANDOL
(MOURVÈDRE)

Languedoc-Roussillon
GRENACHE BLENDS
CARIGNAN BLENDS
ROSÉ
CRÉMANT DE LIMOUX

Corsica
ROSÉ

N

100km   100mi

FRANCE: BORDEAUX

Merlot and Cabernet Sauvignon originate in Bordeaux and are blended into the eponymous Bordeaux Blend. Red wines make up nearly 90% of the production.

CLASSIFICATION OF RED BORDEAUX

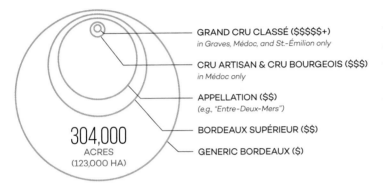

304,000
ACRES
(123,000 HA)

GRAND CRU CLASSÉ ($$$$$+)
in Graves, Médoc, and St.-Émilion only

CRU ARTISAN & CRU BOURGEOIS ($$$)
in Médoc only

APPELLATION ($$)
(e.g., "Entre-Deux-Mers")

BORDEAUX SUPÉRIEUR ($$)

GENERIC BORDEAUX ($)

FINDING QUALITY

Pay attention to vintage and look for wines labeled by their sub-appellation. If you see the term "Grand Vin de Bordeaux" printed on the label, this is typically a producer's best wine.

GOOD VINTAGES:
2010, 2009, 2008, 2005, 2003
2000, 1998, 1990, 1989

TOP WINES OF BORDEAUX

🍷 "LEFT BANK" BORDEAUX

The west side of the Garonne River is predominantly Cabernet Sauvignon. The wines taste of black currant, pencil lead, violet, tobacco, cocoa, and licorice with dense structured tannins. Many will age 20 years.

🍷 "RIGHT BANK" BORDEAUX

The east side of the Garonne River is predominantly Merlot blended with Cabernet Franc. Wines taste of leather, strawberry, fig, plum, vanilla, grilled almonds, and smoke with silky refined tannins. Some will age 30 years.

🍷 CÔTES DE BORDEAUX

Areas close to rivers are called "Côtes" meaning "slope." Wines are Merlot blends that taste of spicy red fruits, green bell pepper, and herbs with grippy bold tannin. Wines age 10 years.

🍷 BORDEAUX BLANC

This blend is mostly Sémillon and Sauvignon Blanc and tastes of citrus, chamomile, grapefruit, and beeswax. Bolder Bordeaux Blanc come from Pessac-Léognan and Graves. Lighter Bordeaux Blanc come from Entre-Deux-Mers.

🍷 ROSÉ AND CLAIRET

Rich and deeply colored dry rosé wines with flavors of red currant, wild strawberry, peony, and rose hips. Clairet ("Clair-ett") was the original style of Bordeaux during the 18th and 19th centuries.

🍷 SAUTERNAIS

A group of dessert wine regions can be found along the Garonne River. The largest appellation is Sauternes, which produces viscous, honeyed, waxy, and peachy Sémillon-based wines.

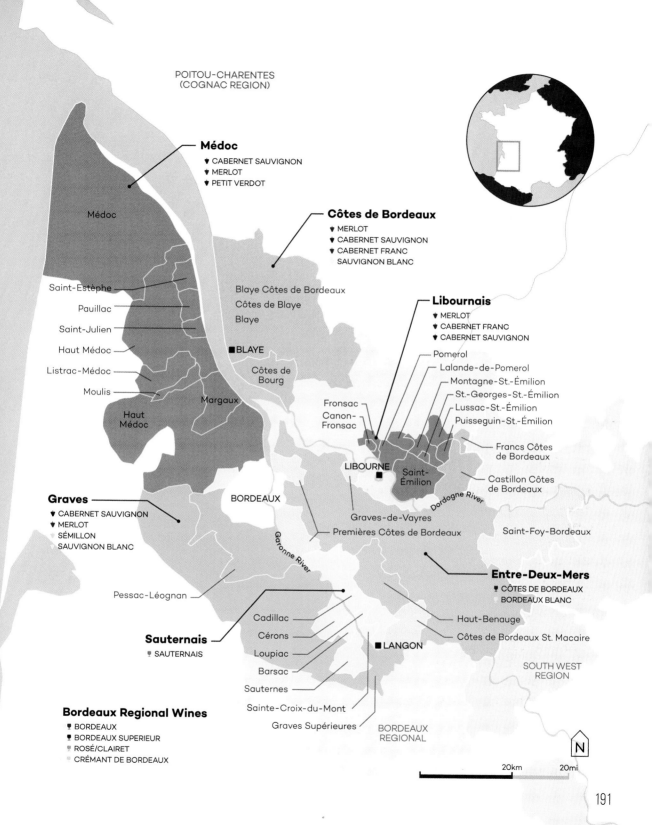

POITOU-CHARENTES
(COGNAC REGION)

Médoc
♥ CABERNET SAUVIGNON
♥ MERLOT
♥ PETIT VERDOT

Médoc

Côtes de Bordeaux
♥ MERLOT
♥ CABERNET SAUVIGNON
♥ CABERNET FRANC
SAUVIGNON BLANC

Saint-Estèphe

Pauillac

Saint-Julien

Haut Médoc

Listrac-Médoc

Moulis

Blaye Côtes de Bordeaux
Côtes de Blaye
Blaye

Libournais
♥ MERLOT
♥ CABERNET FRANC
♥ CABERNET SAUVIGNON

■BLAYE

Pomerol
Lalande-de-Pomerol
Montagne-St.-Émilion
St.-Georges-St.-Émilion
Lussac-St.-Émilion
Puisseguin-St.-Émilion

Margaux

Côtes de
Bourg

Haut
Médoc

Fronsac
Canon-
Fronsac

Francs Côtes
de Bordeaux

Graves
♥ CABERNET SAUVIGNON
♥ MERLOT
SÉMILLON
SAUVIGNON BLANC

BORDEAUX

LIBOURNE
■

Saint-
Émilion

Castillon Côtes
de Bordeaux

Saint-Foy-Bordeaux

Graves-de-Vayres

Premières Côtes de Bordeaux

Dordogne River

Pessac-Léognan

Garonne River

Entre-Deux-Mers
♥ CÔTES DE BORDEAUX
BORDEAUX BLANC

Sauternais
♥ SAUTERNAIS

Cadillac

Cérons

Loupiac

Barsac

Sauternes

Sainte-Croix-du-Mont

Graves Supérieures

Haut-Benauge

Côtes de Bordeaux St. Macaire

■LANGON

SOUTH WEST
REGION

Bordeaux Regional Wines
♥ BORDEAUX
♥ BORDEAUX SUPERIOR
♥ ROSÉ/CLAIRET
■ CRÉMANT DE BORDEAUX

BORDEAUX
REGIONAL

N

20km   20mi

FRANCE: BURGUNDY

Chardonnay and Pinot Noir come from Burgundy. The production is about 60% Chardonnay but Burgundy is most known for floral and earthy Pinot Noir.

CLASSIFICATION OF BURGUNDY WINES

71,000 ACRES (28,700 HA)

GRAND CRU ($$$$$+)
43 crus in Côte d'Or and Chablis only

PREMIER CRU ($$$$+)
684 crus (e.g., "Mercurey 1ᵉʳ Cru")

APPELLATION/VILLAGE ($$$$+)
44 appellations (e.g., "Macon-Villages" or "Mercurey")

REGIONAL WINE ($$$+)
23 appellations (e.g., "Bourgogne Rouge" or "Crémant de Bourgogne")

TERMS

Domaine: a winery with vineyards

Negociant: a brand that buys grapes or wine

Clos: a walled vineyard

Lieu-dit/Climat: vineyard plot name listed on the label

 GOOD VINTAGES:
2013, 2012, 2011, 2010, 2009, 2005

TOP WINES OF BURGUNDY

CHABLIS
Chablis produces mainly unoaked Chardonnay. Wines taste of yellow apple, passion fruit, and citrus, with high acidity. At the Grand Cru level, Chablis is made more toasty with oak.

PINOT NOIR (CÔTE D'OR)
At the Village level, wines taste rustic with notes of mushrooms, potting soil, and tart berries. Premier Cru and Grand Cru wines have moderate tannin with flavors of dried cranberry, candied hibiscus, vanilla, and rose.

CHARDONNAY (CÔTE D'OR)
The Côte d'Or produces mainly oaked Chardonnay. Wines taste of yellow apple, lemon curd, quince tart, vanilla, and hazelnut. Look in the Côte de Beaune for high-quality Chardonnays produced in this style.

CHARDONNAY (MÂCONNAIS)
The Mâconnais makes a light unoaked style of Chardonnay with flavors of ripe yellow apple with hints of lemon zest, apricot, and a zesty finish. Pouilly-Fuissé, Saint-Véran, and Viré-Clessé are the largest wine villages.

CRÉMANT DE BOURGOGNE
A sparkling wine appellation that produces white and rosé bubbly wines with the same method as Champagne. The regional appellation offers exceptional quality for the price.

PINOT NOIR (OTHER REGIONS)
Côte Chalonnaise also produces Pinot Noir with plummy fruit, boysenberries, and clove, along with rustic earthy notes of dried leaves and potting soil. Look for Givry and Mercurey.

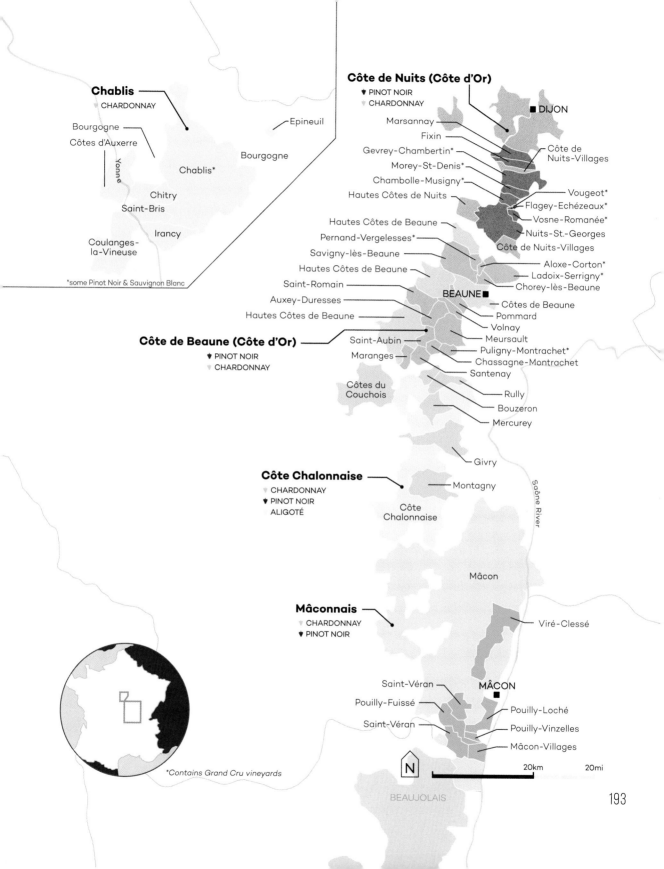

Chablis
▽ CHARDONNAY

Bourgogne
Côtes d'Auxerre
Yonne

Epineuil

Bourgogne

Chablis*

Chitry
Saint-Bris

Irancy

Coulanges-
la-Vineuse

*some Pinot Noir & Sauvignon Blanc

Côte de Nuits (Côte d'Or)
♥ PINOT NOIR
▽ CHARDONNAY

■ DIJON

Marsannay

Fixin

Gevrey-Chambertin*

Morey-St-Denis*

Chambolle-Musigny*

Hautes Côtes de Nuits

Côte de
Nuits-Villages

Vougeot*
Flagey-Echézeaux*
Vosne-Romanée*
Nuits-St.-Georges
Côte de Nuits-Villages

Hautes Côtes de Beaune

Pernand-Vergelesses*

Savigny-lès-Beaune

Hautes Côtes de Beaune

Saint-Romain

Auxey-Duresses

Hautes Côtes de Beaune

Aloxe-Corton*
Ladoix-Serrigny*
Chorey-lès-Beaune

BEAUNE ■

Côtes de Beaune
Pommard
Volnay
Meursault
Puligny-Montrachet*
Chassagne-Montrachet
Santenay

Côte de Beaune (Côte d'Or)
♥ PINOT NOIR
▽ CHARDONNAY

Saint-Aubin

Maranges

Rully
Bouzeron
Mercurey

Côtes du
Couchois

Givry

Côte Chalonnaise
▽ CHARDONNAY
♥ PINOT NOIR
ALIGOTÉ

Montagny

Côte
Chalonnaise

Saône River

Mâcon

Mâconnais
▽ CHARDONNAY
♥ PINOT NOIR

Viré-Clessé

Saint-Véran

Pouilly-Fuissé

Saint-Véran

MÂCON ■

Pouilly-Loché
Pouilly-Vinzelles
Mâcon-Villages

N

20km   20mi

*Contains Grand Cru vineyards

BEAUJOLAIS

193

FRANCE: RHÔNE VALLEY

The Rhône Valley is most known for leathery and fruity Southern Rhône red blends and savory herbaceous Northern Rhône Syrahs.

CLASSIFICATION OF RHÔNE WINES

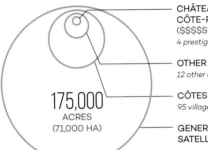

175,000
ACRES
(71,000 HA)

CHÂTEAUNEUF-DU-PAPE, CORNAS, CÔTE-RÔTIE, AND HERMITAGE ($$$$$+)
4 prestige crus

OTHER CRUS ($$$$)
12 other crus (e.g., "Lirac" and "Gigondas")

CÔTES DU RHÔNE VILLAGES ($$)
95 villages

GENERIC CÔTES DU RHÔNE & SATELLITE APPELLATIONS ($)

FINDING QUALITY

Value-driven wines vary in taste year to year, so look for trends on the quality of the vintage overall. You'll see less variation and more age-ability from higher quality producers, particularly in the northern Rhône and the crus.

 GOOD VINTAGES:
2012, 2010, 2009, 2007, 2005, 2001, 2000

TOP WINES OF THE RHÔNE VALLEY

♟ CÔTES DU RHÔNE RED

Some of the highest acclaimed southern Rhône reds have higher proportions of Grenache in the blend. As bold as these wines can be, they're rarely oaked. Flavors range from sweet candied raspberries to leather and bacon fat.

♟ CHÂTEAUNEUF-DU-PAPE

One of the boldest age-worthy southern Rhône blends are made with no less than 13 different grapes. The dominant varieties include Grenache, Syrah, Mourvèdre, and Cinsault.

♟ RHÔNE ROSÉ & TAVEL ROSÉ

Rhône rosé bursts with wild strawberry and red currant flavors. The deeply colored rosés of Tavel are said to have been a favorite of the writer and man's man, Ernest Hemingway.

♟ NORTHERN RHÔNE SYRAH

The birthplace of Syrah offers rich and dense wines that typically have a meaty edge to them along with loads of black currant, licorice, plums, and olives. The finest wines can age for 20 years.

♟ CÔTES DU RHÔNE WHITE

Marsanne and Viognier are the champion grapes of Rhône White. Wines are often citrusy with notes of apple, beeswax, and granite-like minerals. Northern Rhône delivers the boldest whites with notes of almond, white peach, and orange blossom.

♟ MUSCAT BEAUMES DE VENISE

A rarity, Muscat Blanc goes into what the French call a VDN or "Vin doux Naturels"—a fortified dessert wine. Wines are rich with aromas of orchids, candied orange, honey, and tropical fruits.

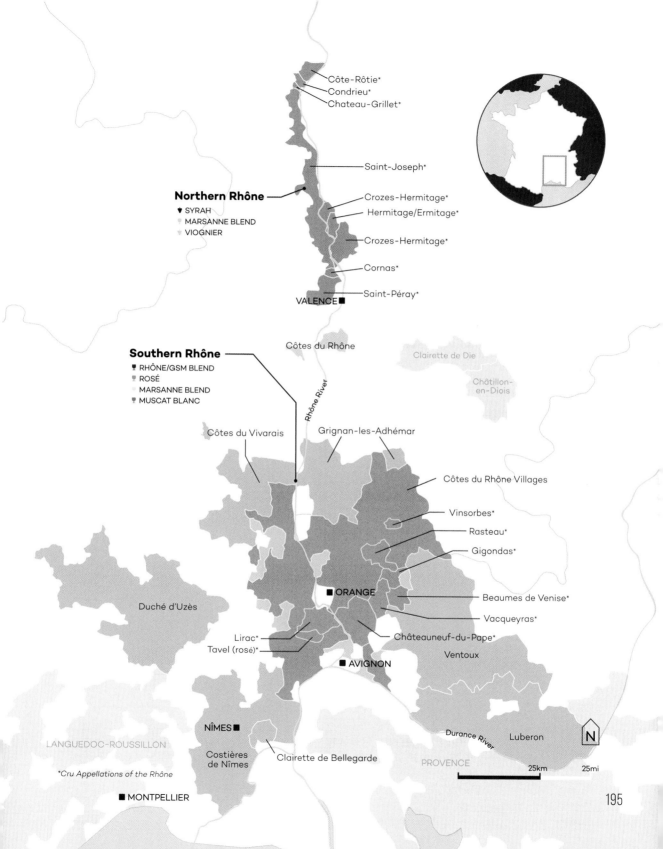

Côte-Rôtie*
Condrieu*
Chateau-Grillet*

Saint-Joseph*

Northern Rhône

● SYRAH
● MARSANNE BLEND
● VIOGNIER

Crozes-Hermitage*
Hermitage/Ermitage*

Crozes-Hermitage*

Cornas*

Saint-Péray*

VALENCE ■

Côtes du Rhône

Clairette de Die

Châtillon-
en-Diois

Southern Rhône

● RHÔNE/GSM BLEND
● ROSÉ
● MARSANNE BLEND
● MUSCAT BLANC

Rhône River

Côtes du Vivarais

Grignan-les-Adhémar

Côtes du Rhône Villages

Vinsorbes*

Rasteau*

Gigondas*

Duché d'Uzès

ORANGE ■

Beaumes de Venise*

Vacqueyras*

Lirac*
Tavel (rosé)*

Châteauneuf-du-Pape*

Ventoux

AVIGNON ■

NÎMES ■

LANGUEDOC-ROUSSILLON

Durance River

Luberon

N

PROVENCE

*Cru Appellations of the Rhône

Costières
de Nîmes

Clairette de Bellegarde

25km   25mi

195

■ MONTPELLIER

Germany

Germany is a cool climate growing region known mostly for Riesling as well as ripe and rustic Pinot Noir.

WINE REGIONS BY SIZE

250,000
ACRES

102,000
HA

◀ RHEINHESSEN
◀ PFALZ
◀ BADEN
◀ WÜRTTEMBERG
◀ MOSEL
◀ FRANKEN
◀ NAHE

◀ RHEINGAU
◀ SAALE-UNSTRUT
◀ AHR
◀ SACHSEN
◀ MITTELRHEIN
◀ HESSISCHE BERGSTRASSE

TOP WINES OF GERMANY

🍇 RIESLING

The top German grape, known for aromatic wines that range in style from dry or "trocken" to sweet ice wine or "eiswein."

- MOSEL
- RHEINGAU
- RHEINHESSEN
- MITTELRHEIN

🍇 MÜLLER-THURGAU

A simple aromatic white wine with peach and floral flavors that is often a touch sweet.

- RHEINHESSEN
- FRANKEN
- PFALZ

🍇 PINOT NOIR

Pinot Noir (Spätburgunder) offers cranberry, cherry, and subtle earthy flavors. Wines are often likened to red Burgundy.

- BADEN
- FRANKEN
- AHR

🍇 DORNFELDER

A simple medium red wine with sweet red fruit flavors, an herbaceous green note, medium tannin, and spicy acidity.

- RHEINHESSEN
- PFALZ

🍇 PINOT GRIS & PINOT BLANC

Germany produces a rich style of Pinot Blanc (Weissburgunder) and Pinot Gris (Grauburgunder) with white peach, citrus, and subtle notes of honeycomb.

- BADEN

🍇 SILVANER

A light dry white wine with high acidity and flavors of citrus zest and green apple.

- RHEINHESSEN
- FRANKEN

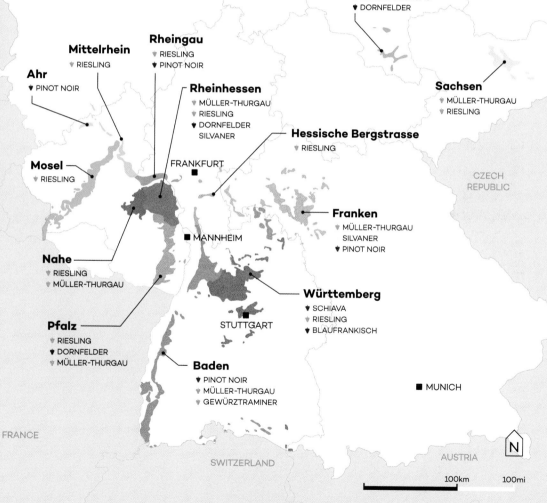

THE NETHERLANDS

BERLIN

Saale-Unstrut
- MÜLLER-THURGAU
- DORNFELDER

Rheingau
- RIESLING
- PINOT NOIR

Mittelrhein
- RIESLING

Ahr
- PINOT NOIR

Rheinhessen
- MÜLLER-THURGAU
- RIESLING
- DORNFELDER
  SILVANER

Sachsen
- MÜLLER-THURGAU
- RIESLING

Hessische Bergstrasse
- RIESLING

FRANKFURT

Mosel
- RIESLING

CZECH REPUBLIC

Franken
- MÜLLER-THURGAU
  SILVANER
- PINOT NOIR

MANNHEIM

Nahe
- RIESLING
- MÜLLER-THURGAU

Württemberg
- SCHIAVA
- RIESLING
- BLAUFRANKISCH

STUTTGART

Pfalz
- RIESLING
- DORNFELDER
- MÜLLER-THURGAU

Baden
- PINOT NOIR
- MÜLLER-THURGAU
- GEWÜRZTRAMINER

MUNICH

FRANCE

SWITZERLAND

AUSTRIA

N

100km   100mi

197

Italy

Italy is known for its concentrated rustic wines. The country can be divided into three major areas, each with a different climate.

1.5 MILLION
ACRES

625,700
HA

WINE REGIONS BY SIZE

◀ SICILY
◀ PUGLIA
◀ VENETO
◀ TUSCANY
◀ EMILIA-ROMAGNA
◀ PIEDMONT
◀ ABRUZZO

◀ CAMPANIA
◀ LOMBARDY
◀ FRIULI-VENEZIA GIULIA
   SARDEGNA
◀ MARCHE
◀ LAZIO
◀ TRENTINO-ALTO ADIGE

◀ UMBRIA
◀ CALABRIA
◀ MOLISE
◀ BASILICATA
   LIGURIA
◀ VALLE D'AOSTA

NORTHERN ITALY

☁ COOL CLIMATE

Northern Italian wines have higher acidity, tart fruit, and herb flavors.
REGIONAL PRODUCTION:

- 🍷 PROSECCO
- 🍷 MOSCATO D'ASTI
- 🍷 PINOT GRIGIO
- 🍷 SOAVE
- 🍷 BARBERA
- 🍷 VALPOLICELLA
- 🍷 BAROLO (NEBBIOLO)

CENTRAL ITALY

⛅ WARM CLIMATE

Central Italian wines have higher acidity, ripe fruit, leather, and clay flavors.
REGIONAL PRODUCTION:

- 🍷 LAMBRUSCO
- 🍷 VERMENTINO
- 🍷 CHIANTI (SANGIOVESE)
- 🍷 SUPER TUSCAN (BORDEAUX BLEND)
- 🍷 MONTEPULCIANO
- 🍷 VIN SANTO

SOUTHERN ITALY/ISLANDS

☀ HOT CLIMATE

Southern Italian wines have medium acidity, sweet fruit, and leather flavors.
REGIONAL PRODUCTION:

- 🍷 VERMENTINO
- 🍷 CANNONAU (GRENACHE)
- 🍷 PRIMITIVO
- 🍷 NEGROAMARO
- 🍷 NERO D'AVOLA
- 🍷 MARSALA

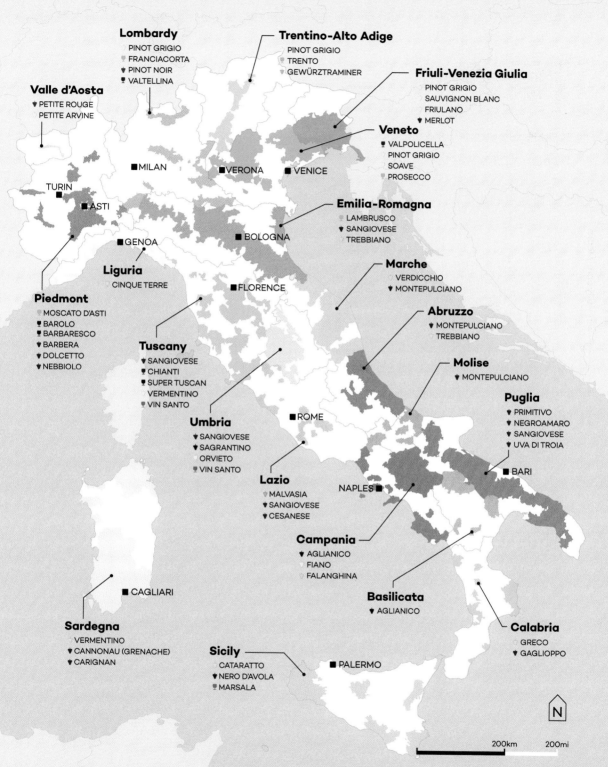

Valle d'Aosta
- PETITE ROUGE
- PETITE ARVINE

Lombardy
- PINOT GRIGIO
- FRANCIACORTA
- PINOT NOIR
- VALTELLINA

Trentino-Alto Adige
- PINOT GRIGIO
- TRENTO
- GEWÜRZTRAMINER

Friuli-Venezia Giulia
- PINOT GRIGIO
- SAUVIGNON BLANC
- FRIULANO
- MERLOT

Veneto
- VALPOLICELLA
- PINOT GRIGIO
- SOAVE
- PROSECCO

Emilia-Romagna
- LAMBRUSCO
- SANGIOVESE
- TREBBIANO

Marche
- VERDICCHIO
- MONTEPULCIANO

Abruzzo
- MONTEPULCIANO
- TREBBIANO

Molise
- MONTEPULCIANO

Puglia
- PRIMITIVO
- NEGROAMARO
- SANGIOVESE
- UVA DI TROIA

Liguria
- CINQUE TERRE

Piedmont
- MOSCATO D'ASTI
- BAROLO
- BARBARESCO
- BARBERA
- DOLCETTO
- NEBBIOLO

Tuscany
- SANGIOVESE
- CHIANTI
- SUPER TUSCAN
- VERMENTINO
- VIN SANTO

Umbria
- SANGIOVESE
- SAGRANTINO
- ORVIETO
- VIN SANTO

Lazio
- MALVASIA
- SANGIOVESE
- CESANESE

Campania
- AGLIANICO
- FIANO
- FALANGHINA

Basilicata
- AGLIANICO

Calabria
- GRECO
- GAGLIOPPO

Sardegna
- VERMENTINO
- CANNONAU (GRENACHE)
- CARIGNAN

Sicily
- CATARATTO
- NERO D'AVOLA
- MARSALA

MILAN
VERONA
VENICE
TURIN
ASTI
GENOA
BOLOGNA
FLORENCE
ROME
NAPLES
BARI
CAGLIARI
PALERMO

200km 200mi

ITALY: TUSCANY

The region of Italy that specializes in Italy's most planted grape: Sangiovese. Wines are spicy and herbaceous when young and more fig-like as they age.

WHAT TUSCANY GROWS

148,000 ACRES

60,000 HA

◀ SANGIOVESE
◀ MERLOT, CABERNET SAUVIGNON, CABERNET FRANC, & SYRAH
◀ CANAIOLO NERO
◀ VERMENTINO
◀ MALVASIA (used in Vin Santo)
  CHARDONNAY
◀ OTHERS

CHIANTI AGING

🍷 2.5 YRS: "GRAN SELEZIONE"
Chianti Classico only

🍷 2 YRS: "RISERVA"
Riserva wines from all 8 subzones

🍷 1 YR: CLASSICO, FIORENTINI, RUFINA
Plus, other subzones labeled as "Superiore"

🍷 9 MO: CHIANTI MONTESPERTOLI

🍷 6 MO: CHIANTI
Chianti, Ch. Colli Arentini, Ch. Colline Pisane, Ch. Colli Senesi and Ch. Montalbano

🍾 GOOD VINTAGES:
2010, 2009, 2006, 2004
2001, 2000, 1999, 1997

TOP DRY WINES OF TUSCANY

🍷 **CHIANTI**

Sangiovese-dominant blend. Aged Chianti wines taste of preserved cherry, oregano, clay pot, sweet balsamic, espresso, and sweet tobacco. Value Chianti tastes spicy and herbaceous with notes of game, red fruits, and tomato.

🍷 **SUPER TUSCAN BLEND**

The colloquial name for a blend that includes nonindigenous grapes such as Merlot and Cabernet Franc. Wines are identifiable from other Tuscan wines by their unique made-up label names.

🍷 **BRUNELLO DI MONTALCINO**

100% Sangiovese with a regional clone called Prugnolo Gentile. Brunello is aged for 4+ years. Wines taste of licorice, cedar, vanilla, fig, and sweet red berries, supported by spicy acidity and moderate tannin.

🍷 **VERNACCIA DI SAN GIMIGNANO**

The "Fiore" Vernaccia wines are dry and minerally, with flavors of lemon, apple blossom, and pear. "Tradizionale" wines are similar to "Fiore" but usually feature a bitter almond note on the finish.

🍷 **OTHER TUSCAN SANGIOVESE**

While Chianti and Brunello are the most well-known Sangiovese wines of Tuscany, there are several other regional designations that also make great Sangiovese:

🍾 CARMIGNANO
Blended 10–20% Cabernet Franc/Cab. Sauvignon

🍾 MONTECUCCO
18 months aging & 34 months aging for Riserva.

🍾 VINO NOBILE DI MONTEPULCIANO
Aged for 24 months & 34 months for Riserva

🍾 MORELLINO DI SCANSANO
Aged for 8 months & 24 months for Riserva

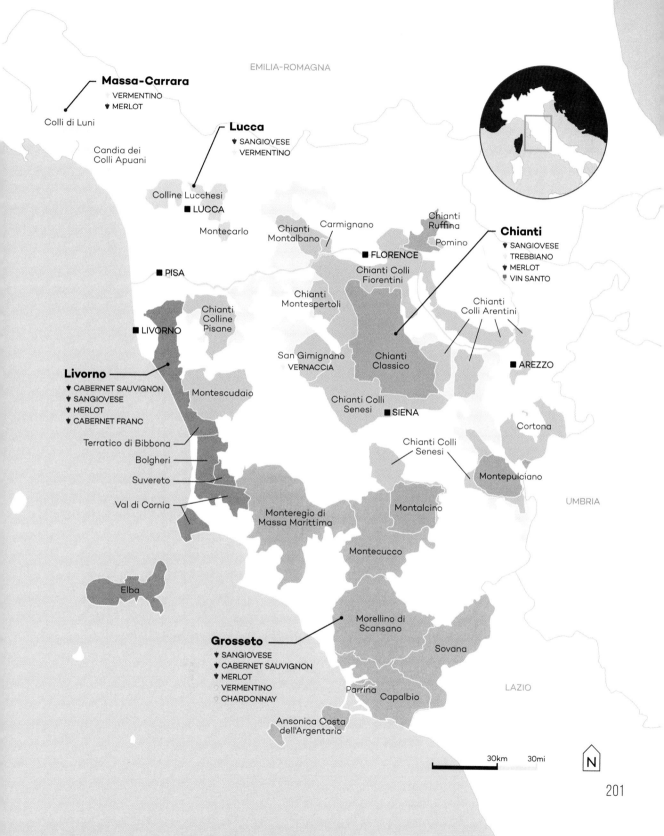

EMILIA-ROMAGNA

Massa-Carrara
♥ VERMENTINO
♥ MERLOT

Colli di Luni

Candia dei
Colli Apuani

Lucca
♥ SANGIOVESE
♥ VERMENTINO

Colline Lucchesi
■ LUCCA

Montecarlo

Chianti
Montalbano

Carmignano

Chianti
Ruffina

Pomino

Chianti
♥ SANGIOVESE
♥ TREBBIANO
♥ MERLOT
♥ VIN SANTO

■ FLORENCE

Chianti Colli
Fiorentini

Chianti
Montespertoli

Chianti
Colli Arentini

■ PISA

Chianti
Colline
Pisane

San Gimignano
VERNACCIA

Chianti
Classico

■ AREZZO

■ LIVORNO

Livorno
♥ CABERNET SAUVIGNON
♥ SANGIOVESE
♥ MERLOT
♥ CABERNET FRANC

Montescudaio

Chianti Colli
Senesi

■ SIENA

Cortona

Terratico di Bibbona
Bolgheri
Suvereto
Val di Cornia

Chianti Colli
Senesi

Monteregio di
Massa Marittima

Montalcino

Montepulciano

UMBRIA

Montecucco

Elba

Morellino di
Scansano

Grosseto
♥ SANGIOVESE
♥ CABERNET SAUVIGNON
♥ MERLOT
♥ VERMENTINO
♥ CHARDONNAY

Sovana

Parrina

Capalbio

LAZIO

Ansonica Costa
dell'Argentario

30km   30mi

N

New Zealand

New Zealand is a cool climate region most known for its intensely flavored Sauvignon Blanc. Expect wines to taste tart, light-bodied, and elegant.

WINE REGIONS BY SIZE

220,000
ACRES

88,300
HA

◄ MARLBOROUGH
◄ HAWKE'S BAY
◄ CENTRAL OTAGO
◄ GISBORNE
◄ CANTERBURY/WAIPARA VALLEY
◄ NELSON
◄ WAIRARAPA

◄ AUCKLAND
◄ WAIKATO/BAY OF PLENTY
◄ NORTHLAND

TOP WINES OF NEW ZEALAND

⚇ SAUVIGNON BLANC

The most important wine of New Zealand explodes with flavors of gooseberry, passion fruit, lime, tomato stalk, and grapefruit.

├─● MARLBOROUGH
├─○ NELSON
└─● HAWKE'S BAY

⚇ PINOT NOIR

Marlborough tends to offer tart red fruit flavors, whereas Central Otago produces wines with ripe raspberry flavors.

├─● CENTRAL OTAGO
├─○ WAIRARAPA
└─● MARLBOROUGH

⚇ CHARDONNAY

Bold lemon and tropical fruit flavors with crisp acidity and usually a touch of oak, which adds toasty caramel and vanilla flavors.

├─● HAWKE'S BAY
├─● GISBORNE
└─● MARLBOROUGH

⚇ PINOT GRIS

Both dry and off-dry styles with notes of apple, pear, honeysuckle, and spice bread.

├─○ GISBORNE
├─○ CANTERBURY/WAIPARA VALLEY
└─○ NELSON

⚇ RIESLING

Wines range from bone-dry with lime notes to lusciously sweet and tasting of apricots and honey.

├─● MARLBOROUGH
├─● CENTRAL OTAGO
└─○ NELSON

♟ BORDEAUX BLEND

A light fruity style with juicy aromas of ripe black cherry, baking spices, and coffee.

├─● HAWKE'S BAY
├─○ NORTHLAND
└─○ AUCKLAND

Northland
- CHARDONNAY
- BORDEAUX BLEND

Auckland
- BORDEAUX BLEND
- CHARDONNAY

Matakana

AUCKLAND

West Auckland

Waiheke Island

Waikato / Bay of Plenty
- CHARDONNAY
- BORDEAUX BLEND

Ormond
Patutahi
Manutuke

Gisborne
- CHARDONNAY
- PINOT GRIS

Coastal Areas

Hillsides

Alluvial Plains

Hawke's Bay
- CHARDONNAY
- SAUVIGNON BLANC
- PINOT NOIR
- RIESLING

Masterton

Nelson
- SAUVIGNON BLANC
- PINOT GRIS
- RIESLING

Moutere Hills

Waimea Plains

Gladstone
Martinborough

WELLINGTON

Wairarapa
- PINOT NOIR
- PINOT GRIS

Wairu Valley

Southern Valleys

Awatere Valley

Marlborough
- SAUVIGNON BLANC
- CHARDONNAY
- PINOT NOIR
- PINOT GRIS

Waipara Valley

Canterbury Plains

CHRISTCHURCH

Canterbury / Waipara Valley
- PINOT NOIR
- RIESLING
- PINOT GRIS

Wanaka

Gibbston

Bendigo

Waitaki Valley

QUEENSTOWN

Cromwell

Alexandra

Bannockburn

Central Otago
- PINOT NOIR
- RIESLING

N

200km   200mi

203

Portugal

Portugal is most famous for Port but also produces excellent dry wines with more than 200 native wine grapes.

WINE REGIONS BY SIZE

554,000
ACRES

224,000
HA

- ◀ DOURO VALLEY
- ◀ MINHO
- ◀ BEIRA INTERIOR
- ◀ LISBOA
- ◀ ALENTEJO
- ◀ DÃO
- ◀ TEJO/RIBATEJO

- ◀ SETÚBAL
- ◀ BEIRA ATLÂNTICO
- ◀ TERRAS DE CISTER
- ◀ ALGARVE
- TRANSMONTANO
- ◀ MADEIRA

TOP DRY WINES OF PORTUGAL

🍇 TOURIGA NACIONAL

Quite possibly Portugal's most important grape, used in Port and dry red blends. Wines offer flavors of black plum, blackberry, mint, and violet.

- DOURO
- DÃO

🍇 TEMPRANILLO

Tempranillo is labeled as "Aragonez" in southern Portugal and "Tinta Roriz" in the north. Wines offer smoky red fruit flavors, cinnamon, and bittersweet chocolate.

- ALL OF PORTUGAL

🍇 ALICANTE BOUSCHET

A rare wine grape that has red skins and red flesh. Wines offer bold black fruit and black pepper flavors with a sweet smoky tobacco finish.

- ALENTEJO
- LISBOA

🍇 TRINCADEIRA

Unique woodsy-tasting wines with notes of red fruit, barbecue smoke, hickory, plum sauce, raisins, kerosene, and chocolate.

- ALENTEJO
- LISBOA

🍇 ARINTO

When young, wines are lean with citrus pith flavors. As they age, they develop flavors of lemon, almond, and honeycomb. Arinto is sometimes aged in oak.

- ALL OF PORTUGAL

🍇 FERNÃO PIRES

An aromatic wine with perfumed floral aromas. Wines are sometimes blended with Viognier to add richer flavors of peaches and honeysuckle.

- LISBOA
- TEJO

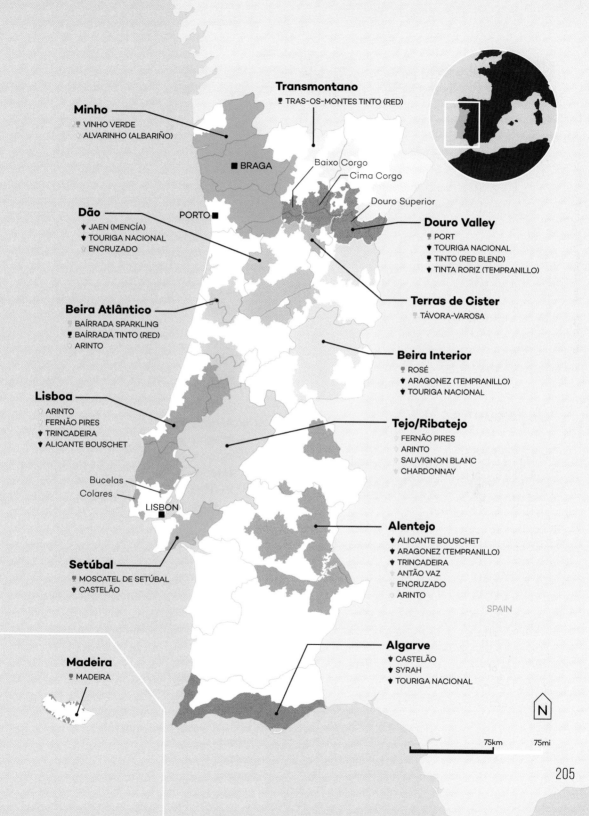

Transmontano
- TRAS-OS-MONTES TINTO (RED)

Minho
- VINHO VERDE
- ALVARINHO (ALBARIÑO)

BRAGA

Baixo Corgo
Cima Corgo
Douro Superior

Dão
- JAEN (MENCÍA)
- TOURIGA NACIONAL
- ENCRUZADO

PORTO

Douro Valley
- PORT
- TOURIGA NACIONAL
- TINTO (RED BLEND)
- TINTA RORIZ (TEMPRANILLO)

Beira Atlântico
- BAÍRRADA SPARKLING
- BAÍRRADA TINTO (RED)
- ARINTO

Terras de Cister
- TÁVORA-VAROSA

Beira Interior
- ROSÉ
- ARAGONEZ (TEMPRANILLO)
- TOURIGA NACIONAL

Lisboa
- ARINTO
- FERNÃO PIRES
- TRINCADEIRA
- ALICANTE BOUSCHET

Tejo/Ribatejo
- FERNÃO PIRES
- ARINTO
- SAUVIGNON BLANC
- CHARDONNAY

Bucelas
Colares

LISBON

Alentejo
- ALICANTE BOUSCHET
- ARAGONEZ (TEMPRANILLO)
- TRINCADEIRA
- ANTÃO VAZ
- ENCRUZADO
- ARINTO

Setúbal
- MOSCATEL DE SETÚBAL
- CASTELÃO

SPAIN

Algarve
- CASTELÃO
- SYRAH
- TOURIGA NACIONAL

Madeira
- MADEIRA

N

75km   75mi

205

South Africa

South Africa is a hot climate region known for full-bodied savory reds and rich fruity whites. Much of South Africa's wine grapes are used for brandy.

250,000
ACRES

102,000
HA

WINE REGIONS BY SIZE

◀ STELLENBOSCH/FRANSCHHOEK
◀ PAARL
◀ SWARTLAND/MALMESBURY
◀ ROBERTSON
◀ BREEDEKLOOF
◀ OLIFANTS RIVER VALLEY

◀ WORCESTER
◀ ORANGE RIVER VALLEY
◀ KLEIN KAROO
◀ OTHERS

TOP WINES OF SOUTH AFRICA

CHENIN BLANC
The country's top wine offers 6 main styles: fresh & fruity; rich & unoaked; rich & oaked; rich & sweet; very sweet; and a sparkling style called Cap Classique.
- PAARL
- SWARTLAND
- STELLENBOSCH

CABERNET SAUVIGNON
Wines are bold and herbaceous with flavors of black pepper, black currant, and earthy notes of graphite and clay.
- STELLENBOSCH
- PAARL

PINOTAGE
Quality producers offer wines with blackberry, raspberry, and plum sauce with a smoky sweet tobacco finish.
- PAARL
- STELLENBOSCH
- SWARTLAND

SHIRAZ/SYRAH
Bolder Syrah wines with spicy flavors of black pepper, licorice, raspberry, and plum sauce.
- STELLENBOSCH
- PAARL
- SWARTLAND

CHARDONNAY
Chardonnay grows well in the cooler southern parts. Wines have baked apple notes, lemon zest, and vanilla flavors from oak aging.
- WALKER BAY
- ELGIN (NW OF WALKER BAY)

SÉMILLON
Wines are rich and full-bodied with flavors of Meyer lemon, yellow apple, wax lips, and creamy hazelnut.
- FRANSCHHOEK
- STELLENBOSCH

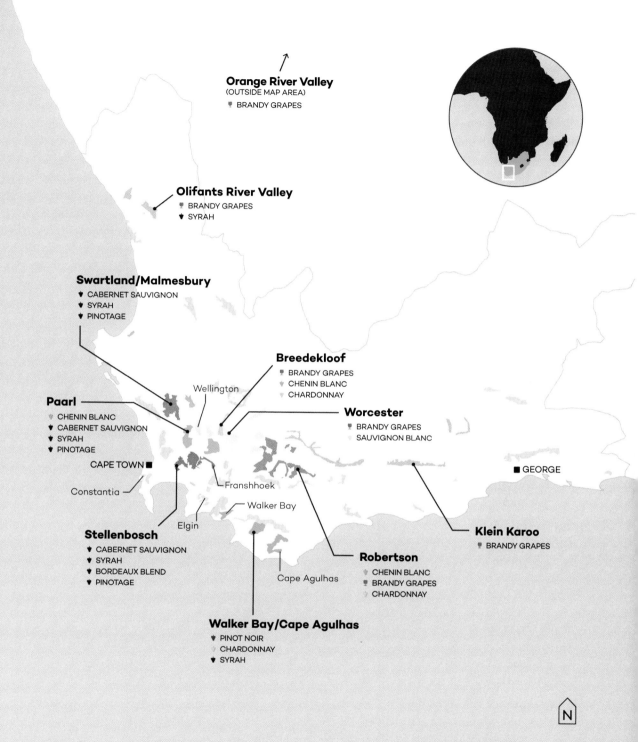

Orange River Valley
(OUTSIDE MAP AREA)
🏆 BRANDY GRAPES

Olifants River Valley
🏆 BRANDY GRAPES
🍷 SYRAH

Swartland/Malmesbury
🍷 CABERNET SAUVIGNON
🍷 SYRAH
🍷 PINOTAGE

Breedekloof
🏆 BRANDY GRAPES
🥂 CHENIN BLANC
🥂 CHARDONNAY

Wellington

Paarl
🥂 CHENIN BLANC
🍷 CABERNET SAUVIGNON
🍷 SYRAH
🍷 PINOTAGE

Worcester
🏆 BRANDY GRAPES
🥂 SAUVIGNON BLANC

CAPE TOWN ■

■ GEORGE

Constantia

Franshhoek

Walker Bay

Elgin

Stellenbosch
🍷 CABERNET SAUVIGNON
🍷 SYRAH
🍷 BORDEAUX BLEND
🍷 PINOTAGE

Klein Karoo
🏆 BRANDY GRAPES

Robertson
🥂 CHENIN BLANC
🏆 BRANDY GRAPES
🥂 CHARDONNAY

Cape Agulhas

Walker Bay/Cape Agulhas
🍷 PINOT NOIR
🥂 CHARDONNAY
🍷 SYRAH

100km   100mi

207

Spain

A region most known for its full-bodied fruity wines with subtle claylike earth notes. The country can be divided into three major climates.

2.5 MILLION
ACRES

1 MILLION
HA

WINE REGIONS BY SIZE

◀ CASTILLA-LA MANCHA
◀ VALENCIA
◀ EXTREMADURA
◀ RIOJA AND NAVARRA
◀ CASTILLA AND LEON
◀ CATALONIA
◀ ARAGON

◀ ANDALUCÍA
◀ GALICIA
▶ PAÍS VASCO
◀ THE ISLANDS

GREEN SPAIN

☁ COOL CLIMATE

Northwest Spanish wines have high acidity, tart fruit, and mineral flavors.

REGIONAL PRODUCTION:

ALBARIÑO
MENCÍA

NORTHERN SPAIN

⛅ WARM CLIMATE

Northern Spanish wines have medium acidity, ripe fruit, and mineral flavors.

REGIONAL PRODUCTION:

CAVA
VERDEJO
GARNACHA (GRENACHE)
CARIGNAN
PRIORAT (GSM BLEND)
RIOJA (TEMPRANILLO)
RIBERA DEL DUERO (TEMPRANILLO)

SOUTHERN SPAIN

☀ HOT CLIMATE

Southern Spanish wines have medium acidity, sweet fruit, and rustic clay flavors.

REGIONAL PRODUCTION:

GARNACHA (GRENACHE)
MONASTRELL (MOURVÈDRE)
SHERRY

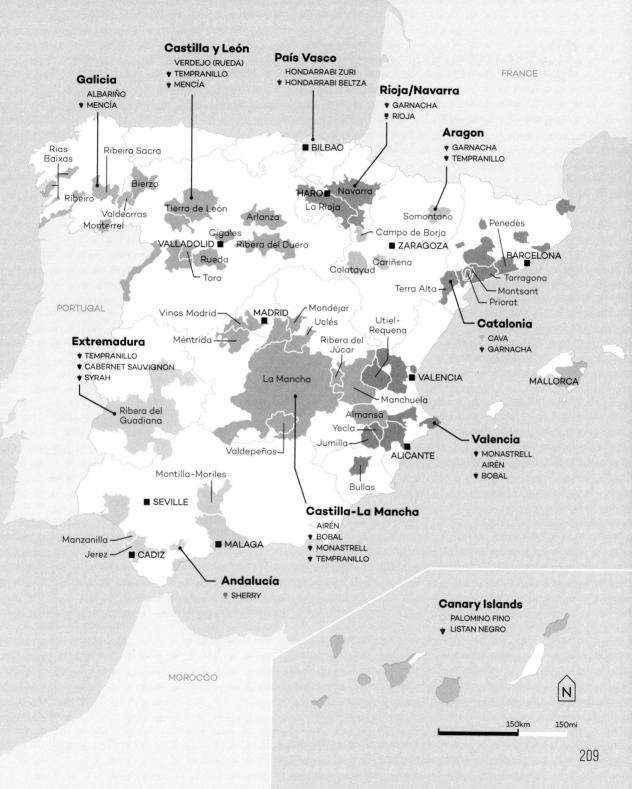

Galicia
  ◦ ALBARIÑO
  ♥ MENCÍA

Castilla y León
  VERDEJO (RUEDA)
  ♥ TEMPRANILLO
  ♥ MENCÍA

País Vasco
  HONDARRABI ZURI
  ♥ HONDARRABI BELTZA

Rioja/Navarra
  ♥ GARNACHA
  ♥ RIOJA

Aragon
  ♥ GARNACHA
  ♥ TEMPRANILLO

Rias
Baixas

Ribeira Sacra

Bierzo

Ribeiro

Valdeorras
Monterrei

Tierra de León

Arlanza

Cigales

VALLADOLID ■ Ribera del Duero

Rueda

Toro

PORTUGAL

BILBAO ■

HARO ■ Navarra
La Rioja

Somontano

Campo de Borja

ZARAGOZA ■

Calatayud

Cariñena

Penedès

BARCELONA ■

Tarragona

Montsant

Terra Alta

Priorat

Catalonia
  ◦ CAVA
  ♥ GARNACHA

Extremadura
  ♥ TEMPRANILLO
  ♥ CABERNET SAUVIGNON
  ♥ SYRAH

Vinos Madrid

MADRID ■

Mondéjar

Uclés

Ribera del
Júcar

Utiel-
Requena

Méntrida

Ribera del
Guadiana

La Mancha

VALENCIA ■

Manchuela

Almansa

Yecla

Jumilla

ALICANTE ■

Valencia
  ♥ MONASTRELL
  ◦ AIRÉN
  ♥ BOBAL

MALLORCA

Valdepeñas

Montilla-Moriles

SEVILLE ■

Castilla-La Mancha
  ◦ AIRÉN
  ♥ BOBAL
  ♥ MONASTRELL
  ♥ TEMPRANILLO

Bullas

Manzanilla

Jerez

CADIZ ■

MALAGA ■

Andalucía
  ◦ SHERRY

FRANCE

Canary Islands
  ◦ PALOMINO FINO
  ♥ LISTAN NEGRO

MOROCCO

150km   150mi

N

United States

The United States is most known for its bold, fruity red and white wines. Three regions produce the majority of US wine.

564,000
ACRES

228,000
HA

WINE REGIONS BY SIZE

◀ CALIFORNIA
◀ NORTHWEST
◀ NORTHEAST
◀ MIDWEST
◀ SOUTHEAST
◀ SOUTHWEST

WHAT IS AN AVA?

American Viticultural Areas (AVA) are grape-growing regions with distinguishing features that allow people to identify quality or taste or other traits of a wine that are unique to its geographic origin. There are over 200 AVAs.

CALIFORNIA

☁/☀ WARM/HOT CLIMATE

California wines have rich ripe fruit flavors and medium acidity. The coastal areas are cool enough for Pinot Noir and Chardonnay.

- ⚲ CHARDONNAY
- ⚫ CABERNET SAUVIGNON
- ⚫ MERLOT
- ⚫ PINOT NOIR
- ⚫ ZINFANDEL

THE NORTHWEST

☁/☁ WARM/COOL CLIMATE

A slightly cooler region than California, producing red wines with higher acidity and ripe fruit flavors.

- ⚫ BORDEAUX BLEND
- ⚫ PINOT NOIR
- ⚲ CHARDONNAY
- ⚲ RIESLING
- ⚲ PINOT GRIS

THE NORTHEAST

☁ COOL CLIMATE

A cool climate region most known for its native American hybrid grapes that survive icy winters. Reds range from slightly sweet to dry and rustic. Whites are zesty.

- ⚫ CONCORD
- ⚲ NIAGARA
- ⚲ ROSÉ
- ⚫ MERLOT
- ⚲ RIESLING

CANADA

■ SEATTLE

Northwest

■ BOSTON

California

CHICAGO ■

NYC ■

■ SAN FRANCISCO

Northeast

Midwest

■ LOS ANGELES

Southwest

Southeast

■ DALLAS

■ MIAMI

MEXICO

N

750km   750mi

USA DETAIL

Okanagan Valley
Similkameen Valley

Washington
- BORDEAUX BLEND
- RIESLING
- SYRAH

■ SEATTLE

Yakima Valley
Horse Heaven Hills
PORTLAND ■

Columbia Valley
Walla Walla

Willamette Valley

Oregon
- PINOT NOIR
- PINOT GRIS
- CHARDONNAY
- RIESLING

Umqua Valley

Snake River Valley

Mendocino County
Lake County
Napa Valley
Sonoma County
Sierra Foothills
Lodi

California
- CHARDONNAY
- CABERNET SAUVIGNON
- ZINFANDEL
- PINOT NOIR
- SYRAH

Grand Valley
■ DENVER

West Elks

SAN FRANCISCO ■

Madera
Monterey
Paso Robles
Santa Barbara

Southwest
- BORDEAUX BLEND
- RIESLING
- SPARKLING WINE
- VIOGNIER

■ LOS ANGELES

Temecula Valley

■ ALBUQUERQUE

Middle Rio
Grande Valley

■ SAN DIEGO

■ PHOENIX

Texoma

Texas High Plains

Sonoita

Escondido Valley

Texas
- BORDEAUX BLEND
- TEMPRANILLO
- MOURVÈDRE

Texas Hill Country

CANADA

MEXICO

212

Michigan
- ♥ RIESLING
- ♥ PINOT NOIR
- PINOT GRIS

New York
- ♥ CONCORD
- ♥ ROSÉ
- ♥ MERLOT
- RIESLING
- ♥ ICE WINE

Lake Michigan Shore

Niagara Escarpment

Finger Lakes

Hudson River

North Fork

The Hamptons

Lake Wisconsin

Lake Erie

NEW YORK

CLEVELAND

CHICAGO

PHILADELPHIA

Outer Coastal Plain

WASHINGTON, DC

Ohio River Valley

Middleburg

Augusta

Shenandoah Valley

Upper Mississippi River Valley

Virginia
- CHARDONNAY
- ♥ BORDEAUX BLEND
- VIOGNIER

Monticello

Midwest
- ♥ NORTON
- ♥ CHAMBORCIN
- ♥ VIDAL
- CHARDONEL

Yadkin Valley

Ozark Mountain

CHARLOTTE

Southeast
- ♥ SCUPPERNONG

ATLANTA

JACKSONVILLE

N

300km   300mi

MIAMI

213

USA: CALIFORNIA

A large and varied region known for bold fruit-forward wines. Three regions make most of California's wine, and each region is suited for different wines.

491,000
ACRES

199,000
HA

WINE REGIONS BY SIZE

◀ INLAND VALLEYS
◀ NORTH COAST
◀ CENTRAL COAST
◀ SIERRA FOOTHILLS
◀ OTHERS

TOP CALIFORNIA REGIONS

● NORTH COAST

The North Coast contains Napa and Sonoma and can be split into two climate areas: the cooler coastal areas and the warmer inland valleys and hillsides.

☀ WARM CLIMATE
Inland areas of Napa, Sonoma, & Lake County

- ♥ CABERNET SAUVIGNON
- ♥ ZINFANDEL
- ♥ SYRAH

☁ COOLER CLIMATE
Coastal areas of Sonoma, Napa, & Mendocino County

- ♥ PINOT NOIR
- ♥ CHARDONNAY
- ♥ MERLOT

● CENTRAL COAST

The Central Coast can be separated into two distinct climate areas: coastal valleys that receive morning fog, and hot, dry inland areas.

☀ HOT CLIMATE
Inland areas such as Santa Barbara & Paso Robles

- ♥ CABERNET SAUVIGNON
- ♥ SYRAH
- ♥ ZINFANDEL

☁ COOLER CLIMATE
Coastal areas of San Luis Obispo & Santa Barbara

- ♥ PINOT NOIR
- ♥ CHARDONNAY
- ♥ SYRAH

● INLAND VALLEYS

The Inland Valleys are hot and dry regions most known for large-scale commercial wine production. The AVAs of Madera and Lodi make 75% of the wine in this area. The region has many old vineyard plantings of Zinfandel, Petite Sirah, Portuguese varieties like Touriga Nacional, and Muscat of Alexandria that have potential.

- ♥ ZINFANDEL
- ♥ PETITE SIRAH
- ♥ MUSCAT OF ALEXANDRIA
- ♥ BRANDY GRAPES

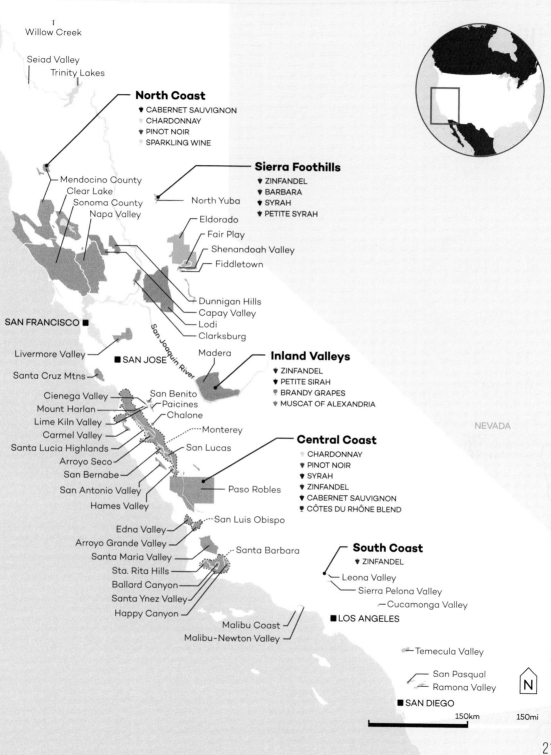

Willow Creek

Seiad Valley
Trinity Lakes

North Coast
- ♥ CABERNET SAUVIGNON
- ♡ CHARDONNAY
- ♥ PINOT NOIR
- ♡ SPARKLING WINE

Mendocino County
Clear Lake
Sonoma County
Napa Valley

Sierra Foothills
- ♥ ZINFANDEL
- ♥ BARBARA
- ♥ SYRAH
- ♥ PETITE SYRAH

North Yuba

Eldorado
Fair Play
Shenandoah Valley
Fiddletown

Dunnigan Hills
Capay Valley
Lodi
Clarksburg

SAN FRANCISCO ■

Madera

San Joaquin River

Inland Valleys
- ♥ ZINFANDEL
- ♥ PETITE SIRAH
- ♥ BRANDY GRAPES
- ♥ MUSCAT OF ALEXANDRIA

Livermore Valley

■ SAN JOSE

Santa Cruz Mtns

Cienega Valley
Mount Harlan
Lime Kiln Valley
Carmel Valley
Santa Lucia Highlands
Arroyo Seco
San Bernabe
San Antonio Valley
Hames Valley

San Benito
Paicines
Chalone

Monterey
San Lucas

Central Coast
- ♡ CHARDONNAY
- ♥ PINOT NOIR
- ♥ SYRAH
- ♥ ZINFANDEL
- ♥ CABERNET SAUVIGNON
- ♥ CÔTES DU RHÔNE BLEND

Paso Robles

NEVADA

Edna Valley
Arroyo Grande Valley
Santa Maria Valley
Sta. Rita Hills
Ballard Canyon
Santa Ynez Valley
Happy Canyon

San Luis Obispo

Santa Barbara

South Coast
- ♥ ZINFANDEL

Leona Valley
Sierra Pelona Valley
Cucamonga Valley

Malibu Coast
Malibu-Newton Valley

■ LOS ANGELES

Temecula Valley

San Pasqual
Ramona Valley

N

■ SAN DIEGO

150km   150mi

215

USA: NORTHWEST

The Northwest is characterized by fruit-forward wines with moderate acidity. The region can be split into two major regions by climate.

WASHINGTON

 WARM CLIMATE

44,000 ACRES

17,700 HA

◀ CABERNET SAUVIGNON
◀ MERLOT
◀ CHARDONNAY
◀ RIESLING
◀ SYRAH
◀ OTHERS

OREGON

☁ COOL CLIMATE

25,000 ACRES

10,300 HA

◀ PINOT NOIR
◀ PINOT GRIS
◀ CHARDONNAY
◀ SYRAH
◀ RIESLING
◀ OTHERS

TOP WINES OF WASHINGTON

🍷 BORDEAUX BLEND

Bordeaux blends from the dry and sunny Columbia Valley area usually taste of raspberry, blackberry, milk chocolate, and mint. Wines tend to have higher acidity, making them taste lighter bodied. High-quality examples will age 10+ years.

🍷 RIESLING

Ranging from dry to sweet, Washington Rieslings offer mouth-quenching acidity and flavors of yellow peach, honey, and limeade.

🍷 SYRAH

At their best, Washington Syrahs offer bold blackberry flavors with notes of olive, black pepper, vanilla, clove, and bacon. The region also produces Red Rhône blends with Grenache and Mourvèdre.

TOP WINES OF OREGON

🍷 PINOT NOIR

At its best, Oregon Pinot Noir has rich spicy flavors of cranberry, cherry, vanilla, and allspice with subtle notes of tarragon. The best wines can be found in the sub-appellations of the Willamette Valley.

🍷 PINOT GRIS

Oregon Pinot Gris offers delicate aromas of pear, white nectarine, and peony. The wines are typically made in a dry style that is zesty and refreshing.

🍷 CHARDONNAY

The cooler climate of the Willamette Valley produces Chardonnay with flavors of yellow apple, lemon, and pineapple with high acidity and cream flavors from oak aging. Unoaked Chardonnay delivers flavors of honeydew, pear, and apple.

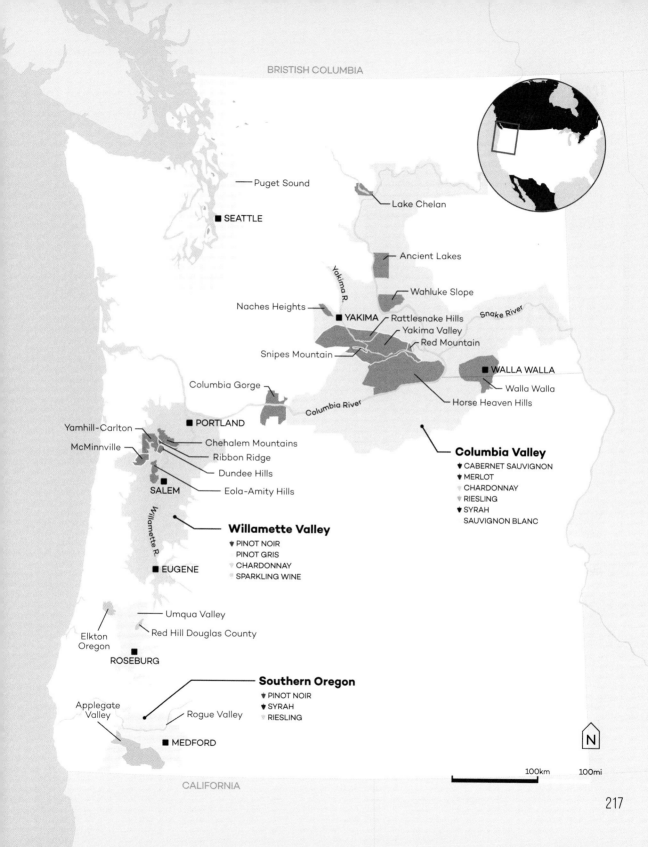

BRISTISH COLUMBIA

Puget Sound

Lake Chelan

■ SEATTLE

Ancient Lakes

Wahluke Slope

Yakima R.

Naches Heights

Snake River

■ YAKIMA Rattlesnake Hills
          Yakima Valley
          Red Mountain

Snipes Mountain

■ WALLA WALLA

Columbia Gorge

Walla Walla

Horse Heaven Hills

Columbia River

Yamhill-Carlton

■ PORTLAND

McMinnville

Chehalem Mountains

Ribbon Ridge

Dundee Hills

■ SALEM

Eola-Amity Hills

Columbia Valley

❦ CABERNET SAUVIGNON
❦ MERLOT
CHARDONNAY
RIESLING
❦ SYRAH
  SAUVIGNON BLANC

Willamette R.

Willamette Valley

❦ PINOT NOIR
  PINOT GRIS
  CHARDONNAY
  SPARKLING WINE

■ EUGENE

Umqua Valley

Red Hill Douglas County

Elkton
Oregon

■ ROSEBURG

Southern Oregon

❦ PINOT NOIR
❦ SYRAH
  RIESLING

Applegate
Valley

Rogue Valley

■ MEDFORD

N

CALIFORNIA

100km   100mi

GLOSSARY

winefolly.com / learn / basics / wine-terms

⚲ ABV

The abbreviation of alcohol by volume, listed by percent on a wine label (e.g., 13.5% ABV).

⚗ Acetaldehyde

A toxic organic chemical compound that is produced in our bodies in order to metabolize ethyl alcohol. It is the cause of alcohol poisoning.

⚖ Acidification

A wine additive process common in warm and hot climate growing regions to increase acidity by adding tartaric or citric acid. Acidification is less common in EU countries and more common in USA, Australia, and Argentina.

⚗ Amino Acids

Organic compounds that act as building blocks of proteins. Red wine contains 300–1,300 mg/L of which proline accounts for up to 85%.

⌖ Appellation

A legally defined geographical location used to identify where the grapes in a wine are grown.

⚗ Aroma Compounds

Chemical compounds with very low molecular weights making it possible for them to be carried into the upper nasal passage.

Aroma compounds are derived from grapes and fermentation and are volatilized by the evaporation of alcohol.

⚲ Astringent

A drying mouthfeel typically caused by tannins that bind to salivary proteins causing them to depart the tongue/mouth. It results in a rough sandpapery sensation in the mouth.

⚖ Brix (symbol °Bx)

Relative density scale for sucrose dissolved in grape juice used for determining the potential alcohol level of a wine. ABV is about 55–64% of the Brix number. For example, 27°Bx will result in a dry wine with 14.9–17.3% ABV.

⚖ Carbonic Maceration

A winemaking method where uncrushed grapes are placed in a sealed vat and topped with carbon dioxide. Wines created without oxygen have low tannin and color with juicy fruit flavors and bold yeast aromas. This practice is common with entry-level Beaujolais wines.

⚖ Chaptalization

A wine additive process common in cool climates where sugar is added when grape sweetness isn't high

enough to produce the minimum alcohol level. Chaptalization is illegal in the United States and common in parts of France.

⚖ Clarification/Fining

A process after fermentation where proteins and dead yeast cells are removed. To clarify, either a protein, such as casein (from milk) and egg whites or a vegan clay-based agent like bentonite or kaolin clay are added. These fining agents bind to the particles and pull them from the wine, making it clear.

⚲ Cru

A French term meaning "growth" which signifies a vineyard area of recognized quality.

⚗ Diacetyl

An organic compound found in wine that tastes like butter. Diacetyl comes from oak aging and malolactic fermentation.

⚗ Esters

Esters are one type of aroma compound found in wine that are caused by alcohol reacting with acids in wine.

⚲ Fortified Wine

A wine that has been preserved by the addition of spirits, typically made of neutral-tasting grape brandy. For example, about 30% of Port wine is spirits that raises the ABV to 20%.

🜔 Glycerol

A colorless, odorless, viscous, sweet-tasting liquid that is a by-product of fermentation. In red wines there are about 4–10 g/L and noble rot wines contain 20+ g/L. Glycerol has been considered to add a positive, rich, oily mouthfeel to wine, however, studies have shown that other traits, like alcohol level and residual sugar, have a greater effect on mouthfeel.

♉ Grape: Clone

Wine grapes are cloned for their beneficial traits much like other agricultural products. For example, there are over 1,000 registered clones of the Pinot cultivar.

♉ Grape Must

Freshly pressed grape juice that still contains the seeds, stems, and skins of grapes.

🍷 Lees Aging

Sediment left in wine after the fermentation from dead yeast particles.

🍷 Malolactic Fermentation (MLF)

MLF is technically not fermentation but a bacterial conversion of one type of acid (malic) to another type of acid (lactic). MLF is common on nearly all red wines and some white wines, like Chardonnay. It is responsible for creating the compound diacetyl, which smells and tastes like butter.

♀ Minerality

Minerality is not thought to be presence of trace minerals in wine but more likely the presence of sulfur compounds, which sometimes taste like chalk, flint, or gravel.

♀ Noble Rot

Noble rot is a fungal infection caused by *Botrytis cinerea*, common in areas with high humidity. It is considered a flaw in red grapes and wines, but in white grapes it is appreciated for adding flavors of honey, ginger, marmalade, and chamomile, making wines sweeter.

🍷 Oak: American

American white oak (*Quercus alba*) grows in the eastern United States and is primarily used in the Bourbon industry. American oak is known for adding flavors of coconut, vanilla, cedar, and dill. Since American oak tends to be more loose grained, it's known to impart robust flavors.

🍷 Oak: European

European oak (*Quercus robur*) is sourced primarily in France and Hungary. Depending on where it is grown it can range from medium grained to very fine grained. European oak is known for adding flavors of vanilla, clove, allspice, and cedar.

♀ Off-Dry

A term to describe a wine that is slightly sweet.

♀ Oxidation

When wine is exposed to too much oxygen, a chain of chemical reactions occurs that alters the compounds in the wine. One of the obvious changes you can sense is an increased level of acetaldehyde, which smells similar to bruised apples in white wine and artificial raspberry flavor and nail polish remover in red wines. Oxidation is the opposite of reduction.

🜔 pH

A figure that expresses the acidity or alkalinity in a substance numbered from 1–14 where 1 is acid, 14 is alkaline, and 7 is neutral. The average range for wine is about 2.5–4.5 pH, and a wine with a pH of 3 is ten times more acidic than a wine with a pH of 4.

⚕ Phenols

A group of several hundred chemical compounds found in wine that affect the taste, color, and mouthfeel. Tannin is a type of phenol called a polyphenol.

♀ Reduction

When wine doesn't receive enough air during fermentation, the yeast will substitute its need of nitrogen with amino acids (found in grapes). This creates sulfur compounds that can smell like rotten eggs, garlic, burnt matches, rotten cabbage, or sometimes positive traits like passion fruit or wet flint rocks. Reduction is not caused by "sulfites" being added to wine.

♀ Residual Sugar (RS)

The sugar from grapes left over in a wine after fermentation stops. Some wines are fermented completely dry, and some are stopped before all the sugar is converted to alcohol to create a sweet wine. Residual Sugar ranges from nothing to about 220 g/L (which is viscous and sweet like syrup).

⚕ Sulfites

Sulfites or SO_2 is a preservative that is either added to wine or present on grapes before fermentation. Wines range from about 10 ppm (parts per million) to 350ppm—the legal US limit. Comparatively, bacon contains nearly double that of wine and french fries contain about 2,000 ppm SO_2.

⚕ Sulfur Compounds

Sulfur compounds affect the aroma and taste of wine. In low levels they offer positive aromas of minerals or some tropical fruits. In high levels they smell of rotten eggs, garlic, or rotten cabbage.

♀ Terroir

("Tear-woh") Originally a French word that is used to describe how a particular region's climate, soils, aspect (terrain), and traditional winemaking practices affect the taste of the wine.

♀ Typicity

A wine that is typical of a particular region or style.

⚕ Vanillin

The primary extract of the vanilla bean is also found in oak.

♀ Vinified

The creation of wine by fermentation of grape juice.

♀ Volatile Acidity (VA)

Acetic acid is the volatile acid in wine that turns wine to vinegar. In small levels it adds to the complexity of flavor and in high levels it causes the wine to spoil.

INDEX

Sources

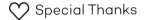

winefolly.com / learn / book / about

Ahn, Y., Ahnert, S. E., Bagrow, J. P., Barabási, A., "Flavor network and the principles of food pairing" *Scientific Reports*. 15 Dec. 2011. 20 Oct. 2014. <http://www.nature.com/srep/2011/111215/srep00196/full/srep00196.html>.

Anderson, Kym. *What Winegrape Varieties are Grown Where? A Global Empirical Picture*. Adelaide: University Press. 2013.

Klepper, Maurits de. "Food Pairing Theory: A European Fad." Gastronomica: *The Journal of Critical Food Studies*. Vol. 11, No. 4 Winter 2011: pp. 55-58.

Lipchock, S V., Mennella, J.A., Spielman, A.I., Reed, D.R. "Human Bitter Perception Correlates with Bitter Receptor Messenger RNA Expression in Taste Cells 1,2,3." *Am. Jour. of Clin. Nutrition*. Oct. 2013: pp. 1136–1143.

Pandell, Alexander J. "How Temperature Affects the Aging of Wine" *The Alchemist's Wine Perspective*. 2011. 1 Nov. 2014. <http://www.wineperspective.com/STORAGE%20TEMPERATURE%20&%20AGING.htm>.

"pH Values of Food Products." *Food Eng*. 34(3): pp. 98-99.

"Table 3: World Wine Production by Country: 2009-2012 and % Change 2012/2009" *The Wine Institute*. 2014. 3 March 2015. <http://www.wineinstitute.org/files/2012_Wine_Production_by_Country_cCalifornia_Wine_Institute.pdf>.

Special Thanks

Kym Anderson
Director of Wine Economics, University of Adelaide

Andrew L. Waterhouse
Professor of Enology, UC, Davis

Luke Wohlers
Sommelier

Tony Polzer
Italian Wine Expert

Geoff Kruth
Master Sommelier

Beth Hickey
Sommelier

Rina Bussell
Sommelier

Sam Keirsey
Washington Winemaker

Cristian Ridolfi
Italian Winemaker

Jeffrey and Sandy

Margaret and Bob

Chad Wasser
Critique

University of Adelaide

University of California, Davis